P9-CPZ-656

After the
School Bell Rings

This book is dedicated:

to three excellent educators, Alvin, Shelby, and Ernest Grant, my brothers

C.A.G.

to Pearl E. Sleeter, a loving mother who taught me by example to believe in people

C.E.S.

and to those teachers, students, and administrators who refuse to accept mediocrity and injustice, and who give their best effort toward making the world a better place for humanity

C.A.G. and C.E.S.

After the School Bell Rings

Carl A. Grant
University of Wisconsin-Madison

Christine E. Sleeter
University of Wisconsin-Parkside

106812

 The Falmer Press

(A member of the Taylor & Francis Group)
Philadelphia and London

UK The Falmer Press, Falmer House, Barcombe, Lewes, East Sussex, BN8 5DL

USA The Falmer Press, Taylor & Francis Inc., 242 Cherry Street, Philadelphia, PA 19106-1906

First published 1986

Library of Congress Cataloging in Publication Data

Grant, Carl A.
    After the school bell rings.

    Bibliography: p.
    Includes index.
    1. Educational equalization—Middle West—Case
Studies. 2. Junior high school students' socio-
economic status—Middle West—Case studies. 3. Sex
discrimination in education—Middle West—Case studies.
4. Children of minorities—Education (Secondary)—Middle
West—Case studies. I. Sleeter, Christine E.,
1948–   . II. Title.
LC213.22.M53G73   1986   370.19′0977   85-29404
ISBN 1-85000-085-9
ISBN 1-85000-086-7 (pbk.)

Typeset in 11/13 Bembo by
Imago Publishing Ltd, Thame, Oxon

Printed in Great Britain by Taylor & Francis (Printers) Ltd, Basingstoke

Contents

Acknowledgements

We were given support and encouragement by many during the various phases of this project, and we wish to say THANKS. Marilynne Boyle we gratefully acknowledge for her valuable partnership throughout the conceptualization, data collection and data analysis phases of the project. Also we thank her for her critical reading and suggestions on some of the earlier drafts of manuscript materials.

A super thanks is given to Margaret Quinlin for her sound advice, critical reading and suggestions on earlier drafts of this project. She is appreciated also for her continuous support and encouragement throughout the project. John Ogbu is deserving of a personal thanks for his wisdom in discussions we had about ideas in the book. We would like to extend our appreciation to Donna Gollnick for her helpful suggestions on an earlier draft of the manuscript, and to Linda McHugh for help in analyzing the observation data. A big thanks is given to Al Hanner and Larry Lucio for their support, advice and willingness to share their thoughts, ideas and wisdom with us.

All the students, teachers and administrators at Five Bridges are deserving of special recognition for allowing us to follow, question and observe them. They were excellent sports. The students in particular became a special source of inspiration that kept us going when we became tired or discouraged. James Steffensen and William Smith must also be thanked for their encouragement and support. They were there when we needed them.

Transcribing the tapes and typing the narrative were the responsibility of several, but four are deserving of special mention: Kay Corwith, Jackie Pettiford, Kathy Weiss and Val Krueger. They persevered with a good sense of humour and commitment through barely audible taped interviews and barely legible handwriting.

Finally, a general thanks to friends and family members who extended moral support and belief in us during our many days on the road to conduct the study, and locked away to write it.

Preface

After the School Bell Rings is written as a response to our commitment to top quality education for ALL students. We know in order to provide top quality education, especially in urban areas, the complexities of school life must be fully understood. These include complexities of school life that are often caused by such factors as social stratification based upon race, class, gender and handicap; constraints and determinants of teachers' and administrators' work; and constraints and determinants of students' school and social life. We have been ambitious in *After The School Bell Rings* in examining race, class, gender and handicap collectively. This ambitiousness is not founded upon arrogance or naïvité, but upon our professional belief that in order to understand school life these factors must be explored collectively. Also, for a similar reason we have examined the school life of all three of the principal groups of actors: students, teachers, and administrators.

We believed that if we observed well, listened well and asked good questions, we could provide an illuminating and unique insight into complexities of school life that would cause discussion and action among educators. We believed that qualitative approaches to studying school life are necessary to understand fully the subtleties and complexities that exist when individuals of different race, class, gender and handicap are brought together *and* the expectation (hope) is that all achieve excellence. Qualitative research (ethnography in this case) when done well can become very beneficial but also very trying. Often we tired of the 5+ hours drive to Five Bridges, observing and interviewing all day, spending until late in the evening preparing for the next work day, and spending most of the following week preparing for the next visit. We believed, however, that it is the understanding of school life that can come from studies such as ours that can be important to improving schools.

After The School Bell Rings is written out of admiration for the *many* teachers and administrators who 'do try' and 'do good'. We respect them. The book is also written out of respect and need of the many students who want to succeed in school and life and are placing their faith and future life aspirations in the hands of the school. We respect them and want them to have every opportunity to succeed.

Chapter 1

Introduction

Why are schools currently under attack? To what extent will this attack make a difference in the quality of schooling all students receive? If schools are not serving all young people equally well, or worse yet, if they are really not serving any of them well, what can be done about it? Educators and many others in society are presently discussing and debating what can and should be done to the education system to help it educate students more effectively. A discussion of this depth and quality is long overdue. It is needed to correct that which is wrong with schools as well as praise that which is right with them.

After the School Bell Rings addresses the quality of schooling in the context of a concept that this country was founded upon — equal respect for all. It is important that the recent discussions in education be examined in the context of this concept to make certain that these discussions do not lose sight of our recent reaffirmation of it. The reports that currently examine what is wrong with schools and suggest agendas for improving them are inadequate in this regard.

A Nation at Risk (1983) sees schools as promoting mediocrity and contributing to a weakening of America's strength internationally. It calls for changes such as establishing a new basic curriculum for all students, raising standards, providing better trained teachers, and providing longer school days and school years and more homework. John Goodlad's *A Place Called School* (1984) sees teaching as mediocre and intellectually bland in most classrooms, curricula as out of balance, and students as denied equal access to good teaching. His agenda for school improvement includes a common, balanced curriculum taught to all students by teachers who are given the time and incentive to improve their teaching skills. The state is called upon to set the goals of its schools, and local schools are to translate those goals into programs for their students. Ernest Boyer, in *High School* (1983), sees a decline in academic standards, absence of leadership, confusion over school goals, and a lack of a unified core curriculum as contributing to the ineffectiveness of the schools. His agenda for action calls for addressing these areas as well as developing a better transition between the world of work and schooling, improving teacher preparation and teaching conditions, and using technology in the classroom. Mortimer Adler's *Paideia Proposal* (1982) calls for improving schools by providing all students equal access to a common curriculum that focuses around acquisition of knowledge, development of intellectual skills, and exploration of values and ideas.

Will implementation of any or all of these proposals solve what is wrong with schools? Do these proposals accurately identify what is needed to promote both excellence and equity?

We are concerned that they do not. If implemented, we are concerned that these proposals will raise the quality of education primarily for those who schools have always served best: white middle class students, and particularly males. Although they address cultural diversity and the historic failure of schools to provide excellence for lower class and minority students, we find their analysis of the relationship between schooling and cultural pluralism in a stratified society to be weak (see Grant and Sleeter, 1985). The approach to excellence and equity represented in these reports is not new, in fact, although many issues they address are recent. Let us review briefly the theoretical orientation taken by different researchers who have examined why schools have not provided well for all young people, and locate these current reports in this context.

Human capital theorists have examined how much success different schools and different amounts of schooling have had with similar student populations (for example, Jencks, 1972; Rutter, *et al.*, 1979). These researchers have tried to identify factors in school that, if modified, can equalize the benefits for students from diverse backgrounds. A few factors such as academic expectations and time on task have been identified, but as yet, this research has not been able definitively to tell us how to close significant gaps in student achievement levels.

Researchers working within the deficiency model have identified the 'deficient' backgrounds some students bring with them as the culprit (for example, Coleman, 1966; Becker, 1977). Their research has sought ways to compensate for deficiencies believed to cause student failure. However, programs such as Head Start that are based on findings of this research have thus far yielded only marginal success.

Researchers working within the culture conflict model have assumed that unequal school outcomes are due in part to cultural differences between teachers and students in learning style, cognitive style, interaction style, prior knowledge, and language (for example, Longstreet, 1974; Philips, 1983; Hale, 1982). They have attempted to identify cultural differences that interfere with school success. Their research has clearly identified cultural differences between teachers and students from minority backgrounds. But it has yet to demonstrate that cultural differences between teachers and students can be eradicated in schools, and that doing so will eliminate gaps in student achievement. In fact, Ogbu (1982) argues that cultural differences between teachers and students are often strengthened in schools in the students' attempts to assert and maintain their own identity within a hostile environment.

The current reports on schooling derive from the human capital orientation. Like earlier human capital theorists, they argue that schools exist to prepare all students to enter society and contribute to it. They trace the poor performance of many schools to factors such as failure to provide all students with equal amounts of the same school experience, failure to distribute good teaching equitably, and failure to provide training in higher thinking processes.

But these reports share weaknesses inherent in human capital theory. They ignore the unequal social context schools prepare the young to inhabit — they ignore inequalities embedded in wage structures, family roles, housing patterns, political processes, and so forth. They ignore research on culture conflicts between school and low income or minority communities and assume that a common curriculum for all students can be developed that will not conflict with the cultural identities of some. They ignore research on cultural and sex bias in the curriculum and in tests. In short, they fail to take seriously the importance of cultural diversity and schooling, and thus do not adequately address why schools so often do not provide excellence for all children.

This book examines schooling and the quality of teaching specifically in relationship to the cultural and gender backgrounds of students. Our analysis is situated within the camp of conflict theory. Conflict theorists argue that society and its institutions are shaped by conflicts of interests among competing groups. Institutions such as schools, rather than serving as vehicles to bring about equality, are used by dominant groups to maintain their dominance (for example, Bowles and Gintis, 1976; Bourdieu and Passeron, 1977; Collins, 1971). Schools in particular sort and select the young for an unequal labor market, and teach the young to accept the idea that unequal distribution of wealth and power is just. Rather than searching for defects in schools that prevent them from benefiting all students equally, conflict theorists seek connections between schooling and our social structure that is stratified based on race, family socioeconomic background, and gender.

We find this last theoretical orientation to be the most compelling. To explain why, and to describe how that orientation will guide this study, let us consider what is usually meant by the notion of equal respect for all, and do so with explicit recognition that we are a diverse and stratified society.

Theoretical Framework

What is meant by 'respect for human diversity'? We took a poll of students in our classes, asking them to write down what this phrase meant to them. The following responses were most common: understanding and listening to people different from oneself, treating each person as an individual, not trying to change other people, and tolerating differences among people. Stated simply, our students saw respect for human diversity as treating people kindly in face-to-face situations, or accepting differences among individuals. But in a society in which people are stratified by differences in culture, race, sex, and academic competence, definitions are limited in three ways.

First, they fail to acknowledge the group membership of individuals in society, and the important role group membership plays in the identities and histories of individuals. For example, when a white male meets a Hispanic female, it is insufficient for each to acknowledge the other only as an individual. Both are also members of ethnic and sex groups that have their own constellations of values, traditions, and experiences. The importance of identifying with enduring human groups has often been underestimated. Today, many social scientists believe people need to define themselves in relation to groups that are more permanent than associations in the workplace or the neighborhood. According to Appleton (1983),

> Close associations, common experiences, and a well-known network of religious and cultural traditions have provided a psychological and cosmological *homes* of reference for human

experience. Individuals find comforting support and order among others like themselves. (p. 45)

Thus, we need to recognize, understand and respect the social groups of which an individual is a member and from which that individual derives identity, in addition to respecting individuality.

Second, it is important to recognize that human differences are not neutral. In the United States today, wealth, power and status are distributed unequally on the basis of race, sex, social class background, and handicapping condition. And, to a great extent group membership forms at least as much of the basis for competition for resources as do individual characteristics.

This conflict in American society has historically been lopsided. Dominant groups maintain control over resources and privileges, and subordinate groups struggle to gain as many resources and privileges as possible. A definition of human diversity must acknowledge the role race, sex, social class, and handicap play in the distribution of our nation's resources and privileges.

Third, the commonly held definitions suggested earlier tend to be very passive. They have a 'live and let live' ring to them. But passive definitions suggest that the customs, traditions, and institutional processes in our society related to class, race, gender, and handicap are not in need of any major change. An individual who fails to be actively involved in changing these customs, traditions, and processes that foster inequality allows it to continue. For example, if a hearing person passively accepts denial of equal access to all public facilities for the hearing impaired, is that person really showing respect for the hearing impaired?

How is human diversity actually viewed and responded to in a school? How is the issue of equality acted on, given the importance group membership plays for both individual identity and society's distribution of resources? And, given the fact that schools credential the young for different positions in a stratified labor market (Collins, 1979), is it possible to view schools as potentially equalizing agents, or do schools in fact help create and reinforce inequality?

These questions suggest conflict theory to be the most fruitful orientation to guide our study. And indeed, prior studies of schools based on conflict theory have shown that schools do actively participate in the reproduction of social inequality, although the focus of prior studies has been limited to only one form of inequality. Thus far, most studies of schooling and inequality in America[1] based on conflict theory have focused on inequality as it relates to social class (for example, Anyon, 1981; Everhart, 1983; Bowles and Gintis, 1976); a smaller number of studies have examined schooling inequality and race (for example, Ogbu, 1974; Wax, 1976). No major study in America has yet been reported that examines closely schooling and inequality as it relates to sex or handicap from a conflict theory perspective. In fact, very few qualitative studies have looked closely at handicapped students from any perspective, a lack which needs attending to. By examining schooling and inequality as it relates to race, social class, sex and handicap within one school, this study takes an ambitious and much-needed examination of schooling in America.

Conflict theory offers a lens for sifting through the phenomena in a school, as well as suggesting links between the school and society at large. But it does not offer a methodology or an orientation for understanding human thinking and behavior on a daily basis. For that, we turned to anthropology. Anthropology helped us examine what happens and how it happens; conflict theory helped us analyze why it happens.

Conflict Theory

Conflict theorists who have built on the work of Weber (1947 and 1968) and Marx and Engels (1947) argue that individuals and groups act primarily on what they perceive to be their own interests. While people may have concern for the interests of others, it is normal to act in such a way that one's own interests, and the interests of groups of which one is a member, will be advanced or at least not jeopardized. But human groups do not all share the same interests and frequently find themselves in conflict with one another. Conflict is not necessarily bad, since it is a normal outcome of the pursuit of varied interests. In fact, conflict is good, according to theorists such as Coser (1956), in that it keeps social systems vibrant.

However, conflict over resources often leads to the domination of some groups by others. Resources are limited within a society, and groups compete for access to and control over them, chiefly power, wealth, and status. Theorists disagree about which of these three is most important; for Marx it was wealth, while for Dahrendorf (1959) it was power. Most agree, however, that competition for power, wealth and status generates great conflict, and that gaining or controlling one facilitates control of the others. Groups use resources they control to maintain and enlarge their control over others, in whatever way they can. According to Michels (1959), '... every human power seeks to enlarge its prerogatives. He who has acquired power will almost always endeavor to consolidate it and to extend it' (p. 207). The result is domination of some groups by others.

Dominant social groups attempt to mask the nature of conflict by promoting consensus on the part of both their own members and members of subordinate groups of the legitimacy and integrity of its dominance. Thus they attempt to shape social institutions — including schools — and the ideology of those institutions in such a way that all will believe that it is in their own best interests to adhere to the social order. Collins (1977), for example, argues that schools can be understood best not by examining the way they teach technical knowledge for jobs and life success, but by examining their roles in teaching and legitimating the values and norms of dominant groups. He writes, 'The main activity of schools is to teach particular status cultures, both in and outside the classroom' (p. 126). By teaching the culture of the dominant group, schools teach children who are members of all groups to see this as *the* legitimate and valued culture.

Subordinate groups usually only partially accept the social order. Deutsch (1973) describes four responses by members of subordinate groups to their subordinate status. One is acceptance of that status as natural — for example, women in many cultures have historically responded to subordination in this way. A second response is an attempt by individuals to escape membership in the subordinate group — members of the lower class who work their way up to middle class status, or blacks who 'pass' as whites make this response. A third is mobilization as a group to change the existing power relationship — the civil rights movement in the sixties, led primarily by blacks, represents an example. As a fourth response, a subordinate group can reject norms and traditions of the dominant group, thereby insulating itself, and develop or strengthen its own culture and rewards — Hargreaves (1967) and Lacey (1970) report working class, low-stream boys who, failing to attain status in school according to middle-class standards, rejected the standards of the school and developed their own based on working class culture.

Conflict theory suggests that we examine the school to see how competing claims for status, wealth and power are made. It suggests that we recognize the fact that society is dominated by those who control economic resources, those who are white, and those who are males. We should then look for ways in which the school helps to

7

reproduce and legitimate their dominance. But we also need to attend to the struggles of subordinate groups. In what ways do schools serve their interests? How do they use the institution of schooling to further their own claims? What forms does that response to dominance take and why? Identifying how subordination is resisted and equality is supported while it is simultaneously being undermined is very important because, as Walker and Barton (1983) point out, this 'will not only provide us with illustrations that certain practices are not inevitable, that procedures are changeable, but also identify points of opposition and entry' (p. 16).

How do we get at the lived experience of people in a school without distorting it to fit our purpose? We turned to anthropology to guide our work.

Anthropology

Anthropologists are interested in studying both the behavior and the shared knowledge of a social group. A central assumption of anthropology is that individuals think and act in a way that makes sense to them. Human behavior is guided by 'cultural knowledge', which Spindler (1982) defines as 'the knowledge participants . . . use to guide their behavior in the various social settings they participate in. Such knowledge is complex and subtle; it includes specific knowledge of social roles and rules, and generalized, usually only dimly conscious, knowledge of categories and management skills' (p. 5). Cultural knowledge includes the structure and content of meanings shared by individuals within a social group, and the sentiments attached to meanings. Cultural knowledge 'encompasses patterns of meaning, reality, values, actions, and decision-making that are shared by and within social collectivities' (Goodenough, 1963).

To make sense of their world, people need to organize the infinite array of phenomena they encounter. Cultural groups develop categories of meaning or typifications of phenomena, and use both linguistic and non-linguistic symbols to refer to these categories. As we grow up in a society, we learn the symbols, categories, and meanings used by others around us; we learn to make sense of the world in ways similar to the cultural groups of which we are members. The result is some degree of continuity of cultural knowledge from one generation to the next, and among different individuals and groups in a society.

It is important to recognize, however, that people do not simply absorb meanings unreflectively. They also actively participate in creating meanings based on new situations or contradictory experiences. Thus, it is important to attend also to intergenerational changes in cultural knowledge, and to variations among different individuals and subgroups. Sometimes newly constructed meanings are idiosyncratic to individuals, but sometimes they come to be widely shared within a cultural group, and form the basis of new kinds of action. Any study of the cultural knowledge of members of a social setting must be sensitive to new and evolving meanings as well as to established meanings that participants hold.

Cultural knowledge, however, is not the whole of a culture. One must also know what people actually do — how they behave in their daily lives. As Pelto (1965) has pointed out,

> Even the best informants, cross-checked against one another, provide the anthropologist with a very distilled, inadequate picture of life in a society. A native might be completely unconscious of, or take for granted, and thus not mention, aspects of his culture that would have great significance to the outside observer. (p. 41)

Thus, it is necessary to observe the social behavior of members of a cultural group in order to identify patterns in their activities and rituals.

Knowing a group's cultural knowledge and the patterns of their behavior does not explain why these exist as they do. What factors helped shape them? The world inhabited by social groups is partially defined by a set of factors we call determinants. Determinants limit the range of experience possible within one's world, and amplify others (Willis, 1977). Some determinants are local-level — experiences in a school may be shaped partially by its budget, the backgrounds of its teachers, the interests of its students, and so forth. But in part, situations and the local-level determinants that shape them are themselves shaped in complex ways by macro-level determinants that include unequal social, economic, and political relationships among race, sex, social class, and handicap groups. By understanding how these unequal relationships take form in specific contexts and in turn affect the cultural knowledge and actions of participants, we will be able to understand why conflict is acted out as it is in a school.

Viewed within a conflict theory framework, cultural knowledge that represents what Gramsci (1971) described as critical insight into the nature of oppression must be examined. Giroux (1981) argues that cultural knowledge is a complex of meanings both justifying present

9

social relationships among groups and questioning those relationships. Cultural knowledge and activity that offer a critique of inequality and oppression is particularly important if we wish to understand how a more just society might be attained.

The study reported in this book will begin by examining the behavior and the cultural knowledge of the students, teachers, and administrators — especially that which focuses on human diversity and on the participants themselves as members of diverse social categories. At issue will be two related questions: How are participants in the school reproducing unequal social relationships? And how are they affirming the notion of equality for all?

This study will also examine local-level determinants of participants' behavior and cultural knowledge, and suggest relationships between those and unequal relationships among racial groups, social classes, the sexes, and handicap groups in society at large. An attempt will be made to probe for data that will show how younger generations can learn to forge a more just society, based on the experiences of the young in the community studied here.

Methodology

This study was conducted in a junior high school located in a working class neighborhood in a mid-western city. The school, Five Bridges Junior High, was desegregated in 1976. At the time of this study, school records reported the racial composition of Five Bridges' 580 students as follows: 0.5 per cent Asian, 2 per cent black, 28 per cent Hispanic, 2 per cent Native American and 67.5 per cent white.[2]

Five Bridges was also mainstreamed in 1976. The only barrier-free junior high in the city, it was chosen to house programs for physically impaired and multiply-handicapped students. About fifteen physically impaired students per year were bused to Five Bridges from throughout the city. The school also had programs for students classified as educable mentally retarded, learning disabled, and emotionally disturbed.

We were interested in studying this school largely because of the rich diversity of its student body. We were also interested because a number of staff members, including the Principal, were trying to make the school more responsive to the diversity of its students. Our final decision lay with the willingness of the staff and particularly the administrators to open their doors to us as researchers. In Chapter 2, this school and its students will be described in greater detail.

An ethnographic case study design was used. This design was chosen to obtain in-depth data about relationships among people in the school and the knowledge they construct about those relationships (their cultural knowledge). It was also chosen to illuminate contextual factors that impinge on those relationships and that knowledge.

Data were collected during a series of visits to the school over a three-year period. These included one two-week visit during August, 1978 and twenty-four two- to three-day visits between September 1978 and April 1982. Data were collected mainly through observation, interviews, and collecting documents.

Two kinds of observations were made: site-specific and person-specific. We made site-specific observations of classrooms, the lunchroom, halls and other places in the school. We made person-specific observations of individual teachers and students, which entailed shadowing individuals for about half of the day, keeping running notes about what the individual did, and asking the individual to explain his or her actions or to give reactions to events that were observed.

Interviews were conducted with all of the administrators, most of the teachers, and a large sample of students stratified by race, sex and handicap. All interviews were taped and later transcribed. Most were guided by interview questions developed for the students, teachers and administrators for that particular visit, but some took place spontaneously.

A wide variety of documents were collected. For example, we subscribed to the student newspaper, collected samples of student work, teacher lesson plans and materials, and memos from the administrators to the staff. We also collected and examined documents produced by the school or school district relating to desegregation and mainstreaming, and newspaper articles written about the neighborhood of the school. A more detailed description of methodology for data collection and analysis appears in the Appendix.

Notes

1 The research tradition in Great Britain has used conflict theory as a way of understanding inequality and schooling to a greater extent than has been the case in America. See, for example, Sharp and Green (1975), Willis (1977), McRobbie (1978), Fuller (1980).
2 These categories underplay the racial and ethnic mix of the student body. Many of the students are children of mixed marriages, which these figures

do not capture. Also, within the Hispanic, white and Asian groups, there is considerable ethnic variety. For example, although most of the Hispanic students are Mexican, some are Puerto Rican, and a few are Cuban. Students classified as white include students who are Egyptian, Lebanese, Syrian and Italian, as well as those of northern European descent.

Chapter 2

The Community and the School

The area of the city from which the junior high school — referred to hereafter as Five Bridges Junior High — draws its students is called Rivercrest. Rivercrest, in a mid-western city, is located along a river, on the side of a hill. It is separated from the rest of the city on three sides by the river and is connected to the city by five bridges. The fourth boundary of Rivercrest marks the city limit separating it from a suburb.

Rivercrest

Rivercrest possesses certain scenic features. It offers panoramic vistas of the downtown and areas adjacent to downtown, and it boasts heavily wooded areas, bluffs and caves. It has several historical buildings that have been recommended for restoration. In addition, brightly painted murals on a few buildings, and a commanding bell tower in a housing project lend interest to the community's architecture.

Local residents distinguish between two neighborhoods in Rivercrest: the lower and the upper bluffs. The lower bluff, often referred to as the flats, is located along the river and is subject to frequent flooding. A former resident explained:

> I remember as a kid along with other kids looking into the mud puddles that were left [from the flooding] and fishing out carp. I always used to ask my mother and father, 'Well, why don't you move out of this area and move to higher land because every year we get flooded out'. And they used to say like everybody else did, 'We haven't got any money to move out, we can't move to a better place because it's impossible for us to move'.

13

The lower bluff has been the initial residence of many different ethnic groups that have migrated to this city. The earliest settlers were French-Canadians retired from the fur trade. They were followed by waves of Russian and European Jewish immigrants in the 1880s. Early in the 1900s Mexicans migrated to the state to work, and many settled in Rivercrest. According to a historian who was a former resident of Rivercrest:

> [These ethnic groups] gravitated toward Rivercrest because that was the cheapest place they could find to live. Not only the cheapest place, but there were certain places in the city where even if you had money people wouldn't allow you to live there because there was so much deep prejudice.

Historically, lower bluff residents, especially those who did not prefer living in a racially mixed neighborhood, moved either up the hill or out of Rivercrest altogether when able to afford it. More often than not, emigrants of Rivercrest were whites. According to a Hispanic resident, 'We [Hispanics] weren't as mobile as some of the white families, and so we were pretty much restricted to moving up the block, so to speak'. Over time, this movement resulted in shifts in the ethnic composition of the neighborhood, with the lower bluff growing in its population of color, and a gradual movement of people of color up the hill. By 1975, about half of the lower bluff population was of color, in contrast to about 10 per cent of the upper bluff population. The dominant ethnic group in the lower bluff was Mexican-American; other ethnic groups included Jewish, Lebanese, Syrian, black, Scandinavian and Native American. In addition, Asians had begun to move into the neighborhood.

Both spouses held jobs in many families. The majority were employed in factory work or other forms of manual labor (for example, butchering, janitorial work, printing), many in the local meat packing plants and a publishing company. Some were also employed as salesclerks, post office employees, firefighters and police officers. A number of young adults were employed in social service agencies such as day care centers and youth employment programs. There were few teachers, no doctors, two or three lawyers, and only a few small business owners.

In 1980, the average household income of lower bluff residents was below the average for the city, although several neighborhoods in the city had lower average incomes than the lower bluff. The estimated median family income for the city was $19,900, while the median income for the lower bluff was $14,304. A newspaper article in which lower bluff residents had been interviewed pointed out that local residents of all colors saw themselves united in a common bond of poverty (Bissinger, 1980). The average income of upper bluff households was somewhat higher. The most extreme differences were found between the lower few blocks of the flats and the few blocks farthest up the bluff, where median family income was $17,610.

Lower Bluff

In 1963, in an effort to expand the city's industry, several blocks of housing along the river were replaced by an industrial park. People were forced to relocate, many to low-income housing projects in the neighborhood. New housing included a public housing project, a federally subsidized residence for elderly people, a private residence for the severely handicapped, and two additional federally subsidized projects. City planners argued that this urban renewal effort benefited Rivercrest, but many adult residents still are bitter about this loss of land and home (*ibid*).

At the time of this study, about 52 per cent of the residents were Hispanic, 2 per cent were black, 2 per cent were Native American and 1 per cent were listed in the census as 'other'. Spanish and English were the two major languages spoken in this neighborhood. About one-third of the residents spoke Spanish only, while another third was bilingual (Helland, 1978). Community residents predicted that Asian languages would gain prominence in this area over the next few years.

Housing in the lower bluff neighborhood consisted of single-family dwellings, apartment buildings, housing projects. Sixty-three per cent of the dwellings housed three or more families. Forty-one per cent of the households were single-member households, and 24 per cent of the households had five or more persons (Polk, 1978). In short, families ranged widely in size, and over half lived in multiple-family dwellings. Most houses and yards were small; some appeared rather rundown, but the majority were clean and in reasonably good repair. Yards with statues of the Virgin Mary in the garden attested to the neighborhood's predominant religion: Catholicism. Several churches served the community, the largest of which played an active role in the cultural life of the community. Another active community service organization, Community House, provided GED (General Equivalency Diploma) classes, health services and recreational activities. Two playgrounds drew the neighborhood's children.

The lower bluff had a small business area that served the entire Rivercrest community. Rivercrest businesses were traditionally small-scale, individually owned shops, some of which had been in operation for several generations. The urban renewal project was reported to have damaged Rivercrest's business. A newspaper account reported that:

> Before urban renewal, a person could walk down [the] street and find a hardware store, barbershops, a bakery, a bank, a movie theater, and a meat market. None of those businesses are around today; a number of them moved out during urban renewal and did not move back. (Bissinger, 1980)

In the early 1980s, local businesses in the lower bluff neighborhood included, for example, grocery stores, a furniture store, restaurants, (a restaurant featuring Mexican and Lebanese food symbolized the neighborhood's ethnic mixture equite well), and bars. However, since Rivercrest had only a few retail and service establishments such as supermarkets and drug stores, the community was mobilizing to secure more businesses.

Upper Bluff

Racial composition was the major difference between the upper and lower bluffs. On the average, the upper bluff was 90 per cent white, although the neighborhood grew increasingly racially mixed as one descended the hill.

There were relatively few multiple-family dwellings in the upper bluff. About three-quarters of the families lived in single-family units or duplexes, most of which were built during the 1940s for single families on moderate to low incomes. Upper bluff households tended to be more uniform in size than lower bluff households (Polk, 1978). As one ascended the hill, one saw a gradual, visible change in the size and condition of houses; houses on the summit of the upper bluff were quite large and obviously more expensive than houses farther down. A park along the summit of the upper bluff was within easy walking distance of the wealthier residents; there was also a playground located in the center of the upper bluff where children from several blocks

played. Adjacent to this playground was a community service organization that served social needs of upper bluff residents. Several
churches were in this neighborhood, one of which housed a Catholic
school. A few small businesses, such as a 7–11 and a Dairy Queen,
were located here.

Lifestyle of Rivercrest

Although Rivercrest had two neighborhoods that differed in racial
composition, residents of the Rivercrest community shared a common
lifestyle. The people of Rivercrest represented different cultural traditions, but their lifestyles became more and more alike as they adapted
to each other. The fact that most Rivercrest families could not afford to
move elsewhere contributed to this. Families had lived in Rivercrest for
several generations. As generations remained in the neighborhood,
similarities in lifestyle overtook differences. For example, most Rivercrest families spoke English, although many families also retained
their native language. Rivercrest residents adapted to the dress and
customs of their neighbors, yet they accepted differences among
families in matters such as religion and food. A newspaper article put it
this way:

> Sure, there are different ethnic groups — Lebanese, Mexican,
> Spanish, Puerto Rican, Swedish, German, Italian and Irish. But
> Rivercresters share a common heritage that comes from ex-
> periencing floods, urban renewal, stickball, and backyard bar-
> beques. (Bissinger, 1980)

The fact that family incomes were not widely divergent also contributed to a similarity in lifestyle. Residents could afford the essentials
but had little remaining for luxuries or major expenses. Most residents
were adequately clothed, but few could afford costly or extensive
wardrobes. Young people could afford low-cost entertainment —
movies, the local rollerskating rink, games of baseball or basketball;
few could afford expensive activities such as trips, private music or
dance lessons. In other words, there were few social class differences
that might compound differences in lifestyle due to cultural
background.

Rivercrest was known for its community spirit and unity on
matters of improvement in the area. As one parent commented:

> We do have pride in our community.... We work at making
> our community a good community to live in and raise our kids.
> A lot of people are willing to work for that.

The Rivercrest Citizens' Organization offered several services and
sponsored community events. Its staff was fluent in Spanish and
English, removing for most residents a language barrier. One staff
member told us 'The majority of people that come in are either Anglo
or Chicano and I've always tried to make my office receptive to both
races'. In addition, the Citizens' Organization had worked actively with
the City Planning Office since 1975 to poll residents and recommend
improvements to be funded by the city. The Rivercrest community
also published a thriving local newspaper that informed residents about
Rivercrest news and upcoming events.

The School

In 1971, the city announced intentions to desegregate its public schools.
A task force was established to develop plans for doing this. In 1976,
the schools in Rivercrest were desegregated by consolidation. The
feeder system for the high school in this neighborhood had previously
consisted of three elementary schools (one in the lower bluff and two in
the upper bluff) and two junior high schools, one of which served the
lower bluff and the other served the upper bluff. This school system
reinforced a division between the upper and lower bluffs, and, to some
extent, between whites and non-whites. A Hispanic adult who attended the school system as a child recalled that:

> We grew up together and got along with each other but yet,
> when you got to [the senior high], you got the feeling that you
> were from [the lower bluff junior high] so that you were just
> kind of out of it. You weren't included — like it was very hard
> to get into student council and other things, and minorities —
> forget it!

Following the desegregation plan, the feeder system was reconstructed
along a 2-2-3-3-4 plan, with each school serving the entire Rivercrest
community. When Five Bridges Junior High opened as a desegregated
school its minority student population came from the following school
areas:

Table 1:   Source of minority students after desegregation

Source of students	School enrollment	Number of minority students	Percentage of minority students
Old upper bluff junior high	411	80	19.4
Old lower bluff junior high	290	135	46.6
Total enrollment of Five Bridges after desegregation	701	215	30.7

Prior to the passage of PL94-142 in 1975, the city was evaluating its programs and placements for special education students with an eye toward mainstreaming them where possible. Part of this evaluation included recommendations for capital improvement of school facilities. A short-range goal was to ensure that at least one or two schools at each level was accessible to physically impaired students; a longer-range goal was to make all buildings accessible.

Five Bridges, an old building, was one of the schools that underwent extensive renovation, for example, constructing a new swimming pool and cafeteria. One member of the Citizens' Renovation Committee for Five Bridges was a contractor who had a physically impaired son. His professional training allowed him to make certain that the renovation made the building fully accessible to physically impaired people.

Five Bridges was mainstreamed in 1976. It was the only barrier-free junior high in the city. This meant that about fifteen physically impaired students per year were bused to Five Bridges from throughout the city. About one-third of the first floor of the building contained classrooms for this program, and physically impaired students were enrolled in regular classes unless they were mentally retarded or unable to communicate verbally with individuals untrained to teach them. Five Bridges also had programs for students classified as educable mentally retarded (EMR), learning disabled (LD), or emotionally disturbed (ED). Enrollment in these programs totaled about forty-five students per year; these students were enrolled one or two hours per day in a special education resource room and in selected regular classes the rest of the day.

Achievement scores at Five Bridges were fairly low. Every year the SRA test in reading, math, and language was administered to all students in the city. In the years 1978–1980 Five Bridges ranked third from the bottom out of twelve junior highs in the city in overall basic skills achievement; this was an improvement over earlier scores. Table 2 shows the national percentile averages of composite basic skills achievement scores for each grade level from 1975–1980. As these statistics indicate achievement at Five Bridges was considerably below the national average.

Table 2: SRA (Science Research Associates) test scores by percentile

	Grade	1975	1976	1978	1980
Composite	7	23	26	29	40
	8	21	21	32	44
	9	18	22	32	35
Reading	7	23	27	25	36
	8	23	22	26	40
	9	23	23	30	34
Math	7	21	24	23	34
	8	20	20	27	46
	9	19	24	32	36

The architectural design of Five Bridges was a variation on the egg-crate design. The school had three floors connected by both staircases and elevators; wide halls and ramps facilitated passage of those who were both ambulatory and in wheelchairs. In addition to thirty classrooms, including band and chorus rooms, science and home-economics labs, graphic arts and woodworking labs, and reading and math labs, the school was equipped with a spacious and well-stocked instructional materials center, a large gym, a swimming pool, a large cafeteria, offices and a community room.

The basic core of course offerings was typical of many junior highs. But the school also had a number of programs and classes that were provided through state and federal funding, including Title I reading and math, ESAA (Emergency School Assistance Act) reading and math, Teacher Corps, Bilingual Education, ESAA World Languages and Cultures Magnet Program, Affective Education and Peer Counseling, and Multicultural Education. Five Bridges also offered some extracurricular activities, which included an elected Student Council, an Intercultural Committee, a yearbook staff, a chess club, a cheerleading squad, and a ski club. After school organized sports were available for girls — basketball, track, volleyball, gymnastics, and softball and for boys — basketball, baseball, gymnastics, wrestling, and track.

Now that we have provided a setting and background for Five

Bridges, we wish to take *you*, the reader, with us into the school. Your visit will allow you to see what we found to be a typical school day. You will begin your visit by becoming acquainted with the students as they talk informally with each other during lunch.

Chapter 3

Students' Cultural Knowledge about Human Diversity

You enter the building as the students are heading for lunch. The halls are teeming with boys and girls clad mostly in jeans, tennis shoes and T-shirts. They move through the halls in small groups, talking, laughing; opening and slamming shut their lockers. Occasionally, one or two students in electric wheelchairs drive by. You follow the crowd into the lunchroom.[1]

As the students take their places at the lunch tables, one cannot but notice that times haven't changed since you were in school — boys and girls are still choosing to sit at separate tables. In fact, sex segregation in schools has been a consistent finding in studies of student social systems (for example, Coleman, 1961; Cusick, 1973; Everhart, 1983; Gordon, 1957; Schofield 1983).

One noticeable difference from times past is the presence of physically impaired students; they are seated at a separate table where two aides are helping them to eat. One wonders if physical segregation at the lunch tables could be a reflection of the social segregation often found in studies of students (for example, Centers and Centers, 1963; Force, 1956; Richardson, Ronald and Kleck, 1974), or whether the LD, ED and EMR students are socially accepted as equals by their peers. Research finds these students are usually rejected by, and lower in status than, their regular peers (for example, Bruininks, 1978; Bryan, 1977; Goodman, Gottlieb and Harrison, 1972; Gottlieb and Budoff, 1973; Iano, *et al.*, 1974).

What strikes you is that, of the eighteen occupied tables, sixteen are racially integrated. Eleven tables are occupied by white and Hispanic students, one by black and white students, and three by students representing at least three different racial groups. Furthermore, at the racially mixed tables students are rarely clustered by racial group. At some tables there are clusters of white or Hispanic students, but these clusters are usually dotted by one or two members of another racial group. This is a particularly surprising occurrence in view of studies of student social systems which have consistently found students to segregate themselves based on race (for example, Achor, 1978; Cusick and Ayling, 1974; Petroni and Hirsch, 1971; Rist, 1979; Schofield, 1983). You decide to wander around and eavesdrop on a few conversations.

Four Mexican girls and two white girls are discussing whether they will go to 'Open Gym' tonight. A white girl addresses one of her Mexican tablemates.

'Hey, Anna, do you suppose Keith will be there?'

The girls giggle and Anna, a cute girl with short black hair, blushes. 'Well, if he is, I'm not gonna play basketball. I don't want him laughing at me.'

Another girl chimes in. 'He sure is cute. I love his baby blue eyes. I bet he calls you up this week.'

'Yeah, and he's such a good basketball player. I know Anna just likes to go to Open Gym to watch him. Hey, Carlos!'

Carlos, a tall, good-looking boy with carefully manicured black hair, approaches and takes a handful of Anna's french fries. He mumbles, 'Keith says hi, Anna.'

'Get your hands outa my fries!' protests the flustered Anna. The students all laugh, and you move on.

You notice a small attractive black girl bouncing in her seat as she carries on an animated conversation with a white girl, a Mexican girl and two Asian girls. They are next to the table of physically impaired students, one of whom is simultaneously carrying on conversations with the black girl and with another girl in a wheelchair. They are discussing the dance scheduled for after school Friday. The black girl invites you to sit down. She introduces the group: her name is Yvonne, and her friends are Delia, Mariko, Cheryl, Pat and Ruth. She explains that she recently moved here from Chicago, and she is teaching her friends here how to dance. Ruth, the girl in the wheelchair, is saying, 'Well, I might come to the dance this time. I didn't go to the last one!'

Yvonne tells her firmly, 'You're coming. Elaine came last time, and she dances good in her chair. We'll teach you won't we, Elaine?'. Ruth's companion, Elaine, giggles. Then Delia, who has finished eating, stands up and demonstrates a dance step, asking Yvonne for help in perfecting it. The two girls form an interesting picture as they hop up and down and kick their feet: petite Delia with her shoulder-length black hair, strikingly pretty Filipino face, and pink embroidered cotton shirt; and chunky Yvonne, with her short curly black hair, captivating smile, in jeans and a shirt tied together by a bright green plastic belt.

Moving down the lunchroom floor, you pause at a table that seats about ten boys. Five are white, four are Mexican and one is black. Some of them are quietly eating and listening as the others discuss last week's football game. A blond boy flicks his milk carton down the table in imitation of a football, and it lands in a Mexican boy's apple sauce. He protests in mock anger, 'Hey, cut it out, Gil, or you can't borrow my records this weekend.' Another boy says to him, 'Ernie, is it true Laura gave you back your ring?'. Ernie looks flustered. 'Aw, I don't care about her, anyway.'

A red-headed boy exclaims, 'That's not what I heard! I heard you were gonna beat up the new guy she's been seeing'.

Ernie shakes his head. 'He just likes her 'cause she's got a good body and long blond hair. And I don't care. I'm taking Maria to the party at your house this weekend.' The boys all hoot and holler at this announcement.

Hal, the red-headed boy, wanders over to you and asks who you are. You explain, and ask him if these are the boys he is friends with.

'Naw, I just eat lunch with these guys. Are you gonna be in third lunch? One of the guys I hang around with is in third lunch, and you should say hi to him. You can't miss him. He's got light hair, and he's in a wheelchair, and he sits at that table with a couple of Mexican guys.' You thank Hal for this recommendation.

The bell rings, and the students who are still eating gulp down their food, take their trays to the dumping area, and leave, soon to be replaced by the next hungry crowd of students.

By the end of lunch, you are more puzzled than anything else. Is what you just witnessed characteristic of the total school program? Is this school a model of multicultural and mainstreamed education? Does this mixing indicate a genuine appreciation and affirmation of human diversity? Or, is it just happening today — will tomorrow be more consistent with the findings of other studies of student social systems? Perhaps these students are like a boiling pot with the lid on: the appearance of harmony is there, but the slightest incident could trigger an explosion.

This chapter responds to these questions. It reports the kinds of relationships Five Bridges students formed with each other across race, sex and handicap lines. It also describes and discusses the ways in which the students viewed these human differences, plus other differences they recognized among themselves. It focuses on how the students viewed their own diversity, but it also offers a glimpse at how they viewed themselves in an unequal social system that is stratified based on race, sex, class and handicap.

The data for this chapter are based on interviews with and observations of a sample of fifty students. They were equally divided between girls and boys; they included students who were Asian, black, Egyptian, Mexican American, Native American, Puerto Rican, white, and mixed Mexican/white. In addition, they included students who were physically impaired, and learning disabled and/or emotionally disturbed. This sample was selected during lunch, since virtually all the students were in the lunchroom then and could potentially be selected as interviewees. We randomly picked groups of students eating lunch, and sat with them while they ate and talked. On this basis, we selected students who were willing to talk with us for series of in-depth interviews. These were not the only students we observed and talked with, however. In classrooms we observed the entire class, and frequently chatted informally with other students in order to check our emerging findings.

Kinds of Friends

As our trip through the lunchroom illustrated, there was friendly mixing among the students. How intimate were interracial friendships? Friendships between handicapped and non-handicapped students? What kinds of friendships did girls and boys form? Before answering these questions, we will explain how friendships at Five Bridges were classified. There is a difference between choosing a person as a best friend, and choosing that person as one of many acquaintances. The students talked about five different kinds of friendships: best friends, friends one does many things with, friends one does some things with, girl/boyfriends, and non-romantic girl/boy friends.[2] We will describe each of these kinds of friends briefly so that the degree of intimacy in students' intergroup friendships is clear.

Three kinds of friendships were with members of the same sex. These included a best friend, friends one does many things with, and friends one does some things with. Distinctions among these three kinds of friends depended on two factors: the level of trust and intimacy between two individuals, and the number of things one does or the amount of time one spends with that individual. Some students spoke of one particular person they trusted most or got along with best — this person was termed 'best friend'. Only about half of the students named a best friend. The best friend plus the friends one does many things with will be referred to as 'close friends'. Students also named friends they saw in school only, at home only, in sports only, etc.; these are designated as 'friends one does some things with'.

Two kinds of cross-sex friendships mentioned by students were girl/boyfriends and non-romantic friends. Non-romantic friends typically included members of the opposite sex that the student had known for a long time and talked to in school, but did not date.

Several students did not name any friends in one or two of the categories. For example, some students who had many acquaintances at school had few or no close friends. Conversely, a few students talked extensively about two or three close friends they saw constantly, but mentioned no one else. Several students said that they were not yet interested in the opposite sex, so all their friendships were with members of the same sex.

Student Cultural Knowledge

As shown in the opening tour, the students' lunchroom conversations revolved around what they were going to do that night or that weekend, sports, the opposite sex, food and upcoming events in the school. Within the context of these discussions, topics relating to the students' own diversity sometimes arose. For example, the girls and boys discussed their latest romantic interests partly in terms of physical appearance, which is in part racially determined (for example, Laura's blond hair). Their discussions also reflected criteria for evaluating members of the opposite sex (for example, hair color, body build). Sometimes their discussions included physical impairment; for instance, Yvonne discussed dancing as it related to both students who could stand and those in wheelchairs.

Most of the students did not directly talk about human diversity as a topic in and of itself. Yet, because they were a diverse student population, they had some beliefs and perceptions about diversity that helped them make sense of each other. All the students, as they talked about life at Five Bridges, referred to human characteristics that served as symbols of meaning to them. A human characteristic becomes a symbol when meaning is attached to it that transcends individual cases. For example, hair color is a symbol to a person in whose view blonds, brunettes, and redheads are distinctly different categories of people sharing certain characteristics (for example, blonds have more fun). Some of the symbols used by Five Bridges students were related to race, handicap, gender and social class; others were not.

Let us now look closely at the kinds of friendships students formed across race, handicap and sex lines, and at their cultural knowledge about race, handicap, gender, social class and other differences they considered important.

Race

Earlier we questioned the depth and durability of the interracial interactions we observed in the lunchrooms. Were the students merely being polite to one another because they were in the same room together, or did they form friendships that extended beyond the boundaries of the lunchroom and the school?

Before examining students' interracial friendships, we should point out that the students saw Mexicans as being a racial group distinct from whites. Most of the Mexican and Puerto Rican students at Five Bridges had black or dark brown hair and light brown skin. They referred to any student of this description as 'Mexican', and as a member of a particular racial group, unless they knew that student was not Mexican (usually such a student was Native American or Puerto Rican). The Puerto Rican students saw themselves as being related to but not the same as Mexicans. Broadly speaking they classified themselves as Hispanics or Latinos, distinct racially from whites, but further distinguished their own ethnicity. Students also recognized Native Americans as a distinct racial group, as well as blacks and Asians (who were often called 'Chinese' or 'Japanese' regardless of their actual ethnicity).

Friendship Patterns

As mentioned, the most intimate friendship formed by students with members of their same sex was the best friend. Half of the students talked about a best friend; of these, two-thirds of the best friendships were interracial. Who were some of these interracial pairs? Bill (Native American) and Ricky (white) named each other as best friends. They were neighbors and had known each other several years; they also had some classes together, so they were in each others' company several hours every day. Sue's (white) best friend was Lisa (Mexican); although they lived quite a distance from each other, they first became close in school. Now they not only spent time together in school, but also visited each other's houses and did things together on weekends. Carlos (Mexican) named Alvin (black) as his best friend. As two of the school leaders, they shared many interests and tastes; they visited each other's homes, double dated and were on sports teams together. Rakia (Egyptian) named Tracy (Italian/Native American) as her best friend. They played together after school, went shopping on weekends and were planning a summer trip to visit Tracy's relatives in California.

We asked the students who their close friends were and what race they were—who they 'hung around with' both in and outside school. Three-quarters of the students named close friends of more than one race. Figure 1 illustrates the racial composition of a few of the students' friendship sets.

Figure 1: Racial composition of friendship sets

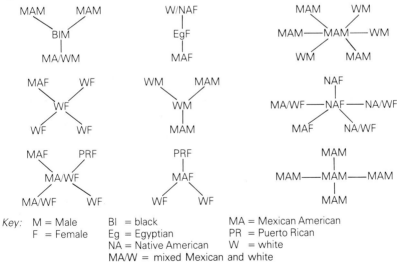

Key: M = Male   BI = black   MA = Mexican American
      F = Female   Eg = Egyptian   PR = Puerto Rican
                 NA = Native American   W = white
                 MA/W = mixed Mexican and white

A third kind of intimate relationship is the romantic girl/boyfriend. Studies of adolescent dating have noted interracial dating to be relatively rare (for example, Petroni, 1971; Porterfield, 1978; Schofield, 1983; Stuart and Abt, 1973). To find out how much interracial mixing there was at Five Bridges in romantic girl/boyfriends, we asked students who their girl/boyfriends were. Fifty per cent of the pairs students named were interracial. Hispanic male white female was the most common pairing. This was followed closely by all-white pairs, and all-Hispanic pairs. Assorted other combinations were also named. We noted that the relatively small numbers of black, Native American, and Asian students made it impossible for a large number of pairs to include members of these groups, although members of these groups did engage in interracial dating. We also discovered that many of the white boys had not begun to date yet, although most of those who did date had dated more than one race.

Thus, it appears that the students in the lunchroom were not interacting just because they were in the same room together. Their interracial interactions reflected close interracial friendships that they had formed with each other. If their behavior demonstrated close bonding across racial lines, how did the students actually perceive and think about race?

Race (Skin Color) as a Symbol of Meaning

We all attach some symbolic meaning to skin color. It symbolizes particular racial stereotypes for some, power and status for others, and to still others it symbolizes beauty. What did skin color symbolize to these students?

The students at Five Bridges overwhelmingly believed that a mixture of colors of people was interesting; it symbolized harmony, and having fun. For many, this symbol had sufficient salience to be mentioned spontaneously when the kids at school, one's friends, the community, and the social structure of the school were described. For example,

> R^3: Tell me about the different kinds of kids at Five Bridges.
> *Juan (Mexican):* There are a lot of different kids at Five Bridges. There are a lot of different races, Mexicans, blacks, Chinese — and we all get along good. One person is not singled out from another and everybody is welcome.

Several students said that being with a mixture of races was more interesting than they thought being with one race only would be. For instance:

Gayle (white): In our [neighborhood] we have all different [races], we've got Mexicans, Chinese and whites; we have them all.

R: What difference would it make if there were more whites living someplace than more different colors living someplace?

Gayle: It seems like when we all get together we think of different things to do. We don't do the same thing everyday.

Two Five Bridges students talked about joking with each other about their racial backgrounds. For example:

Hal (white): In our gang we have a black, Mexican, and we're gonna have a Korean. None of my friends are prejudiced here.

R: Do you guys joke around about what color you are very much?

Hal: Yeah. Kenny is always calling me 'carrot top' and stuff, and I'll call him an 'imported African' or something. We just goof around. Mike, sometimes I'll start calling him a 'teepee liver' or something like that. No one means it, we just goof around. Like Pat, he's Canadian, and we call him 'bacon lips.'

Of the students interviewed, only one was hesitant about accepting this symbolic meaning of mixed colors. While he spoke about Five Bridges students getting along, he also said that if fights result from racial mixing, it should not be attempted.

The views on color of upper bluff and lower bluff students were compared. Since the upper bluff was less racially mixed than the lower bluff, the researchers wondered if there would be a difference in the way students viewed mixed colors. There was not. No matter what neighborhood they lived in, with the exception of one sample student who lived in the upper bluff, students shared common cultural knowledge about the symbolic meaning of mixed colors.

For some students, a particular color symbolized the kind of girl or boy they were most interested in dating. For example, Pam (white) and Grace (Mexican) commented very positively that the neat guys were usually Mexicans, but qualified this by noting that personality counted more than color. Robin (Native American) said she had dated mostly whites, but any color was okay. Delia (Asian) noted that 'black guys are kind'. 'the guys with the blond hair are stupid', and 'some of the Mexicans here like girls to look at them'. Three students (two black and one Egyptian) commented that black girls at Five Bridges seemed to prefer Mexicans and whites, although a fourth (Mexican) believed blacks prefer blacks. Doug (white) preferred white girls, and Carlos (Mexican) preferred blonds, although he had had girlfriends of several different colors.

Though there was disagreement over which if any color was most preferred, there was high agreement that one should be able to choose a girl/boyfriend without regard to color. The following exemplified the perception of all but a small minority of the sample students:

> *R:* Is there mixed dating in this school? Do boys, black boys, go out with white girls, or Hispanic girls, or —
> *Alvin (black):* Yeah.
> *R:* How do people take that, is that accepted?
> *Alvin:* Yeah, they go out with all kinds of colors.
> *R:* What do you think about that?
> *Alvin:* I think it's pretty bad.
> *R:* You like it or dislike it?
> *Alvin:* I like it.
> *R:* Why?
> *Alvin:* 'Cause I get to — I went out with all colors: black, Mexican, and white.

The belief that one should be able to have girl/boyfriends of any color was so accepted among the students that two new students commented that they had changed their minds about color and dating. For example, Frances (black) talked about her changed perception:

> *R:* Are you going to date just black boys, or what?
> *Frances:* Nope. I'm not just gonna date black ones.
> *R:* Are you going to date just who you want to?
> *Frances:* Yeah, regardless of race.
> *R:* How long have you been thinking like that?
> *Frances:* Since I already came here. . . . I guess cause when I was in Chicago I didn't think about anything else because I was only with black boys, that's all I was really with when we lived in Chicago. But in this school you've got all the different kinds of races, it's not only black, it's four or five different ones.

Only one sample student said that cross-sex relationships should be between people of the same color:

> *Greg (white):* I still think that the white people should stay with the white people and the black with the black and the Mexican with the Mexican. I don't think that we should get all scrambled

up and stuff. If they really *want* to be, I don't care —

R: Why? What reasons?

Greg: I don't know, it really doesn't look right. Like a black guy and a white lady. It really doesn't look right, does it? Do you think it does?

We were struck that all but a few students we talked to were very positive about racial diversity. They enjoyed their diversity. They did not ignore it, they were not blind to it — they joked about it and talked about it in very friendly ways.

This did not mean, however, that Five Bridges' students did not have stereotypes for some racial groups; a few students did. Although most students stressed the importance of getting to know individuals and disregarding color, four of our sample students said they saw being black as symbolic of certain traits and two mentioned stereotypes for Asians. For example:

Anna (Mexican):   Blacks sometimes treat people mean.

Hal (white):   Mostly black people always hold grudges against white people.

Kristen (white):   Some people don't like them [Asian people] because they think they eat like dogs. People always say they're going to come and get your dog and eat them.

Carmen (Puerto Rican):   They're [Asians] kind of weird. I don't know them, that's why.... They're really shy and quiet. I'm kind of scared to go up and say hi.

Furthermore, Delia (Asian) mentioned that some people in her neighborhood avoided her and her Cambodian neighbors. Since South-east Asians were newcomers to the area, these biases were just beginning to surface. Whether many students actually believed stereotypes about Asians was difficult to assess at this time. But while a few students believed a few racial stereotypes, most did not stereotype blacks, Hispanics, Native Americans and whites, and overtly rejected stereotypes voiced by others (such as parents or the media).

We were interested in learning how the students viewed race outside of personal interactions. In particular, we wondered how much attention they paid to the historic traditions of their different racial groups, to the issue of status among racial groups, and to race relations in society. Probing these areas gave us insight into the sense students made of race in this society, and of their own location in a racist social structure.

About one-fifth of the sample students very clearly associated race with cultural traditions. They were aware of the many components to a cultural tradition, and were interested in learning about their own traditions as well as those of other groups. For example, Rakia is Egyptian; she is Moslem and bilingual. During interviews she frequently referred to both her own and others' cultural backgrounds.

> *R:* You said that Sara was Mexican and German: how do you know she is?
>
> *Rakia:* I asked her because she looks Mexican. I've seen her dad and he wasn't Mexican and her mom is Mexican. I asked her if her dad was German and she said yes.
>
> *R:* How important do you think a person's background is?
>
> *Rakia:* It's important.
>
> *R:* Do you intend to pass down your Egyptian background to your kids?
>
> *Rakia:* Yes.

> *R:* Do you feel you have learned about different cultures being here?
>
> *Rakia:* I learned about Catholics and their religion and I learned about the Philippines. Do you know Delia? I talk to her and she tells me about her country and everything. . . .
>
> *R:* Give me an example.
>
> *Rakia:* Like, they say they take communion. They told me about it because I didn't know what they meant. Now I know what it means.

Juan's mother was white and his father was Mexican. He had made an effort to learn about both his Mexican and his white heritage. For example:

> *R:* How much do you feel you know about the Mexican culture?
>
> *Juan:* Probably more than expected because my dad is Mexican and a lot of the people I go to school with have families that speak Spanish. They want to keep the Spanish culture in their home. So I think I know a little more than what is expected.
>
> *R:* What do you think is expected of you?
>
> *Juan:* Like, the language. I think my dad and my grandma think

that I should know a little about the language and a little about
the people that are important in Mexico. Like when I come in
and I know that a certain city was completely demolished in a
certain year, they are really surprised.

Juan was also somewhat curious about other cultures. He talked about
aspects of black culture learned from Alvin, one of his close friends:

> *Juan:* Like they use different English from us. They have diffe-
> rent names for different things. Like when me and Carlos talk,
> we say something in Spanish and Alvin will say something the
> way he says it. Carlos can come up to me and say something in
> Spanish and I'll know what he's talking about. Alvin could
> come up to me and say the same thing Carlos said, but the way
> he usually says it, maybe the way he picked it up from the place
> he lived before, I won't understand what he's saying. Then, like
> I know some of the foods, like they like to eat chitlins and stuff
> like that. Alvin likes that stuff. I know that I've tried it. I've
> tried grits and everything and it's good. In ways of food and
> family life I know what it's like. When it comes to language I'm
> lost.

Half of the students expressed only mild interest or curiosity in
cultural traditions. And in this area they expressed greatest awareness
of language and food. During an interview, Larry (Mexican) only discussed the Spanish language when comparing Texas with his own state;
he saw no need to learn more about the Mexican culture than that
which he required to function in Rivercrest.

> *Larry:* Down in Texas everybody practically speaks Mexican or
> Spanish because it is one of the states that they do it in. That is
> where most of them [Mexicans] live. Most everybody speaks
> Spanish there. My dad and my mon speak Spanish because that
> is where they came from but nobody else in my family does
> because we were all born right here.

The rest of the students did not seem aware of or interested in
cultural traditions of different racial groups. When asked about cultural differences among racial groups, the following responses were
typical:

> *R:* Why are [Mexican kids] similar to you?
> *Pam (white):* Lisa, I know from her they don't eat the Mexican
> meals. They just eat ours and that. And they just act the same.

35

> *R:* Do you learn very much about Mexican kids from Mexican friends?
>
> *Robin (Native American):* I don't really pay attention.
>
> *R:* Do you feel they learn very much about Indian kids or maybe about the Chippewa culture when they are at your house?
>
> *Robin:* I don't think so. We're just like everybody else. We don't do what the original Indians do like dress up in Indian clothes.

Most students assumed that the norms, values, and daily practices in Rivercrest were 'the' culture. They were not concerned with the life styles their predecessors brought to this country and fought to maintain. They recognized and accepted variations in some cultural items such as language and food, but otherwise seemed uninterested in culture and lacked knowledge about it.

Cultural interest is not automatic when different racial groups mix. In fact, we wonder if the cultural homogeneity among the students, despite diverse racial backgrounds, may obscure the fact that different groups historically have defined diverse world views and systems of values. Lacking knowledge of their own heritage, the students were unaware of what they would lose by failing to keep that heritage alive.

Race can symbolize status. Given that the races are not equal in status in the larger society, one might expect to find race symbolic of status in a student social system. But, when asked if any racial group ran things in school or was most popular, only one student (the student body President, who was Mexican) named Mexicans; the rest of the students stated that no color ran things or was most popular. In fact, when asked, 'How would you define racism in society?' some students responded in terms of their views on status among racial groups:

> *Kristen (white):* Do you mean when different colors are fighting?
>
> *R:* Or like white people basically running things.
>
> *Kristen:* I don't like that. Everyone is always equal here.

> *Hal (white):* I don't know what you mean. Do you mean discrimination against other people?
>
> *R:* Not just on a person-to-person basis, but like one racial group having more opportunity, more money, more power.
>
> *Hal:* I don't think that should be, I think they should be equal.

When asked they perceived race relations in society at large, most students demonstrated relatively little knowledge about it outside their neighborhood. They talked about racial tension in specific places or involving a specific racial group, but did not articulate a general picture of race relations in society as a whole.

> R: How about if you went to another state, ... would you expect to see people who are different colors getting along the same as they do here?
>
> Hal (white): I don't think there would be much difference. Unless it was mostly a black state or Mexican or something like that, then there might be some problem. If I moved to another place like New York, I don't really think so....

Only one-sixth of the sample students said they perceived race relations in Rivercrest as exceptional rather than typical of race relations in society in general. They discussed race relations in the following ways:

> Lupe (Mexican): Everywhere you go you'll find prejudice. If you stay in Rivercrest you won't. My brother has experienced it and he's really prejudiced now because of what they did to him in Michigan.

> Robin (Native American): I don't think it's the same. I don't think they get along very well.
>
> R: How do you know?
>
> Robin: I don't but that's what I think.... I heard in one school there was blacks against whites. They don't get along.

Some students associated racial tension with older generations only. For instance:

> Kristen (white): [My parents] don't care if I have friends, they just don't want me to go out with different colors. Like they don't want me to go out with a black person or marry a black person. It's just the way they grew up, and the way I've grown up is different. The world is changing.

But most students believed that the racial harmony of Rivercrest was typical. They were unaware or never verbally indicated that the society they were living in had racial problems. How would these problems affect their lives? To what extent would they develop the analytical skills necessary for dealing with the problems associated with with race in the larger society?

Handicap

During the lunchroom tour you noticed handicapped students were part of the crowd; you also noticed some communication between non-handicapped and handicapped students. What kinds of relationships did handicapped and non-handicapped students at Five Bridges form with one another, and what did handicap symbolize to each of these groups?

We asked some learning disabled and physically impaired students to tell us about their friends. Their friendship sets followed a variety of patterns. For example, two LD students, Ricky and Bill, talked about doing things with each other, although each named a long list of other LD and non-LD friends and both seemed to lead fairly active social lives. Larry (LD) had a network of friends typical of many non-handicapped students in the school. He talked comfortably about other non-LD boys he knew, the non-LD boy who was his best friend and why, and a girlfriend he had had for a few months. Hugh (LD), on the other hand, had few friends. He was noticeably vague and uncomfortable when asked about his social life, and sometimes responded with inappropriate answers that seemed to serve the purpose of getting attention. He brooded during one interview over a lost girlfriend, but was vague about things they had done together at an earlier time or what happened to her.

Ruth was a cerebral palsy student in a wheelchair. Three of her friends were physically impaired students with whom she had attended school for years. She also had a few non-handicapped friends, such as Yvonne, whom she talked to in school. The only friend she saw at home was a non-handicapped girl in her neighborhood, but Ruth reported that this girl was younger than she, and their interests were divergent — 'She still plays with dolls!'.

Phil also had cerebral palsy, although he could walk. His closest friend was another physically impaired student who walked similarly to him. Phil interacted comfortably with both handicapped and non-handicapped students, but he preferred talking with adults. One could classify him as a loner — 'I drift in and out of groups' — yet this seemed to be due more to Phil's preference than to his own lack of social skills.

Doug was paralyzed from the waist down and in a wheelchair; he had many friends of both sexes, none of whom were physically impaired. In fact, Doug avoided other physically impaired students. Although he lived across town, he regularly spent much of his out-of-school time in Rivercrest with his friends, often sleeping over at Hal's home.

While there was no visible tension between mildly learning handicapped and other students, there was tension between physically impaired and non-impaired students, especially at the beginning of the study. On occasion, mean pranks were pulled against wheelchair students (physically impaired students who could walk were rarely the target of these pranks). Some non-impaired students called wheelchair students names as they went down the hall, and on occasion sneaked up behind them grabbing their wheelchairs. One non-impaired student pointed out that some people teased those in wheelchairs because they thought they were helpless, and were often surprised when the victim chased his/her assailant down the hall in the wheelchair. However, since the implementation of the mainstreaming program, the number of pranks decreased considerably, and as Phil aptly remarked at the time of this study relationships between the two groups were 'cordial'.

Handicap as a Symbol of Meaning

Before examining handicap as a symbol of meaning, we would like to share the students' feelings about mainstreaming physically impaired students. When asked how they felt about going to a school that has handicapped students, a few students said they were very pleased that physically impaired students were in their classes. The following comment is illustrative:

> *Sharon:* I think they should be in our school. I don't think they should be put into a separate school.

The majority of the students did not have strong feelings one way or the other. The following responses were typical:

> *Juan:* It didn't really bother me or affect me.

> *Carlos:* I don't mind. I just mind my own business, they are there to learn, too.

A few students expressed some reservation about having physically impaired students in the school. For example:

> *Shirley:* Well, I don't mind them in my classes, but I'll tell you what really gets to me though is in lunch, because I just like to

sit a couple tables away from the handicapped and I always sit towards the front where the handicaps are, and sometimes when I watch them eat, I just get sick. Because they spit it out and yuck.

Greg: It felt kind of weird seeing people going down the hallways in wheelchairs. It was a change.

None of the students voiced a strong objection to having physically impaired students in the school.

When the physically impaired students were asked how they felt about being mainstreamed, they unanimously expressed positive opinions about it.

Ruth: I like it better. I used to know only handicapped kids and I like it better to know other kids because I make friends really easy, but if there is nobody to make friends with, you can't.

Elaine: It's pretty good, really.
R: Why?
Elaine: Well, for one thing, Ruth and I and Ellen came over here and half of the time the kids are pretty decent.

Phil: I'm pretty much treated like everyone else. It's not even an effort to interact with me, it's just done.

As an oppressed group, the handicapped have historically been closeted away unless as individuals they could survive in 'normal society'. Making the school barrier-free represented a change in what was considered normal. The handicapped students we interviewed had been conscious of their oppressed status, and were enthusiastic about being allowed to join their non-impaired peers at school. Some of their peers shared their enthusiasm, feeling that seclusion of handicapped people was wrong. Others were more tentative — they were willing to accept the handicapped as long as it did not disrupt the world they saw as normal.

How, then, did they see diversity based on wheelchairs, limps, and assignment to special classes? Surely not in the same way as they embraced racial diversity, since to them the world was normal when it was inhabited by different racial groups — they were not tentative about racial integration.

Most non-impaired students did not mention handicapped or

physically impaired students unless directly asked about them. This could suggest that most did not think about handicap. However, when asked, the students articulated rather definite perceptions of the physically impaired.

Most non-impaired students divided their physically impaired peers into two categories, which they called 'handicaps' and 'normal'. A 'handicap' was described as being 'like us', but limited in one or more ways (although as students got to know handicapped peers, their perceptions changed). The limitations mentioned included:

1 Inability to talk

R: How would you define being handicapped?

Richard: Well, like some people not being able to talk, or not being able to wheel themselves around.

R: Have you gotten to know more about handicapped people here?

Kristen: Yes, when I was in sixth grade I didn't know anyone and I thought they were different, they weren't real people or anything like that. I didn't think they could talk normal. But they're just like normal people.

2 Not intelligent

Becky: Like, Bruce, I have him in science right now, and he was only in three weeks, and they took him out. And we asked the teacher why he got tooken out, and she said, he knows more than you guys. You can imagine how I felt, you know, how dumb do you think I am?

R: I guess ... that you were surprised that he was smarter.

Anita: I almost thought that handicaps wouldn't be as smart because they're handicapped. But now that they're here in my own school, I find out that they can be even smarter.

3 Not sociable

Hal: They keep to theirselves, they don't talk to nobody, they say you keep to yourself and I'll keep to mine, and that's how all of them are.

Carmen: They just want to live in their own little world. They just don't want to meet anybody.... It seems to me like they have their own friends and so I stick with mine.

4 *Want extra attention and privileges*

Maria: Them handicaps aren't fair because let's say you're walking down the hall and they just hit you and run you down and then say, 'Well, stay out of the way', like they're perfect. And some of them ditch class, like Mary, she never went to class and she never got in trouble for it just because she is a handicap.

Gayle: At first it seemed like they got their own way with the teachers, but after you think about it they need the extra attention.

5 *Need help, need friends*

R: How did you get interested in trying to understand handicapped kids?

Jo Ella: They needed a friend. Like if I see someone getting beat up I can't help, but I get a warm feeling towards them and I have to be their friend.

R: Why did you pick the [school service job] you picked [aide in physical education class for the physically impaired]?

Hugh: I like the kids and the teacher. I just like helping out the handicapped.

6 *Can't engage in physical activities kids enjoy*

Pam: They can't really go outside because you know if they go down to Rivercrest and they have to run for some reason, they ain't gonna be able to make it, you know, so it's better off if you know they hang around by theirselves and they ain't gonna get hurt that way because they're with each other. And you can't hang around with the ones in a wheelchair 'cause they can't go nowhere. In school you know they got to go down in the elevators. You can't walk with them in the halls and it's hard to be a friend with them if you never see them 'cause they're always in the back halls or you know in the elevators.

Juan: They're no different than anybody else. It's just that they can't do as much as we can.

R: When you say they can't do as much as you can, what do you mean?

Juan: Like they can't play sports.

It is important to note that much of the knowledge non-impaired students had about their physically impaired peers was inaccurate. It seemed to be formulated on the basis of casual observation and possibly stereotypes learned elsewhere. But as long as students accepted their inaccurate beliefs, their own conception of what normal people are like could remain intact, and their tendency to ignore the handicapped gained legitimacy. The two groups could coexist in the same building without understanding each other.

A few non-impaired students had physically impaired friends. In contrast to the majority of their peers who viewed the handicapped as people 'like us but who can't ...', these students did not see physical impairment as symbolizing anything in particular. Yvonne was an example of such a student:

R: In the school you have a number of handicapped kids; what do you think about those kids?

Yvonne: I think they're just people.

R: Do you have any friends among these kids?

Yvonne: Yeah. Two girls in a wheelchair and one who can walk. They wanted me to work with them. All of them know me because I was at their party for the handicapped. I danced with them in their chairs and stuff. It's a lot of fun being around them. They're no different than anybody else.

Yvonne's conception of what normal people are like was broader than that of most of her peers. To her being human did not depend on one's ability to walk or perform fine motor movements: not only did normal people come in different colors, they came with different physical conditions.

Three physically impaired students were widely classified by their non-impaired peers as normal, since the symbolic meaning for 'handicapped' did not fit them. How were these students viewed, and what diferentiated them from other physically impaired students? Doug avoided associating himself with other physically impaired students, and overtly tried to be like the 'regular' kids. For example, he went to the skating rink with everyone else on Friday nights. His peers described him thus:

> *Richard:* I wouldn't really call him handicapped. He gets around. He's like everyone else.

> *Hal:* He's not really handicapped. He's not crippled or nothing. But it's just his legs are dead.

Fannie (physically impaired and EMR) walked awkwardly, but got around the building. She was usually smiling at people. In the interviews, students commonly mentioned that 'everyone' knew her, and several said that they talked to her on the phone. As two students described her:

> *Hal:* Do you know Fannie? She talks to everybody and she socializes with people and stuff.

> *Ricky:* She just got back from surgery. She's nice, she always chases me in Mrs. Smith's room every morning.

Phil considered himself intellectually superior to his age-mates, but made an effort to blend in with them — whether physically impaired or not — while at school. In fact, he had a talent for talking about whatever anyone was interested in, gearing his language and sense of humor to the level of sophistication of those around him.

Thus, being physically impaired was only part of the definition of 'handicapped'; a person could be physically impaired and still not be seen as handicapped. It seems those physically impaired students who escaped classification as 'handicaps' were the most socially outgoing, suggesting that students saw social skill as a necessary component of normal humanity. Furthermore, the most socially assertive students were best equipped to 'prove' they were normal human beings, since the burden was on them to establish their common humanity.

The physically impaired students had quite diverse perspectives, however, about what it means to be 'handicapped'. Ruth had cerebral palsy; she had been in a wheelchair all her life. To her, handicapped meant struggling to learn to walk. Phil viewed having learned to walk as a hurdle he had mastered, and a larger hurdle than most other people his age have faced. Although his walk was awkward and he lacked some fine motor coordination, he did not see himself as handicapped.

> *Phil:* It doesn't impair me, I can do anything I put my mind to.
> *R:* Then it doesn't seem to be too much of a handicap.

Phil: You're only as handicapped as you decide you are.

Doug accepted much of the stereotype his able-bodied peers had of 'handicaps', but differentiated himself from handicapped kids:

Doug: Some people think handicapped people are kind of screwed up, and if you hang around with them you are too in a way....

R: You say that being with the handicapped kids embarrasses you.

Doug: Sometimes. I would never hang around with them. I would never call them up ... I think of myself as normal.

The physically impaired students had somewhat different perceptions of non-impaired kids. Ruth and Elaine categorized non-impaired students as either nice or mean, and felt that the student body was split about equally between these two categories. However, they described 'mean' students as being mean to most of their peers, not only to students in wheelchairs.

Ruth: They make snide remarks at me. They make them at everybody, really.

Ruth: Sometimes the boys tease you, but I'm getting used to that. It used to really bug me....

R: So the girls don't tease you. How do the girls act?

Ruth: They are usually pretty helpful if you need help.

Elaine: Except for the rowdy ones. They don't care about anyone.

Ruth and Elaine also saw 'mean' students as sometimes being nosy:

Ruth: They don't ask really about cerebral palsy, they ask, like, how do we get dressed, and do your mom and dad help you get dressed, or how do you go to the bathroom.

Elaine: That's the favorite one.

R: How do you feel when they ask those kinds of questions?

Elaine: It's like they're being nosy.

Ruth: But they really aren't because they don't know. Usually I just explain it.

Elaine: Some of them are trying to be nosy.

Thus, Ruth and Elaine saw their world dominated by equal numbers of nice, concerned non-impaired people, and mean, ignorant non-impaired people. They clearly did feel subordinated to the non-impaired world: they spent considerable time discussing the social structure in us–them terms.

Phil had many non-impaired friends and generally believed the students at Five Bridges were nice, but he also pointed out that 'they complain a lot about the wheelchair people running them over'. Unlike Ruth and Elaine, Phil did not describe his non-impaired peers in terms of their behavior toward him as a handicapped student. Neither did Doug, who thought of regular kids as his friends. Although he did not like a few regular 'smart alecks', he felt very positively toward non-impaired students, especially those who were popular. Since both Phil and Doug were seen as normal, they did not see themselves as members of an oppressed group in the school, and did not describe non-impaired students as oppressors. However, both were aware that handicapped students were an oppressed group — they had simply escaped classification as members of that group.

When asked to describe other kids at Five Bridges, physically impaired students — including Phil and Doug — were the only ones to differentiate between handicapped and non-handicapped before making further distinctions. Regular students did not mention the handicapped at all as a kind of 'other kid' unless they happened to be friends with them. This suggests that physically impaired students perceived the social structure of the school in a rather different way from non-impaired students. Their own handicap was very salient to them and defined their place in the social structure.

Earlier it was noted that academic or mental difficulties are often ridiculed by students. Did membership in a special education class or the labels LD, ED or EMR symbolize anything to the students at Five Bridges?

Of the non-special education students only a few were heard to refer to academic slowness in a derogatory way. For example, one student used the term 'mental' to describe a person who acted strange, in her opinion. Another commented that LD students were slow and therefore she would not want to be in that class, although she did not mind it if her friends were LD. Most of the students either did not know what the special education classes were, or if they knew, considered them part of the 'normal' course offerings. When asked what they thought about LD, ED or EMR kids, the following comments were typical:

> *Kristen:* I don't know, it's just like normal. It's just that they need more help.

Hal: Who are they?

R: Mrs. Smith's class.

Hal: I don't know.... I don't know nothing about them. In school the only thing that I worry about is my grades. Just as long as I pass.

Comments by LD students coincided with these perceptions:

R: Nobody put you down or said anything about it during the time you were in LD?

Larry: They just asked me what I was doing in there.

R: How do you like being in LD?

Ricky: It's fun.

R: Why is it fun?

Ricky: Because they have the right teachers for it.

R: Do kids ever make fun of you or anything for being in LD?

Ricky: No.

R: How do you feel about being in LD?

Hugh: Pretty good. I'm getting good grades out of it. It's a nice class. The teacher is really nice. I have some friends going there.

R: Does anyone ever tease you about being in LD?

Hugh: No.

Being in a special education class for academic reasons held no importance for Five 'Bridges' students, other than the fact that the academic work of special education students differed from that of their peers. This feeling was summed up nicely by one student:

R: Do you see them as different from the other kids?

Anna: During school, yeah, but out of school, no. You're sitting there talking to all your friends about your work and they come with their work. But out of school we don't talk about work, we talk about sports and all that.

Thus, while visible impairments were invested with some symbolic meaning that legitimated an unequal social structure, non-visible academic difficulties were not. To the students it was normal that different people learned academic material with different degrees of competence. This suggests that they did not see academic skill as having a distinct or a valued pay-off. They did not see academic ability as a basis for inequality in their own social system or elsewhere.

Gender

In the lunchroom the boys and girls sat at different tables. To what extent did they segregate by sex in their daily life in and out of school? What kinds of cross-sex friendships did the students form with one another, and how did they perceive gender and sex differences?

Friendship Patterns

The students segregated by sex in school whenever given the opportunity to decide where to sit or with whom to work. But, even though students tended to sit with members of their own sex, they did not ignore the opposite sex. In class, in the lunchroom, in the halls, and after school, boys and girls talked, flirted and called each other on the telephone. We asked the students to specify who their cross-sex friends were, and to describe the nature of those relationships.

The majority of cross-sex friendships were romantic in nature. About three-quarters of the students named a girl/boyfriend. In some cases, this was the person they dated; in others, the girl/boyfriend was someone 'I like', but did not necessarily see outside school, or someone 'I walk around with after school'.

Only one-third of the students mentioned cross-sex peers with whom they had close but not romantic ties. Of those, half (both boys and girls) said little about this/these person(s), and specified that this person was *only* a friend. The other half (all girls) referred to groups of boys in their grade who they had known a long time, with whom they did things and enjoyed talking. These girls often selected boyfriends from this group.

Thus, it appears that Five Bridges students were not radically different from students reported in other studies when it came to cross-sex mixing. Their close friendship ties were primarily with members of their own sex, and most cross-sex ties were romantic in nature. Non-romantic boy-girl friendships tended to be with peers the individuals had grown up with and probably saw as sister-like or brother-like figures.

Gender as a Symbol of Meaning

The symbolic meanings attached to gender have generally related to psychological and physical characteristics, what is expected of people, and what they have an opportunity to do. What symbolic meanings did the Five Bridges students attach to gender?

A substantial majority of the students interviewed said they believed in equal opportunity for both sexes. When asked if boys and girls should have an equal opportunity to do the same things, most students of both sexes agreed they should:

> *Bill:* Boys and girls should do the same things, like if boys do something they shouldn't say that girls can't.

> *Frances:* Yeah, like grocery shopping and ironing and washing.

Since most of the students verbalized a belief in equal opportunity for both sexes, it would seem that gender symbolized little to them in terms of social roles and expectations. Some prodding revealed this not to be the case. In the context of talking about things such as jobs, sports, grades, household chores and dating, many students verbalized roles and expectations that gender symbolized to them.

Several students talked about characteristics and abilities of boys and girls. About half of the students (including both male and female students) believed physical strength and skill in sports were characteristic of the male sex. For example, when asked, 'What does it take to be considered masculine?' some of these students responded in terms of physical fitness and athletic ability, such as:

> *Carlos:* I guess you have to be big. You have to be good in sports and school.

In talking about sports, some also said that boys had more general ability than girls.

However, not all students believed boys are necessarily superior in sports, and some spontaneously voiced their belief that either sex can excel in sports and in strength. For example:

> *Larry:* Girls can do anything they want. I know some girls that can do a lot better than boys in sports. Some boys get mad because girls embarrass them when they are better.

> *Carmen:* My brother thinks that I am really weak but then he couldn't move the couch and I changed the whole living room by myself and he said he was really surprised.

A few students mentioned what they believed were characteristics of the female sex. Being female meant concern for looks and dress, cooking and smartness. They remarked in this way:

R: What does it take to be a real feminine girl?

Carmen: I don't know. Like wear dresses and keep your hair real nice.

R: Are there some things you think girls can do better than boys?

Tony: Cook, girl stuff.

R: Are there some things you think girls can do better than boys?

Juan: I think girls are even smarter than boys.

There were also several students for whom gender symbolized no particular abilities or traits. As two boys put it:

R: What do you think it takes to be really masculine?

Ricky: Just to be yourself.

R: So any guy is masculine.

Ricky: Yeah.

R: How about feminine?

Ricky: If they be theirselves. That's all you have to do.

Phil: You don't have to do anything special to be feminine. That does not consist of doing a certain activity for a certain amount of time.... There's not much difference in purpose here between the men and the women.

R: What do you mean?

Phil: They're all here to get educated.

Most of the students subscribed in theory to equal opportunity for both sexes. But, as has been shown, several did not expect boys and girls to show the same abilities in all areas. We probed student feelings about a sexual division of labor at home. Since many of the girls viewed domestic chores differently than boys, girls' and boys' perceptions about this matter will be reported separately.

The girls did not agree with each other on the extent to which gender should define domestic chores. A few girls who experienced a division of labor based on gender at home were angered by what they perceived to be an inequity. They described their anger like this:

Carmen: The boys work outside in the garden and they rake the grass and stuff and then we [my mom and I] have to do the housework inside. Sometimes I'd like to rake outside too. My mom told all my brothers that when they are 14 they can stop doing the dishes and my brother is only 11 and he stopped doing the dishes. He is supposed to do them on weekends and that is when we get days off and he doesn't do them.

R: What do you think of that?

Carman: I think that that is not fair at all. I think I get mad.

Grace: So far in the last couple of months I haven't been getting along with neither my mom or dad. All I do is fight and get mad and stuff like that. . . .

R: What have you been disagreeing with them about?

Grace: Like my little brother never does nothing. I say, Look, he never does anything, and my mom says, So what, you're the girl, you're the one who is supposed to do. He never washes dishes, I always have to wash dishes, and I say, Give me a break once in a while, let him do the dishes. She says, No, no, you're the girl, you have to do them. So I have to do them.

R: Is there a lot of things that they have at your house that they say boys do this and girls do this?

Grace: The girls have to wash the clothes and the boys have to take out the trash and stuff like that. That is about the only thing they do is throw out the trash. Make trouble and make a mess.

R: How do you feel about being the one who is supposed to do all this stuff?

Grace: I get mad all the time. I usually come to school mad because of that.

Several other girls who experienced a division of labor by sex at home did not necessarily accept it, but neither did they express anger about it. For example, one mentioned offering unsuccessfully to switch jobs with her brother:

Rakia: I do mostly everything, me and my mom. My dad works on cars and everything and my brothers work out in the yard. They say I get the easy jobs because I'm in the house and they are in the yard. I told them that I would switch with them, like shoveling snow, and they don't want to.

A few girls explicitly advocated dividing domestic labor based on gender:

R: What do you think about who in the house should do the housework type stuff?

Gayle: The woman should clean up the house and the man should do the outside work and make repairs.

R: Why do you think it should be divided that way?

> *Gayle:* The outside work seems like it would be harder and men are always stronger. A lady can fix the house how she wants.

> *R:* Do you ever think that you might want to switch things?
> *Sue:* No.
> *R:* How come?
> *Sue:* I'm just used to cleaning the house. It's easy. . . . It wouldn't be as good if I did the yard and he did the house.
> *R:* Why?
> *Sue:* I wouldn't be able to do all the yard work.
> *R:* Why?
> *Sue:* I just wouldn't. If I go outside I get cold right away and I have to come back in.

Finally, a few girls lived in homes in which everyone did everything around the house. These girls believed that this was a good system. They did not compare it with one based on traditional sex roles, but saw no reason to advocate anything different from the system they were experiencing.

Some of the girls had initiated talking about domestic chores because they were angry about it. In contrast, none of the boys initiated this topic, and none voiced anger or resentment about their end of the chores. The majority of boys accepted a traditional division of domestic labor. Typically, these boys said they were expected to shovel snow, take out trash, and keep their rooms clean. Their sisters did dishes, housecleaning, sometimes laundry, and sometimes cooking. The following discussion illustrates these boys' feelings about this system:

> *Hal:* Doing the dishes, that's a girl's job. Doing the harder work like moving around stuff, men should do. All I know is stuff for women to do that men shouldn't do.
> *R:* You don't know what the men-type stuff is?
> *Hal:* No, because women can do just as much as a man can, almost.
> *R:* Can a man do just as much as a woman can do?
> *Hal:* Yeah, but they shouldn't, the easier stuff should be for women.

A few boys reported no division of labor by sex at home. These boys did not seems to mind doing general household chores, and did not divide chores by gender.

The boys and girls saw boundaries clearly drawn between male and female roles, and associated mainly with each other socially in sex segregated groups. But the ideology that supports oppression based on sex was riddled with holes. Only about half of the students actually believed men are by nature strong and women are weak. It is especially fascinating to consider Hal's statement that 'women can do just as much as a man can' — but that men *should* do harder things and women *should* do easier things.

It appears that the students — especially the girls — were on the brink of challenging institutional sexism, but had not yet formulated enough of an insight into its injustice to restructure their own regard for themselves and each other and the roles cast for them at home. This is apparent when we look at their views about work roles and boy-girl relationships related to dating.

When asked about work roles, the students overwhelmingly said that males and females should have an equal opportunity to choose the jobs of their choice, and that no job should be restricted on the basis of sex. Only a few students believed that, while most jobs should be open to both sexes, some jobs were too hard or inappropriate for one sex. For example:

Anna: I think boys should do construction work.
R: Any other work that boys should do and girls shouldn't?
Anna: Lineman.

Gayle: Women shouldn't be truck drivers and lifting heavy crates. It seems like they couldn't handle a heavy machine.
R: What kinds of jobs do you feel like women should do that men shouldn't do?
Gayle: Taking care of kids for a daycare center or nursery.

We asked the students about their future work aspirations (students were asked this question during different interviews to check the reliability of their answers). The boys aspired to these jobs and careers: doctor, state patrol officer, football or hockey player, military, pilot, truck driver, high school teacher, computer technician, printer and salesperson (several did not name any aspiration, saying they were unsure). While these jobs have traditionally been held by men, there are few traditionally female jobs from which to pick.

All the girls said they intended to work, and most were specific about what kind of work they wanted to do. Table 3 depicts their aspirations, classified according to whether they have been traditionally held by women or men. As this table shows, the girls' aspirations tended to move away from traditionally female-dominated careers.

Table 3: Girls' career aspirations

Traditionally held by women	Not traditionally held by women
Hairstylist	Lawyer
Cosmetologist	Veterinarian
Stewardess	Psychiatrist
Secretary	Archaeologist
Model	Accountant
Teacher	News reporter
Nurse	Conservation officer
	Medical doctor

However, when it came to the jobs students actually held (summer or afterschool jobs) — and many of them had not yet held a job — there was a greater adherence to roles traditionally dominated by one's own sex. For example, several girls babysat but no boys did. Boys delivered newspapers and worked with cars, while girls did not. Both sexes had restaurant jobs and outdoor help jobs. This may indicate a discrepancy between students' ambitions and their actual behavior, or it may reflect only what kinds of jobs were made available to them at that time.

Thus, the girls aspired to future work roles as if these roles had never been associated with gender. As a group, the girls were ambitious, and had given job aspirations some thought. It is more difficult to assess the boys' responses. As a group they were less sure what they wanted to do than the girls, and less willing to break out of traditional sex roles in the work world.

Courtship is an arena in which sex roles have historically been clearly designated. Traditionally the male pursues the female, and the female waits to be chased, or if the female likes a male, her pursuit must be handled such that the male believes he is the one doing the chasing. However, to some extent these traditional roles are changing and both sexes are overtly pursuing the opposite sex. The Five Bridges students were just in the process of learning courtship conventions. Did their beliefs about equal opportunity for both sexes extend to this realm of social behavior?

The girls when asked generally had opinions about who should do what related to dating, but their opinions were often tentative. Several girls mentioned that girls should be able to call boys on the phone, but then qualified this by saying that they themselves would not do it, that girls were usually too shy to call boys, or that girls should not ask boys for dates if they do call them. For example:

R: Do you feel like girls should call boys as much as boys call girls?

Linda: Sometimes, if they ask them to call them. . . .

R: Do some girls call boys without being asked?

Linda: Yeah.

R: Is that okay?

Linda: It's okay.

R: Do girls ever ask boys to go out?

Linda: One girl did. . . .

R: How do you feel about girls asking boys out?

Linda: I don't think boys like it.

R: Would you?

Linda: No, I'd be too embarrassed.

When asked about who should pay for dates, some girls said either sex should, and some noted that boys usually do. Some of the girls who had experienced a boy paying her way did not automatically accept this practice:

R: Does he pay your way into the places?

Linda: Yeah. I feel stupid, though.

R: Why do you feel stupid?

Linda: Every boy I ever went out with, we never went out places where we had to use money. We'd just go swimming or something and we didn't have to pay.

The fact that girls sometimes protested when the boy paid was also mentioned by a few boys.

In contrast to the girls, when the boys talked about dating, they felt very definitely that the boy should ask for the date and pay for it. For instance:

R: Do you think a girl should pay if she goes out on a date with a fellow?

Juan: No.

R: You say that very firmly. What are your thoughts?

Juan: A girl shouldn't have to pay for nothing if we go out on a date.

R: And also you don't think a girl should ask you to go out on a date?

Juan: No. . . .

None of the boys who dated advocated equal opportunity when it came to asking for dates or paying for them. But they did not see this as a put-down toward women. On the contrary, they viewed the male role as a special treatment extended to females. In their view, to allow girls to initiate dates and pay for them not only threatened their own sense of control — it also went against what they considered to be traditionally right and wrong procedures associated with dating. The girls might have felt funny accepting the role expected by the boys, but not to accept it meant risking the boys' admiration and interest, as well as violating what they had learned was the girl's proper behavior.

Why is it that the girls were definite about future work ambitions but tentative about courtship conventions, while the boys were reversed? Most likely the boys accepted their dominant position and viewed girls not as equals but as subordinant adjuncts to their own lives. The demands their future role as breadwinner would exact on them were not yet real to them, so they saw no personal reason to question unequal sex relationships. The girls saw a reason every day at home when they cleaned up after their brothers, but had not yet abandoned the mythology of romance surrounding their own subordinate role. So they attempted to please the boys when it came to courtship, even though it made them feel 'funny', and saved their dreams of independence for later when presumably romance and self actualization in the work world would somehow be reconciled.

Social Class

Given the way students generally dress today, clothing differences as one possible indication of student social class student social class differences would not be readily observable in a lunchroom tour. However, a brief tour of the community on the way to school would inform you that the students at Five Bridges were by and large members of the working class. Studies of working class students (for example, Willis, 1977; Everhart, 1983; McRobbie, 1978) have found that they usually see themselves as eventually employed in the kinds of jobs held by their parents, and at times they even glorify manual labor. How did the students at Five Bridges view their present social class position and did they aspire to jobs or lifestyles associated with a higher social class?[4]

Symbols of Meaning Related to Social Class

We asked students about money, work and college. Few Five Bridges students spontaneously mentioned money or work as symbolizing differences among people or their own identities and goals. For the most part, when they did mention money and/or work, it was in the context of immediate concerns such as getting an allowance or getting an after-school job. A few students also talked about girls who spent more money than others on clothes, but this was not a big topic of concern.

Sample students were asked to plot their families on a continuum from rich to poor, and explain why they saw themselves at that point. With only one exception, the students marked themselves on or near the middle of the line, offering reasons such as the following:

Kristen: We are not poor and we are not rich. My father has a good job and I got everything I need.

Greg: We are just an average family.

Ricky: We have money, but we don't have a lot of money.

When asked how they viewed people wealthier than themselves, most students responded that the people had worked for it, although a few attributed wealth to luck. The students also replied that richer people were basically no different from other people, although some students noted that rich people have more family problems. When asked how they viewed people poorer than themselves, students were divided, either feeling sorry for them and wanting to help, or feeling they should go to work. They saw poor people as no different from other people except in terms of financial level, and a few believed poor people are happier and have fewer problems than rich people.

In short, the students had an incomplete conception of social class and of their own oppression based on class. They seemed unaware of the access to economic resources that they lacked, and of the powerlessness and low social status that accompanies their social class background. In fact, in attributing family problems to wealth, a few blocked themselves from considering the possibility that they were oppressed, and celebrated their own social class status.

Did the students aspire to jobs that would be of a different social class from those held by their parents? Table 4 depicts students' responses to our questions about their aspirations in terms of the kind and amount of post-high school training that would be required.

Table 4:   *Students' future work aspirations*

	Girls (%)	Boys (%)
Postgraduate training required (for example, lawyer)	33	5
B.A. required (for example, teacher)	17	5
A.A. required (for example, police officer)	7	5
Technical training required (for example, accountant)	10	5
Semi- or unskilled (for example, model, truck driver)	13	15
Military	—	30
College to play sports, unsure about career goal	—	20
Get married and not have job	—	—
Don't know or response hard to classify	20	15

As this table indicates, the girls as a group aspired to careers that require greater professional training than the boys. Over half of the girls said that they planned to go to college; this included those whose career ambitions required college as well as most who were unsure about their ambitions. Two who planned to be lawyers said they had done some reading on this career, and were aware exactly how much college education they would need; the other girls were less specific about the college preparation they would need. The girls who aspired to jobs that require technical training planned to attend a local technical institute after high school.

In contrast, few boys talked about college in relationship to their career choices. Half of the boys who talked about college said that they wanted to go to college to play sports, but were vague about what they would study in college or what they would do after college. One was beginning to reconsider this ambition as he realized that few athletes actually 'make it' to the pro's. The rest of the boys were non-specific about preparation for their futures, commenting either that the junior high school was doing a good job of preparing them, or that junior high does not offer the classes they need (for example, an aspiring pilot cannot learn to fly in junior high). Given most of the future ambitions they named (for example, joining the military, driving trucks, working on cars), the boys' answers were consistent with these goals.

Since over half of the Five Bridges sample students expressed interest in a career that would require post high school training, and since most, if not all, this training would require expenses, an effort was made to determine the extent to which the students were preparing themselves financially for their future goals. A few students stated that their parents planned to support their college education; however, given the income level of the community it can be assumed that most parents would have a difficult time paying college expenses for their children. For example, the following students with college ambitions talked about family money problems in the course of interviews:

Shirley: Right now we're flat broke, you know, and if the college up here won't be free for me I might have to go back down to Oklahoma.

Lupe: I really wanted to get a job. My sister works and everybody works in our family and I wanted to work and get my own stuff. My mom has a lot of trouble paying for stuff as it is.

We asked students who had after-school or summer jobs whether their money was being spent or saved. Most replied that they spent it on clothes, entertainment, snacks, records and so forth. About half said that they saved (or tried to save) money, principally for a car, Christmas gifts or a trip. Only one specifically said she had tried saving her money for college (college was competing with a car, a trip, and a stereo).

Did the Five Bridges students perceive money as something they would need to achieve their ambitions? Most did not seem to. It can be speculated that, since most of their parents had not gone to college, the students were simply unaware of the financial requirements they would have to meet.

That girls in a working class school have higher work ambitions, as a group, than boys is not a new finding (for example, Coleman, 1961; Fuller, 1980). But it is an important finding that has not been adequately discussed. As we stated earlier, many of the girls were dissatisfied with their present lives while the boys were not. Recognizing the drudgery of housework, the girls aspired to something more fulfilling. But at the same time, both sexes liked their community and did not dream for a future that was radically different from the present. Rather than uniting across the sex lines to examine the conditions of their lives and the viability of school as a way of improving those conditions, they lined up against each other for future battles over domestic chores. The girls were correct in seeing sexism as oppressive to their humanity, but were naive in failing to recognize classism as oppressive also. And, later in this book, as we discuss the schooling the students were receiving it will become abundantly clear the extent to which classism was erecting barriers to the personal fulfillment of students regardless of sex.

Students' Categories for Their Own Diversity

When you were looking around the lunchroom, watching and talking with students, you were guided by researchers' ideas about which aspects of human diversity are important. But had you asked a student tourguide to tell you about the kinds of kids in this school, you would have found out about the categories the students used to define their own diversity. Since these were the criteria students used most often to differentiate among themselves, these seem to be symbols that the students saw as constituting significant human differences. Let us take a closer look at each of these symbols of human diversity.

Gender was the main category the students used to differentiate among themselves, often citing gender before making further distinctions. Of a sample of twenty-eight students, twenty used gender as an important distinction.

Social visibility was the second most important difference and was used by eleven out of the twenty-eight students. Socially visible 'popular people' could be recognized by their membership in Student Council, the 'fun' social activities they engaged in, their friendliness with 'everybody', and their style of dress. Most of the time they wore jeans, shirts or sweaters, and tennis shoes (which had to be Pumas or Nikes); sometimes they dressed up in skirts and heels or nice pants. Several girls in this group wore makeup, and some of the boys looked as if they had spent considerable time and money on their hair. They walked through the halls in clusters, talking and laughing. In class, many of the 'popular people' made more contributions to class discussion than other students. As social leaders, they often planned and organized social activities other students participated in. Most dated regularly:

> *R:* What makes these guys popular?
> *Tony:* They always get the girls.

Being good in sports was also named by six sample students as a symbol of status. It has already been noted that several students saw athletic ability as a symbol of masculinity. The popular boys were also good in at least one sport, and popular girls frequently were active in gymnastics or track, and liked to play basketball or softball.

The reverse of social visibility was social invisibility. 'Bores', 'drags', 'out-of-it's', kids who 'don't do nothing' or who 'don't talk to no one' were identified as a category of socially invisible peers.

Hal: I don't try to be a drag, that's for sure. That's the only thing I worry about, being a drag.

Of course, nobody described him/herself as a member of this category — this seemed to be an amorphous category into which students put others they did not know well and did not see engaging in any social activity.

'Getting in trouble' was the hallmark of another category of students. A particular kind of boy whose behavior frequently got him in trouble named by four students was called a 'hard guy'. 'Hard guys' liked to fight others and assert their own physical power. Girls who got in trouble for talking loudly and saying inappropriate things to teachers were called 'big mouths'. It seemed to be fairly well known who the 'big mouths' were; in fact, Kristen who was described as a 'big mouth' by others used this term in an interview to describe herself. Three other sample students also used this category, naming roughly the same people as belonging. Some of the girls explained that there was a fine line between having fun (which was accepted) and being a 'big mouth' (which was not), the difference was talking back to teachers or other authority figures, and repeating stories about her friends to other students.

Six sample students saw smoking pot as a symbol of difference among their peers. None said that they themselves smoked, but talked about a group who did. In fact, one student saw this as the major characteristic differentiating Five Bridges students. On the other hand, according to several students, only a handful of kids smoked pot.

Seven sample students named good students as a category of peers. Of our sample, only Phil placed himself in this category, explaining that his brain was his greatest asset. A few talked about a particular kind of good student: the 'teacher's pet'. Teacher's pets were not looked up to, as the following statement shows:

Kristen: [Teacher's pets] get too involved in it. There is a difference between doing a lot of stuff in school or just doing what you're supposed to do.

Finally, five sample students named handicap as a category for describing their peers. Three of these were physically impaired students, who saw handicap as an important distinction. The other two were non-impaired students who had a physically impaired friend.

All categories share one attribute: they are defined by social behavior displayed, and not by traits or circumstances born with or acquired by an individual. If a person displays friendly behavior, he or she is generally liked. If a person is socially active, he or she is known and considered popular. If a person is not seen in social gatherings, he/she is designated a 'bore' or an 'out-of-it'. People whose social behavior is noticeably obnoxious are termed 'troublemakers', 'big mouths', 'hard guys', or 'smart alecks'. To the Five Bridges students, what people did was more important than what they looked like or what their family was like. It is no accident that Doug, Phil and Fannie escaped classification as handicapped — they were all socially active. This suggests that Five Bridges students believed one could achieve any kind of social image and reputation by controlling one's own behavior, and no one should be excluded from status, popularity, or friendship on the basis of ascribed characteristics such as race, sex, social class or handicap.

Student Cultural Knowledge and Cultural Capital

To what extent were the Five Bridges students contesting inequality and showing active respect for human diversity? Within their own social system, they demonstrated active respect for differences based on race and learning handicap, and were moving toward respect for differences based on physical impairment. They still held stereotypes about and structured their social system around differences based on gender, and around social behavior and social skills. Overall the students spoke positively about each other, and did not see great status differences among themselves. The resources they saw as contributing most to the good life were friends, family, and fun, none of which were particularly scarce or invited competition to control.

However, the students knew little about human diversity outside of their immediate environment. At this point in their lives they were unprepared to challenge structural inequality or social stereotypes. They did not seem to see limits on their own futures posed by their subordinate group membership. But neither had they the awareness nor knowledge that would enable them to hurdle barriers thwarting personal success, or to collectively challenge barriers to equality on a larger scale. What kinds of limits might be placed on the students' futures? Were they entering the school with characteristics that might hinder their attempts to realize their own ambitions?

Schools sort and prepare students for different work and status roles (see Spring, 1976). We are all quite aware that students are regularly tested or otherwise evaluated based on what they know. Too often we forget that the knowledge schools teach and use to evaluate student performance represents the knowledge and experience of the white middle class. Young (1977) has termed this 'high status knowledge', and has likened it to private property which some people have in much greater amounts than others, and can use to extend their control over additional property, status, or power.

Bourdieu and Passeron (1977) point out that access to high status knowledge depends on the cultural capital one brings from home. 'Cultural capital refers to the socially determined tastes, certain kinds of prior knowledge, language forms, abilities, and modes of knowing that are unevenly distributed throughout society' (Giroux, 1981, p. 77). While all children come to school with a fund of cultural capital, they do not all come with the cultural capital valued by the white middle class, and that is the cultural capital on which school knowledge — high status knowledge — is built. Schools evaluate students based on their cultural and linguistic inheritance in order to assess their educational potential. Schools do this formally through IQ or achievement tests, and informally through teacher assessment (Rist, 1970).

Bourdieu argues that students who bring to school a relatively large share of the 'right' cultural capital are usually favorably evaluated in school, placed in the highest ability groups and tracks (for example, college preparatory classes) and taught relatively large amounts of high status knowledge. Students who do not bring the 'right' cultural capital with them to school are usually deemed as having less potential, and are consequently taught less status knowledge than their 'high potential' peers.

Besides bringing cultural capital from home, students can also seek it out either by taking more academic courses (for example, science, math) or by conscientiously exposing themselves to it in the form of books, travel and so forth. Academic courses provide students with the kinds of information that they will see on school tests and increase their chance of being evaluated by the school as academically able. Similarly, by reading the 'right' books, acquiring the tastes and manners of the white middle class, becoming conversant with their literary and art forms, and so forth, one can improve one's chances of being viewed as intelligent, and can therefore improve one's access to educational credentials and informal networks of influence. But, to do these things one must be aware of their importance and given guidance regarding what knowledge will in fact have the greatest pay-off.

Cultural Capital and the Five Bridges Students

We examined students' exposure to middle class cultural capital and high status knowledge both in and out of school. In Chapter 5 we will look at what they were being taught in school and in Chapter 6 we will see what they were getting out of what they were taught. Here we will describe the students' experiences outside school that would help them broaden their fund of cultural capital.

We asked a sample of twenty-four students stratified by race and sex a series of specific questions about their exposure to cultural capital valued by the middle class through attendance at museums, plays and concerts and through reading, private lessons and travel. We realize that there are many additional ways students can be exposed to white middle class cultural capital outside school, but we selected these as indices of their exposure because these were relatively easy to gather valid and reliable data on, and these are measures used by Bourdieu (1977) in his research.

The majority (fourteen) of the students had been to a museum only once in their lives. Six students said they had been a few times, three had been a number of times, and one had never been. Of the twenty-three who had attended a museum, ten had gone with a class in school (most said this was in elementary school), five had gone with family members, three with friends, one with a church group and four did not specify who they were with.

We asked them about their attendance at concerts. We found it very interesting that ten of the students specifically defined concert to mean rock concert, so we followed up our question to find out what kinds of concerts they had been to. Sixteen said they had never been to a concert of any sort outside of the school building (a few did mention required attendance at band concerts in school). Five had attended a rock concert once, one had attended several rock concerts, one had attended a Salvation Army band concert, and one had attended several different kinds of concerts at the city's orchestra hall.

We asked the sample if they had seen plays in a theater. Nine never had. Nine students had once, five had a few times, and one did not respond to the question. Of those who had been to the theater, three had gone with a school class, two with an adult friend, two with the family, one with a recreation group when she was in the hospital, one with a friend and five did not specify who had taken them.

We asked the students about their reading habits, beginning with a question about their use of the public library. Nine of the students said they did not go to the public library at all, nine went on rare occasions, two went often and four got books from sources other than the library. We asked the students to talk more specifically about their reading habits. Half clearly indicated that when they read, it was with reluctance. For example:

Gayle: I get a headache from reading.

Juan: I don't like to read.

Lupe: It's hard when I read ... I've never read a whole book in my life and I'm in ninth grade.

R: How often do you read books?
Hal: Not too often. Only on Thursdays when we need them for reading.
R: Do you ever read at home or outside of school?
Hal: No.

The other students indicated having some interest in reading, and they told us about the kinds of books they read. The girls read primarily romance stories about teenage girls. Some students, both male and female, read thrillers and mystery stories; two — a girl and a boy — were reading science fiction books. One student said she read a wide variety of books, and was currently reading *To Kill a Mockingbird*. One of the girls who read romance books went on to tell us,

Robin: I read books that my mom and dad don't like. Like a 16 year old gets pregnant. They're kind of interesting.
R: Do you keep them hidden?
Robin: My dad found one and told me not to read it, but I did anyway.

Twenty students said they read magazines. Half of these were girls, and all but one read either fashion/glamour magazines (for example, *Seventeen, Cosmopolitan*) or women's magazines their mothers subscribed to (for example, *Better Homes and Gardens*). The one exception told us she read magazines like *People* and *Us*. Of the boys, half read sports magazines such as *Sports Illustrated*, a third read automechanics magazines such as *Hot Rod* and the rest read news magazines such as *Time* and *Newsweek*.

We asked the students about reading the newspaper. Five said they did not read it at all; only two students said they read it every day. The other students said they sometimes read parts of the newspaper, particularly the sports section and the movie section.

> *R:* Do you ever read the newspaper?
> *Larry:* Not really, just to see what is showing at the movies.

> *Rakia:* I just see it lying on the table and just look at the picture and if it looks good then I'll read the middle part.

> *Carmen:* I started reading it since yesterday because I was looking for an article in the newspaper about politics. It's really kind of boring.

A few of the students said that they only read the newspaper in connection with classwork.

> *Phil:* I've started to read the newspaper regularly because this trimester I signed up for a world affairs class. We read certain stories in the newspaper everyday. Normally, I don't read the newspaper.

We also asked the students if they had taken any private lessons. Only four had. One used to take guitar lessons but quit, one used to take trumpet lessons but quit, one went to a private gymnastics camp one summer and had also taken four months of piano lessons at one time, and the fourth was taking hockey lessons. For the most part their participation with lessons had been short lived, and there was no follow-through to develop their skills in that area.

Finally, we asked the sample students where they had traveled. Eight had not been out of the state; another two had not gone farther than an adjacent state. Three had traveled in the midwest and six had been to the east coast, west coast or south. Three had been out of the country: one to Europe, one to Egypt and one to Mexico. Two did not respond to the question. Most of their travels were for the purpose of visiting relatives, although a few students said their families took trips to vacation and see the country.

We tallied each of the twenty-four sample students' responses to the above questions, and found only three students who had what could be called fair exposure to cultural capital outside the school. These were students who had been to museums or plays with some frequency, traveled to different parts of the country, read a variety of materials, and perhaps had taken private lessons. Two more students had limited general exposure, and the other nineteen had very limited general exposure to cultural capital. Either these students were exposed to it through two or three channels only with some frequency (for example, reading and museums only), or were infrequently exposed to it through a variety of means. But none of the students had had experiences that would help them develop a well-rounded fund of cultural capital outside the school.

There are several interpretations and programatic recommendations one could make based on this information about the students' cultural capital. One could decide that the Five Bridges students were hopelessly behind and uninterested in academics, and proceed to teach them small amounts of simple material in an effort to acquaint them with a traditional school curriculum, but not prepare them for future success in the education system.

One could, on the other hand, see it as essential to expose the students to the 'right' cultural capital in large doses, giving them the knowledge, attitudes and manners that it takes to succeed in a biased school system. Since several students mentioned attending museums and concerts through school functions, we can assume that they would be agreeable to greater school efforts to provide this exposure, although we are not sure they would automatically see the point of it and take full advantage of it.

A slightly different tactic one could take would be to find out what the students did know and value and build on that. This tactic would assume that the students were perfectly intelligent people whose experiences and knowledge were legitimate bases for intellectual growth. Of course, if one were to take this approach one would need at some point to provide the students with the knowledge, language, and attitudes they would need to 'make it' in the system, since intelligence and thinking ability alone does not guarantee success on school assessments of potential.

In the following two chapters we will look at the sense the teachers and administrators made of the students — their diversity and their educational potential. We will also examine the school experience they provided for the students, and we will ask whether this was the most appropriate and fair experience to provide for these young people.

Notes

1 The following lunchroom tour is based on notes and transcripts from observations and visits with students in the lunchroom over a three-day period.

2 Although these were distinct categories of friends in the students' cultural knowledge, students used a variety of terms to refer to these categories. For example, what we have termed 'friends one does many things with', students termed 'who I hang around with', 'friends' (with additional description of what one does with them), and 'our group'.

3 R denotes researcher.

4 Although we examined friendship patterns across race, handicap and sex lines, we did not do the same for social class since there was little difference in social class among the students.

Chapter 4

The Administrative Team

There is wide agreement that a school's leadership plays an indispensible role in establishing and developing a strong and effective program (for example, Goodlad, 1975; Lipham, 1976; Purkey and Smith, 1982). The leadership in most schools is made up of its administrative team, of which the Principal is the key figure. At Five Bridges, the leadership team comprised three administrators and the two counselors, who were both formally and informally acknowledged as part of this team by the administrators and the teachers.

Our interest in human diversity and social inequality suggested that we focus on the administrative team's leadership in establishing an educational program. We, along with most Americans today, would hope that that program would be both academically excellent and equitable. The twin themes of excellence and equity have been accepted by many educators and sectors of the public as dual yardsticks for judging schooling in America. For example, Boyer (1983) wrote:

> Equity and excellence are connected. Expanding access to the nation's schools must be seen as only the first step toward opportunity for all. . . . Equality (should) be advanced as the *quality* of education is improved for *every* student. (p. XII)

Similarly, when presenting a need to upgrade the academic excellence of America's schools, *A Nation at Risk* includes the statement that excellence be distributed equitably: 'All, regardless of race or class or economic status are entitled to a fair chance and to the tools for developing their individual powers of mind and spirit to the utmost' (p. 8).

Both academic excellence and equity are goals that should be explicitly addressed in a school like Five Bridges, especially given the diversity of its student population. This chapter will describe how the administrative team viewed the academic program, and took into account race, class, gender and handicap. It will specifically examine how they saw various factors related to their work: the community and the students, the school's program objectives and their own strategy for reaching those objectives, curriculum and instruction, the teaching staff, and each other. We will then reflect on and critique their goals, beliefs, and behavior, and assess their potential for leading the school toward establishing a program that would actively promote excellence and respect for human diversity.

The People on the Administrative Team

Thomas Wilson was Principal of Five Bridges. Thomas was a 45 year old white male who had come up through the teaching and administrative ranks of the city school system. A native of the state, he was a former industrial arts teacher who was also a student council adviser. It was while serving in that role that, with the encouragement of his former Principal, he became interested in school administration. He saw 'administration as a position where you could have more influence on a troubled school'. As a Vice Principal, Thomas had experienced working in a school that was undergoing voluntary desegregation. After serving as Vice Principal for several years, he was asked to accept the principalship at Five Bridges in 1976. Thomas had completed his MA while earning his administration credentials, and was in the process of completing his PhD in educational administration.

Jerry Springs was the Assistant Principal. He was a 39 year old white male. Jerry had spent two years as a Peace Corps volunteer after completing college. Upon returning to this state, he got a job as a math and science teacher. Jerry's reasons for becoming interested in educational administration were similar to Thomas': he felt 'that the role of the Principal is kind of a key role and that you can influence a lot easier and make more of an impact overall in education'. Upon receiving his MA in educational administration, Jerry served as an administrative intern in one of the inner city schools. He was then appointed Assistant Principal at another school, where he had a great deal of responsibility for, and contact with, low income and minority students. Jerry was subsequently given the assistant principalship at Five Bridges.

Marjorie Arnold was the school's administrative intern. She was a 34 year old white female. Marjorie was a product of a Rocky Mountain state where she had taught before moving to this state. Her teaching experience in her home state had included some contact with Native American students. After moving to this city, Marjorie taught in two different schools for two years each; one of the schools was in the inner city and had a substantial black student population. Marjorie applied for the internship at Five Bridges because she felt she was ready for a change from classroom teaching. She took several courses in educational administration, but had not yet completed a degree in it.

Anthony Ruiz was one of two school counselors. He was a 30 year old Mexican male who had grown up and spent most of his adult life working in the Rivercrest community. He had received his MA in counseling and guidance, and was pursuing a PhD in educational administration, since he hoped to become a school Principal in the future. Most of Anthony's work experience had been in human relations and counseling: he had been a group facilitator in a regional training center, an organizer for a teacher training program and the Director of a social agency for pre-delinquents. Anthony had pursued a career in counseling because he 'had such poor counseling as an undergraduate and in high school'. He was committed to remain working with students in the Rivercrest community.

Sarah Ziegler was the other school counselor. Sarah was a 46 year old white female who had taught physical education, grades K-12, in several different midwestern states over a twenty year period before going into counseling. Four of those years were spent teaching in Little Rock, Arkansas, during its famous desegregation crisis; it was here that Sarah had her first sustained contact with black students. It was a process of learning about minority students by experience with no in-service help. From Little Rock, Sarah moved to this city, where she continued teaching physical education, teaching for a few years in a school with a large black student population. The head of the counseling department for the city suggested that Sarah become a counselor. For Sarah, this decision was a 'traumatic experience' because she felt like she was abandoning a field she believed in, but she was motivated by an interest in counseling. Sarah completed a MA in counseling and now, after a few years of counseling, she said that she loved it. Five Bridges was Sarah's first experience with a Mexican student population, and again, she told us that she had mainly been learning by experience.

Just as we introduced you to the students by taking a tour of the lunchroom and eavesdropping on conversations, we will acquaint you with the administrators and counselors in a similar fashion. Thomas greets you in the office at 7.30 a.m. He is standing at the office door with Jerry Springs, who is getting ready to make a regular morning tour of the building. Thomas explains, 'Two of our teachers are absent today and subs are on the way. Jerry's job is to make sure they get settled in. Come on, Let's check the calendar to see what's up for the day'.

Thomas' calendar shows that he has an observation of a teacher who is on probation during second period, a meeting with a teacher during third, and a Principal's meeting at the district office at 2.00. 'Good', he comments, 'that will give me some time to get caught up on paper work during first period'.

'What kind of paper work do you usually do?'

'Oh, writing memos and filling out reports. That is one thing with the federal programs that we have here. With Title I, Bilingual, ESAA, Teacher Corps, there are quite a few reports that need to be done. That doesn't necessarily mean that I have to fill them out, but I have to look them over and sign them.'

You offer to leave Thomas to his paperwork and rejoin him second period. You walk over to Marjorie Arnold's office. She is just finishing a phone call with a parent. She explains that she is trying to resolve a fight that occurred the day before. She says, 'One of the main functions of my job is maintenance and firefighting. I deal with problems that erupt on the spot to make the teachers' job easier. I like it — it makes me feel important'.

Marjorie is interrupted by the appearance of two students in the door. They silently look at you and Marjorie introduces you. Then she motions them to sit down, saying, 'I like your shoes, Valerie. Are they new? Now, why don't you tell me what happened yesterday?'.

You leave and walk across the narrow hall into Jerry's office. He is pouring over some papers. 'Scheduling', he says. 'This is one of my main responsibilities. First of all, I start by sending to the teachers a form in which I enquire what subjects they are interested in teaching for the next trimester. I've got those back, now I'm compiling this information for the computer.'

'Looks very time consuming.'

'It is, especially since we have to do this three times a year. Here, I'll show you. I have to add up all the courses for each grade level available each hour and have the right number of courses in order to cover the students. Then I have to juggle things around, keeping in mind who has a required prep when, and that sort of thing. It's like a big puzzle. First hour is usually a good time to work on it because things are usually quiet then.'

'Are you also involved in discipline?'

'Oh, yes. You could spend 150 per cent of your time on this and discipline. I don't, but I easily could.'

'What else do you do?'

'I'm heavily involved with the special ed program. I meet with student support teams and sit in on a lot of IEP (Individualized Educational Program) conferences. I talk a lot with the special ed coordinator in the building. We discuss whether a kid is having a problem in the program and what alternative program would be best for that kid. We converse quite regularly. Also, the Pupil Problems Committee which I chair takes a lot of time. It's the discipline committee for the school. Its job is to consider any student who is referred who is having problems or not making it in school.'

'So your main role is discipline?'

'My main role is to be supportive of the Principal. You do what the Principal delegates to you. Thomas has me do discipline and scheduling. He also has me do some evaluations of new teachers, but just a smitchen of that.'

You thank Jerry for his time, and rejoin Thomas as he is on his way to observe a teacher. He explains that it is hard to find time for teacher observations. You go with him into the classroom as the period starts. After a few minutes, he gets up and leaves and returns fifteen minutes later. He stays the rest of the period, then briefly talks to the teacher, making an appointment to see her later.

Then he heads back to the office, explaining that a department chairperson is coming in to talk about the budget. 'I generally try to make myself available to staff, too, who have any kinds of problems. Any individual concerns or problems, I like them to feel free to come and talk.'

You pop back into Marjorie's office. She comments that she has been busy all morning with 'irregularities', or disciplinary referrals.

'One thing I try to do is help the kids feel okay about themselves. Starting out with "you're an OK person". Making sure the kid knows that, no matter what they do. "What you did is not okay at all, and I may be fuming and screaming at you, but you're an okay person."' She talks for a while about some discipline problems she has been involved with. Then she tells you it is time for lunch duty.

Accompanying her to the lunchroom, you encounter the rest of the administrators and the two counselors. Lunch time is when they are often all visible in the halls, lunchroom, or patrolling the smoking area. You fall in behind Anthony, asking him what he does when he is patrolling the area.

'I'm not so much patrolling as being available to the kids and getting a feel for them that day. I feel if the students come to me they are usually comfortable in knowing me and they usually have confidence in me. I try to deal with that situation — it could be out in the hall, it could be in the cafeteria, it could be in my office. Part of my responsibility for kids is also doing things outside of school, so a lot of times I'll be down at the teen center or football games or whatever.'

'So you don't really monitor to discipline, more to counsel?'

'Officially, I'm not involved in discipline. Unofficially, I spend about a third of my time on it, because you can't separate it from personal or school problems.'

As you and Anthony walk along, you notice that he greets each student by name, often chatting personably with them. He comments, 'That one, Carlos — I need to kick him in the arse to get him to work. He's bright, but lazy. He tried signing up for two physical education classes and two woodshops — I enrolled him in English, science and computers and told him he'd better buckle down if he wants to go to college. I have to counsel with parents a lot too. Often parents don't perceive their kids fairly. Either they think they should be doctors and lawyers and I know the student has limitations, or they can't picture their son or daughter in a field like that when the kid really has it'.

'It probably helps your job, being from the community.'

'I personally wouldn't want to work anywhere else', he replies. 'I often think about the people I've grown up with, and I often visualize the opportunities that the kids have now, that the people in the past didn't have. I like to think of myself as a role model for these kids — showing them they can make it and hopefully without as much of an uphill struggle as I had. I also try to help the minoirty kids understand how to deal with majority people — give them another way of looking at them rather than just thinking of them as being a racist.' As you walk, a woman approaches you and Anthony says, 'Have you met Sarah, the other counselor?'

Anthony introduces you to Sarah, and tells her he was orienting you to the work of the counselors. He excuses himself, saying he has to attend a meeting to refer a student for special education.

'I gather you also spend most of your day with students?'

'We have kids that come in all the time. You never know exactly what the day is going to bring. I had a little girl in the seventh grade who came in before lunch, she's had problems off and on. She's got problems with her family —.' And Sarah is off into a story about this little girl, and about how she worked with the parents and the girl to resolve the problem. 'They come in with all kinds of problems. And sometimes parents call in with things. They sometimes want us to get — this sounds like a very mundane task, but it's one that has to be done — homework for a kid who's home sick.'

'What's the main thing you personally try to work on?'

'Encouraging the kids — especially the girls — to think about different career objectives. The woman's position in society is close to my heart and I want to try to do something. But I've gotta be honest. I don't do that much unless the situation presents itself. When a kid comes in or parents come in to talk about careers, I push them to think big. But I tend to get bogged down by all the things that come up every day, and I get lax in that area.'

You sit in the counseling office for the rest of the afternoon. It is a busy place, populated by student helpers, students coming in for schedule changes or help with problems, and students dropping by to say 'hi'.

As soon as the last bell has rung, Marjorie comes for you and takes you to a classroom in which a few students are sitting. 'This is detention', she explains. 'Those who broke school rules have to spend time in here after school. I monitor detention most of the time. Sometimes Jerry does it, but I usually do it.' She sits down and whispers to you, 'My feet hurt like hell. I'm up and down all day, in the halls between every class and in the lunchroom all during lunch, and by this time of day I'm ready for a comfortable pair of loafers'.

'Why don't you wear loafers?' you ask, noticing her one-inch heel pumps.

'I think image is important. For dealing with kids and parents and business people who come in, I think clothing is important. I haven't learned to deal with what to wear on my feet, to tell the truth.'

As you leave the building at 4.00 you leave Jerry and Marjorie making phone calls to parents. Thomas has returned from his meeting and is conferring with Anthony, and Sarah is somewhere in the building talking with a special education teacher. Your feet are tired too, and you empathize with the Five Bridges administrators and counselors, who will not be leaving the building for another hour or so.

Perceptions of Human Diversity

Equity has been associated with excellence in examining schooling in the last few years because educational opportunities, as well as many other opportunities and resources, have historically not been distributed equally. Students such as those at Five Bridges have been denied access to a good education in many schools. We wanted to find out how the administrators at Five Bridges viewed race, gender, social class and handicap, and then to examine how that understanding was used to design and provide leadership for an instructional program for the Five Bridges students.

The Five Bridges staff participated in an in-service institute before the start of the school year in 1978. During the in-service institute they were administered a Likert-type attitude assessment scale to determine participants' beliefs about race, class, handicap, and sex (see the Appendix for information about the scale). Questions in each area asked for opinions on curriculum and general policy issues, general knowledge about that aspect of human diversity and acceptance of stereo-types.

As a group, the administrators and counselors scored quite high on this scale, agreeing or strongly agreeing with non-biased and non-stereotypic statements, and disagreeing or strongly disagreeing with those that were biased or stereotyped. On the race subscale, they agreed that schools should not be thought of as a melting pot. They agreed that texts contain few stories about minority group members for reasons other than a lack of good stories within minority cultures, and that experiences such as celebrating Puerto Rican Independence Day or taking a trip to Chinatown insufficiently represent non-whites in the curriculum. They disagreed most over issues related to bilingual education. Both Thomas and Anthony strongly supported the policy of teaching students in their native languages. Jerry, Marjorie and Sarah all gave contradictory responses to questions about language, for example saying that people in the US should learn *in* American English, but at the same time being unsure if total immersion is the best way to learn English, and rejecting the idea that non-English speakers should be treated as handicapped learners.

On the sex subscale the five agreed on most of the questions. For example, they agreed that sexism is learned behavior, that raising children is equally the responsibility of both parents, that neither sex is inherently better in math or reading and that women with children should be able to work outside the home regardless of whether motivated by financial need. Jerry disagreed with the other four on a few questions: he was not sure whether using language like 'chairperson' instead of 'chairman' is nonsense, while the other four believed it is not; he felt that most children from single-parent homes are more difficult to teach than children from two-parent homes, while the others rejected that idea; and he was not sure whether men have more of the top jobs because they are more ambitious than women, while the others were sure this was not so.

On the class subscale, all five agreed that lower class experiences should not be left out of the curriculum, that lower class parents are just as good as middle class parents as role models at home and aides in the classroom, and that children from lower class homes are not inherently poorer learners than middle class children. They also agreed that people on welfare are not lazy, and that the free lunch program should be continued. However, Sarah accepted some stereotypes about the lower class that the other four rejected: she believed lower class students have less desire to work and prize education less than middle class students, and was not sure whether lower class families are culturally deprived. Jerry believed lower class students cause more behavior problems in school than middle class students, while the other four rejected this idea. Finally, Marjorie was simply unsure about several school policy matters the others agreed with: for example, she was not sure whether schools in low socioeconomic areas should receive extra funds to broaden students' learning experiences, or whether student teachers should spend some time teaching in a lower class school.

All five expressed positive attitudes about the handicapped, agreeing for example that children with handicaps should have equal access to community programs including schools, and that attitudes rather than money is the main block mainstreaming is facing. They also agreed that handicapped students should not simply be left alone, and that they should be provided with varied learning experiences, including field trips. Thomas disagreed with the other four about curricular implications of mainstreaming: while the other four believed the curriculum should include information about different handicapping conditions including devices used by handicapped people, he did not. Also, Sarah believed money would be wiser spent on programs for the gifted than the handicapped during times of money shortage, while the others did not.

On the basis of the administrative team's prior experience with diverse student populations, one might wonder whether they had the background to lead the school toward a program that affirms human diversity. But on the basis of their responses to questions about their attitudes toward human diversity, one is optimistic. For the most part they rejected stereotypes based on race, sex, social class and handicap, and believed that these should not be allowed to hinder a person's chance to 'make it'. This seemed to be the sort of leadership team that would be committed to designing an educational program that would promote the interests of all students regardless of group membership.

To what extent did the administrators' positive regard for human diversity translate into their establishing and leading a school program that was academically excellent and equitable to minority as well as white students, working class students, both sexes and handicapped students? Let us now examine their cultural knowledge and actions related to the school and community and goals for the school.

The Community and School

The way in which the administrators and counselors carried out their daily work was guided by their cultural knowledge about the community and students, and about the school and specific elements of their jobs. In addition to observing them work, we interviewed them at length about these things, and also about their goals for the school and the strategy they believed was most effective for achieving those goals. We did this because we wanted to move beyond the daily routine, to see what sort of leadership the administrators and counselors were attempting to exert over the long term. First, let us see how they viewed the community and students.

Rivercrest Community

Many educators, such as James Coleman (1966), have discussed the importance of the home as an influence on how well students do in school. Recognizing the importance of its impact, school staff members usually have some knowledge and beliefs about their students' homes, and the kind of influence those homes and the wider community exert.

Thomas Wilson and Anthony Ruiz shared similar views about the Rivercrest community. Thomas described the community as one of the school's main strengths. Its strength stemmed from its isolation, its sense of cohesion and pride, and its families' sense of responsibility and concern for family members.

> I don't feel that this community is affected by the other kinds of social pressures as much as other parts of [the city].... I think that the parents in the main keep closer tabs on their kids than in general.... This community is working very hard to upgrade its appearance and maintain that.

Thomas also described the community as 'really quite stable', since many adults grew up and remained in Rivercrest and therefore felt some sense of loyalty to it.

Thomas saw a need for developing a working relationship between the school and the community, and for involving community members in more than just a spectator role. On several occasions he commented that he hoped to get parents working with each other to improve the school, and hoped they would take some leadership in doing that. To promote a more active school-community relationship, Thomas helped plan and initiate several activities which he often discussed, such as a community council of parents in the entire Rivercrest schools feeder system, and a school community pride day. The major community-related problem Thomas saw was the fact that it was blue-collar, and parents did not sufficiently encourage or help their children to break out of blue-collar work aspirations.

Anthony was a native of Rivercrest, and a strong advocate of the community. Like Thomas, he saw its isolation from the rest of the city as a positive feature. Thomas saw the community's isolation cutting it off from problems elsewhere; Anthony saw it drawing community members together. Anthony also saw the racial and cultural diversity of Rivercrest's population as a strength. He described it as a rich, positive background students brought to school with them. His involvement with the community was very personal. Since he knew most community residents, as well as their beliefs, values, and needs, he saw himself as a community spokesperson in the school. He said that the adults in the community 'are constantly reinforcing my activities here in Rivercrest and it makes me realize that there is more of a need for people like myself'.

Jerry Springs and Sarah Ziegler shared many views about the community, which differed in emphasis somewhat from those of Thomas and Anthony. Jerry saw two major strengths in the community. One strength was a respect for authority on the part of both young people and adults. He pointed out that 'you have kids who have been taught at home that you respect your elders, and they carry it into the school. I think that is one of the reasons we have quiet hallways and kids that generally, when you tell them to go to class, they go'. A second strength was its support for education. Jerry described the community as one that believed in education. However, he felt that it was difficult to get community members involved with the school because they tended to see teachers as knowing what was best for the kids, and preferred to leave school matters up to the teachers.

Jerry was also quite specific about problems in the community:

> We've got a lot of lower socioeconomic class kids with problems that are attendant to that — broken homes and all kinds of problems with alcoholism or whatever drug problems and so forth.... The kid can be respectful but underneath they can really be hurting.... We see some evidence of kids getting slapped around a lot and that kind of thing.

Jerry qualified this negative evaluation of the community by commenting that most of his contact with parents was related to discipline problems, which could skew his perspective.

Sarah echoed many of Jerry's remarks. She too described the parents as being supportive of education, although she did not consider them reluctant to become involved with the school.

> I think these are very concerned parents. I think the parents in this community really want to have total control. They want control over who is hired as our Principal, what we teach.... I think they're active in the educational process. We call parents a lot when something happens. They are always very happy to be called. They want to help.

Sarah described home problems of the students in much the same way Jerry had. Commenting that 'they have a lot of home problems', she too linked poverty with problems such as alcoholism and 'slapping them around a little', although she added that many of the students have 'got nice families'. Sarah too intimated that her knowledge about problems in the community may relate to her role as one who helps students with problems in school: 'If it's a crisis situation, then they'll tell you what's going on'. When there is no crisis, the students are 'pretty private people just like anyone'.

Marjorie Arnold didn't often comment on the community. When she did, she spoke positively about it, describing it as 'one of the least inner city of inner city schools', 'kind of a sheltered area' in which 'parents are really concerned about how their kids are doing' and residents share 'some real feelings of belonging'.

Thus, the administrators and counselors shared a generally positive view of the community. However, they evaluated different features of the community favorably due to the nature of their contact with the community. Anthony saw strengths in the community's personal relationships and sense of belonging it gave to its diverse members. Jerry and Sarah, on the other hand, evaluated its merits and weaknesses partly on the basis of how the community influenced their jobs. They were positive about the parents' support for education and the students' respect for authority — these things facilitated the schooling process. They were aware of and felt negatively about home factors related to poverty that seemed to have adverse effects on students. In between these two orientations was Thomas — he was not a member of the community but had some active involvement with it and appreciated its sense of pride and determination. He was also aware of factors that contributed to or interfered with the work of the school, such as the community's stability and isolation which produced a congenial student population, and its blue collar orientation which he believed held its young people back.

How would these perceptions of the community help shape the administrators' goals for the school's instructional program? To Thomas and Anthony, the interests of the community were salient. They saw the community in terms of its cultural traditions, its economic problems, its human bonds, its racial makeup. They saw these as central to the school's mission, which was why they were continually attempting to build bridges between the school and the community. To them, the instructional program of the school could not be separated from the cultural identity of the community and its oppressed economic status.

The other three administrators did not see the community as central to the mission of the school. Marjorie did not think very much about the community at all. Jerry and Sarah thought about it primarily as it affected their ability to carry out a job they defined for themselves apart from the community. They came into the school as outsiders with an idea of the school's agenda, which we will describe shortly. The Rivercrest community helped them carry out this agenda by teaching the young obedience; it got in the way when home problems deflected students from concentrating on schoolwork. It is interesting that Sarah saw parents as wanting to control the school, but did not take the time to find out what that control would mean, nor take steps to develop parent participation in the school's program. Parents were to be contacted about individual student problems, but not involved in planning out the school's instructional program.

Students

The student population at Five Bridges was more diversified than it is in many schools, and presented the administrators with human differences each was still learning to deal with. Jerry was in the process of learning to deal with physically impaired students. His role as Assistant Principal made him an active member of IEP teams as well as the school's main disciplinarian. He explained that he had negligible training in dealing with physically impaired students, and that they 'sometimes presented unique student problems' that most people don't face, 'such as running into other students in their wheelchairs'. Jerry talked about having to learn when it was or was not appropriate to treat them like other students.

Marjorie talked about learning to feel comfortable around non-white students. She told us that during her first year of teaching, she had a Native American student in class. She commented that, 'He had to be six feet tall. I was scared to death'. Since then she had taught in another multiracial school before coming to Five Bridges. She said she was overcoming her fear of minority students by:

> Teaching. Being involved with students. Being confronted by students. Getting to know students and adults that are not all white. Going through some hard times, not knowing what to do. Being aware that I would react differently if the students were white and dealing with that.

She was also in the process of learning to feel comfortable around handicapped people. She said that she used to have a hard time disciplining handicapped students, and often left this to Jerry until she learned from him how to handle handicapped students. Now she had learned to feel 'fairly comfortable' around handicapped students by having contact with them, but that 'drooling really bothers me'.

Sarah mentioned on a number of occasions being concerned about sexism, especially as it related to students' aspirations. She said that she had 'a good feel for the gals', and tried to push them into thinking about various career opportunities. She had less experience when it came to other dimensions of diversity, as noted earlier. For her, the students were a good learning experience.

> Our number one strength, we're not all white, we've got handicapped, Mexican-Americans, we have EMR students, and I find that a very nice situation. . . . I've learned a lot about physically handicapped. I've learned to appreciate them and accept them as just plain people who have a lot of desires and senses of humor and all those interesting things that normal people have. Of course, I've come to understand Mexican-American kids. I've never had any association with a Mexican-American before this and so I feel that I know them a lot better.

Anthony had spent most of his life in Rivercrest, which was racially integrated, and his younger brother who had recently died had been physically handicapped. He had learned to feel very comfortable around people who were of different racial groups and who were handicapped. However, he held some traditional views about women that he was trying to work through.

> I've gone to a few workshops since I last talked to you, but the last one that I went to was one on minority women. And it was really interesting. It reinforced a lot of what so-called feminists had been telling me why I'm a chauvinist pig.

In relation to his role as a counselor of students from different home traditions, especially Mexican girls, Anthony felt a dual responsibility — to be fair both to the Mexican tradition that encouraged women to remain in the home and to the feminist movement. He said he felt a need to 'open the door for the girls here but let them decide whether or not to walk through it'.

Thomas felt very positive about the diverse student population at Five Bridges. However, unlike the other four, the way he carried out his role in the school did not put him in direct contact with students. Therefore, he did not have feelings of discomfort or tension that he was trying to work through in dealing with them. In fact, he saw remaining at a distance a strength:

> I talk to kids in the hall. I don't get to know enough of the kids by name. Sometimes Jerry and Marjorie are in a situation that is a little sticky that they want me involved in, or want me to talk to a student. In one sense, I want to try to get as close to the kids as I can and in the other sense, it's kind of good to have a person that isn't all that close in contact with all the kids all of the time.

In addition to discussing specific aspects of diversity that characterized the students, the administrators often described characteristics of the students as students. The main characteristics they described were the students' respect for authority, their compliance, and their non-aggressiveness. For example:

Thomas: I think that the greatest percentage of our kids respect the community and the school. I think they see it as an avenue that is preparing them for life.... They're very workable.

Jerry: The students come to school with some respect for authority and so there is a built-in factor for them to listen to you.

Marjorie: In general, I think they are pretty non-aggressive. They pretty much let things happen. They are very cooperative individually.

Sarah: Maybe in their homes they've learned that there is still patriarchal/matriarchal law there, and they know that they have to follow the rules, and if they don't they have to accept punishment. I think that they accept it in a very nice way. I think kids here are very courteous.

There was agreement that discipline was not a major problem, therefore. Although students did misbehave on occasion, most misbehavior was attributed to inability to do the classwork, teacher insensitivity, or the occasional normal flair-ups among peers. Also, the administrators pointed out that few discipline problems were racially motivated. They agreed that only a small number of students were habitual trouble-makers; most students were usually obedient and willing to follow school rules and teacher expectations.

They also talked about the students' academic abilities and future aspirations, although this seemed to occupy less attention than did students' behavior. With the exception of Anthony, there was a general feeling that most of the students were not strong academically and that their future aspirations were not very high. Sarah was the main one to lay the blame for this on the students' homes, which is consistent with views she expressed in the attitude survey.

Jerry: Our main task is remediation because we are dealing with a large number of kids who have just come in with the minimum of academic skills.

Sarah: These kids are not raised in an atmosphere where they prize the academics. With the guys there is no two ways about it. Their physical abilities are probably the most important, and with the girls, unfortunately, I don't think they are all that tuned in.

All five administrators also, however, realized that there were some bright kids in the school. Anthony believed this included a fairly large percentage of the students; the others seemed to feel this group was a smaller minority. Anthony had entered counseling because, as a former Five Bridges student, he was aware of the lack of encouragement and help Rivercrest students were usually offered. He explained how poorly the students' respect for school served them in the long run in that their academic needs were not met:

> In our family it was always thought that if teachers treat you respectfully, if you get good grades, if they tell you you're a nice boy, that's all there is — that's all you need for an education. And then when you leave and you realize that what they teach you isn't the way it is ... it hurts. You feel degraded, you feel like you've been taken in.

All five administrators agreed on two points about the students: they were respectful of authority and school rules, and they were behind in their basic academic skills. But after that, their viewpoints diverged. Jerry, Sarah and Marjorie saw remediation as the primary need of the students, and doubted that the students had potential for much academic success beyond that. Thomas and Anthony, on the other hand, saw remediation as only a first step, not an end in itself. They thought about the students in terms of their life chances after graduation, and were deeply concerned that remediation alone would not prepare them for anything other than unskilled or semiskilled labor. Anthony in particular saw the students' respect for the school as a help only if the school was committed to offering them much more than remediation. But he feared it was not, and the other administrators' comments about the students supported Anthony's fear.

When schooling is seen as an avenue of social mobility, students believe it is in their best interests to comply with school authorities. But school authorities often see students as unable or unmotivated to excel because they come to school with poor academic skills. They see the school's main job as remediation, and are not optimistic that the majority of the students will leave school equipped to compete for the good life with peers who have better academic skills in the more affluent schools. Students in some schools respond to this hopelessness by rebelling or leaving school. At Five Bridges, the students trusted the judgment of the school. They dared aspire to a wide variety of professions, and saw the school as serving their best interests. Let us now examine what the administrators believed should be the academic program for these students.

The School's Academic Program

Broad school goals were mandated by the District Office and the Teacher Corps contract. More specific objectives were selected at the school building level based on these broad goals. At Five Bridges, school program objectives were proposed by the building administrators and ratified by the faculty. Five Bridges had four school objectives: improving reading and mathematics scores, providing an articulated curriculum, implementing education that is multicultural and improving the school climate. Improving reading scores and implementing education that is multicultural were the objectives that received the most active attention. What were the administrators and counselors' thoughts about each of these two objectives?

All five strongly supported the objective of raising reading and math achievement. Under Thomas's leadership, they encouraged teachers to address students' reading needs in their daily classroom lessons. They also were very supportive of the school's Title I reading and ESAA remedial reading and math programs: they allocated these programs ample space and supplies, and facilitated the assignment of low skilled students to these programs. They also allocated money and in-service time to help the staff as a whole acquire and learn to use materials at the students' reading levels.

Thomas's efforts to involve the staff in working toward this objective were rated favorably by the other members of the administration. For example, Jerry commented,

> Every opportunity [Thomas has] gotten, he's called to the staff's attention that the SRA test scores are going up, he's encouraged the staff to send homework home at least once a week with the kids, these little kinds of things. He's talked it up at staff meetings, we've got tremendous potential here and these kids are better than we give them credit for academically. I think some of that is starting to get across to people.

The second school program objective was to implement education that is multicultural, which Thomas defined as 'developing within the educational program opportunities and experiences where whoever is present can interact normally and naturally with and about folks from all cultures in a comfortable and non-threatening way. Education that is multicultural is education that teaches about cultures'. Thomas saw it as including in the curriculum the contributions of women and handicapped people, as well as different cultural groups. He wanted to see this being done in each classroom: 'I could see a teacher from any discipline conveying that from the perspective of their discipline'. He also saw education that is multicultural as showing respect to students of different backgrounds, treating their interests, values, and ideas with respect. He hoped each teacher would 'develop an atmosphere in a classroom where any youngster could ask any kind of meaningful question, which would be dealt with respectfully'.

Thomas, Jerry, Anthony and Sarah stressed attention to different racial groups in the curriculum. (Marjorie did not specifically bring this up in discussions with us, although she was strongly in favor of this on the attitude assessment and non-verbally supported the idea when it was voiced by other people.) They particularly emphasized the importance of including the Spanish language and the Mexican culture. The school's efforts in this area were an annual Mexican-American week, and a bilingual program. All five felt very positive about these programs, but commented that they were not enough. Anthony was the most articulate about this need:

> The 80s is the decade of the Hispanics. To me that's something that would be such a significant theme for the school, what they can build on that alone. When I was in school it was strictly black and white. It really gave you an idea or the feeling that we [Hispanics] really didn't exist, and to me just knowing as a student the focal point of the country, where it's going, the alternatives and options that it's going to provide for some of our kids, just that alone would cause a lot of real neat head trips for our kids.

In addition to stressing the importance of race in the curriculum, gender was often stressed by Marjorie and Sarah, handicap by Jerry and social class by Anthony.

Thomas was the main person who articulated the school objectives and who provided the strategy for reaching them. He described his overall strategy as: 'to go with those who are going, and not worry about those who don't'. This meant encouraging staff members who showed interest in an objective to become actively involved in working toward it and in helping other staff members with it.

> The way I try to develop things within the staff is to get the people who will do things to do things, and then share that with other staff. And letting the staff know that I support that kind of thing and encourage it. And in some cases, I will go directly to a staff member and ask them to get involved.

He tried to involve staff members with the building objectives in several different ways. He encouraged individual staff members to do specific things, talked about the objectives at faculty meetings and at other opportune times, encouraged the departments to incorporate these objectives in their instructional plans, asked each staff member to speak to these objectives in their own course objectives for each trimester, and provided workshops related to these objectives. For the multicultural objective, he also secured funding for specific programs: Teacher Corps, Bilingual Education and ESAA World Languages. Although Thomas was hesitant about turning people off by forcing staff involvement in working toward the building objectives, he expected some involvement on the part of all staff members, hoping that it would be voluntarily offered. For example, speaking of the multicultural objective, he said, '. . . this is a building activity, not just an individual teacher activity . . . everybody has to be involved, not just the few who might want to do something new'. However, it was never clear exactly what would happen to those who did not become involved.

The other members of the administrative team all agreed that Thomas's leadership strategy for the reading and math objective was appropriate, since they saw the staff as being supportive of it. However, they grew critical of this strategy for leading the building toward the multicultural objective. From the first, Anthony warned that Thomas's leadership strategy was not directive enough to gain active support from many teachers. Early in the study, Jerry began to join Anthony in criticizing this strategy for the multicultural objective. Following a workshop that was partly devoted to education that is multicultural, Jerry commented:

> It was turned over to a couple of people that were at the meeting and it was done so low key and so unexciting that it was — I don't know. I think if you are going to get people to do

something, it has to come on a little stronger. I've told Thomas and I think he agrees, and he says he's going to do it, but I don't know if he's going to find the time. One way to make sure that everyone's going to do something about it is to make sure that you have an individual conference with everybody and they have to tell you what they're doing in their classes.

Jerry was referring to the fact that few teachers were actively doing much in support of the multicultural objective. He attributed this to lack of interest as well as to the fact that many of the teachers had taught for a long time, and had seen 'principals come and go and come and go and new ideas come and go', and saw no need to take this new objective seriously. He believed the Principal should delegate specific responsibilities, such as observing in classrooms, to the other administrators, and provide time for them to carry out those responsibilities. Anthony joined him in advocating classroom observations, adding that 'I would make my position well known. I would be much more assertive and I wouldn't give people the options of having to do certain things'.

The administrators talked about additional ways of improving the academic program at Five Bridges. One, which they acted upon, was to ensure that all students had equal access to the curriculum, regardless of race, sex or handicap. In an effort to ensure equal access, they assigned students to core classes by a computer that was programmed to randomize students by race and sex. Special education students were manually scheduled to ensure equal access and placement with sympathetic and interested teachers. Anthony explained that before his arrival at the school (which was before physically impaired students were assigned to it) LD, ED and EMR students were in special education classes for most of the day. He had insisted that they had as much right to be exposed to the regular curriculum as anyone else, and that they should be in special education classes only for basic skill remediation. The school subsequently began to mainstream these students.

The administrators also mentioned a need to provide more for academically advanced students. For example, Jerry talked on two different occasions about his ideas for an academic program for gifted students. No such program was initiated, however. Anthony tried to meet this need as best he could through scheduling students into classes. He believed that the students, both the bright ones and the not-so-bright, did not know what they should be doing academically to prepare for their futures apart from attending school. He worked carefully with each student, getting to know his or her aspirations and abilities; he assigned them to classes to try to ensure that those with college potential — and he believed that a great number of Five Bridges students fell into this category — were taking the academic classes they would need later.

Thomas and Sarah mentioned ideas for developing students' interest in a wider range of career opportunities. Thomas believed students would benefit from first-hand experience with people in careers different from those of their parents; however, he said a limited field trip budget hindered efforts to provide this. Sarah commented that the Mexican girls needed a 'whale of a lot of push' to aspire to something more than secretarial work, and said that she was working with some of the girls, although her plans to develop a career guidance center in the counseling office were slow in being implemented.

All five administrators believed that the mode of instruction used in classrooms should be diversified, and should promote active student involvement. With the exception of Marjorie, they specifically pointed out that instruction in Five Bridges classrooms did not include enough diverse teaching strategies, nor strategies that promoted active student involvement. For example:

> *Thomas:* If I had a choice I would select some staff who would be teaching in a more open ended approach to get the students to think more on their own, make decisions for themselves on their own. They do get some of that but I would like to see a few more staff members more open to that.

> *Jerry:* [I would like to see] more group activities, shared learning, cooperative learning type things, getting out of the classroom once in a while. It is varying what you do from day to day and within the day to keep the kids' interest up, individualizing a bit, providing several different levels of things for kids to do, bringing in some education that is multicultural. We've got a lot more teachers here oriented not so much to straight lecture — they wouldn't last, the kids won't put up with straight lecture very much — but to a lot of worksheet stuff and a lot of 'Do the questions at the end of the textbook'. It's the easiest way to teach.

Diversifying teaching strategies was not made a building objective, and it was not formally acted upon. The administrators provided a workshop for teachers on cooperative learning and encouraged teachers who attempted diverse teaching strategies, but otherwise did not push this.

Ideas for improving the academic program that were voiced by the administrators were not acted upon much primarily because the administrators did not have a plan for developing curriculum beyond the formal school objectives. Thomas encouraged interested teachers to develop new courses or modify old ones; having done that, he took a passive role in curriculum development and left most of it up to the teachers or counselors to carry out, saying:

> If the counselors will see a need for a particular type of class or course offering, we talk about it, who could best do that, and then either Jerry Springs or I would talk to them, or the counselors will talk to them, and then that starts them thinking. It may not be a totally different course offering, just changing what is happening within a particular course.

Jerry was most active among this group in initiating curriculum development. For a while during this study, he had daily PA announcements made in English and Spanish; and he noted events, holidays and celebrations important to different cultural groups. Jerry also saw a need for supervizing the instructural program by giving direct help to teachers in their classrooms. He recalled an incident in which he had helped a teacher, and the teacher had 'just about jumped out of his chair' embracing the instructional help offered. Jerry contended that 'there are a lot of people who want you, they want me, they want Marjorie, they want a counselor, they want somebody to come in and tell them how they can work with a situation'. However, daily maintenance activities occupied most of the administrators' attention, and long-range plans for acting on ideas beyond the building objectives were not established.

The administrators placed considerable responsibility on the staff for improving the school's academic program. We will first examine their perceptions of the staff and of each other as leaders, before providing an analysis of the academic program and their leadership.

The Staff

Thomas, Jerry and Anthony talked about the history of the staff at Five Bridges on a few occasions (Marjorie and Sarah were relatively new in the building and had little first-hand knowledge about the staff's history). Thomas explained that, before the schools in Rivercrest were desegregated, 'when a teacher couldn't function anywhere else in the district he was sent to Five Bridges. That was Siberia. You never heard from him again'. According to both Anthony and Jerry, supervision in Five Bridges was poor then and the staff got used to doing things as they pleased. When Rivercrest's schools were desegregated, Thomas inherited much of this staff plus others from the senior high who were transferred due to a reduction in force but had enough seniority to be placed where they chose. Thomas was slowly able to add new people to the staff, but he commented that many of them came in at 'ground zero when it comes to working in a low income school in a multicultural setting'.

At the time of this study the administrative team had mixed feelings about the staff. Sarah voiced the most consistently positive opinion, saying that 'we have a really neat faculty' who is 'very tolerant', 'willing to try things', and willing to 'take the bull by the horns'. Anthony voiced the most negative opinion. Although he recognized a few good teachers on the staff, he frequently commented about characteristics of the staff that distressed him. For example, when asked about strengths and weaknesses of the school he cited many of the staff as a weakness, saying that they depended too much on dittos in their teaching: 'I think if the ditto machine ever broke down we would have to close the school, and that would be more serious than a snowstorm!'.

Both Thomas and Jerry gave contradictory global evaluations of the staff. For example, Thomas on one occasion commented that 'they are like a bunch of students — you have to spoonfeed them'; on another occasion he pointed out that they had come a long way, and rated the staff as one strength of the school, noting their 'willingness to try things — I think each in their own field is good'. Thomas also commented that the staff was 'looking for ways to get involved' in school programs, but that 'there has to be a security base before they would really step into [a new program] and get involved'. Jerry saw the staff as 'interested in kids' and 'willing to put some time in to try and do a decent job as a teacher'. But he also saw them as 'remarkably jealous and petty', as 'thinking more in terms of good for my room and area rather than thinking of the whole school and what is good for the school'. Jerry remarked that teachers dreaded 'having anybody come in their classrooms and watch them' in a supervisory capacity even though at the same time they may genuinely want help. Marjorie gave no clear opinion about the staff. She commented positively about junior high faculties, but not specifically about the staff at Five Bridges.

Besides discussing the staff in general, the leadership team would often discuss the staff related to specific issues, such as discipline and expectations of students. Jerry, Anthony and Sarah agreed about the teachers' procedures for handling student discipline. They believed that the teachers didn't want to deal with their own discipline problems, but preferred to send them to the office. Jerry's comment captures the feeling of the three: 'One of the biggest problems here right now, I think, is the willingness of everybody to dump discipline problems on myself and Marjorie and not take any responsibility themselves'. The reason he offered for their unwillingness was that:

> Most teachers, when you really get down to it, expect to teach and not deal with [human behavior]. They haven't been taught how, they're very uncomfortable with it, they tend to be very arbitrary, tend to react on their emotions, and in the junior high especially, we have a lot of kids that are sent down just because the teacher has had it.

The two counselors were the only ones who talked specifically about the staff's expectations of the students, and both agreed that their expectations were low. Sarah compared Five Bridges with a middle class school she worked in before, commenting that at Five Bridges, '. . . teachers just expect that [students] are not going to produce'. Anthony told us that few staff members talked to the students about college or their futures, and that he had been accused by several of being 'too conscientious about the academic part' in scheduling students into classes.

Anthony, because of his Hispanic background and dual role as a counselor and member of the administrative team, had a particular perspective about the staff that the other counselor and administrators did not voice. He perceived the staff in relation to their race and social class backgrounds, and he saw clearly how their predominantly white backgrounds limited their perspectives. He pointed out that 'there are certain racial attitudes about some staff', and that 'a teacher that is white, coming into the school, would be accepted more readily' than a minority. He also believed his Hispanic background often caused the staff to become anxious and uneasy around him. He said they treated him as Mexican when it suited their purposes, but when he voiced a viewpoint they did not like or disagreed with, they regarded him as no more Mexican than they were and tended to pass off what he had to say. Anthony often wondered out loud how he should respond to the staff, given that he was one of the few Hispanics on it.

Perceptions of Each Other

How did the administrators and counselors view each other? How well did they communicate and get along with one another? Over the course of this study these five individuals had numerous opportunities to let their hair down and describe what it was like to work with each other.

To an individual, they described one another and their relationship using such terms as 'hard worker', 'supportive', 'no power struggles', 'nonsexist', and 'mutual respect'. Sarah's comment captures well their general feeling about working with Thomas: 'Thomas Wilson is the kind of guy [with whom] you can speak your piece ... you are not looked down on.... He is really an easy guy to work for'. Marjorie was very pleased with her relationship with all of the members in this group and, especially, the non-sexist attitude of the Assistant Principal. 'I think they are very supportive. I think Jerry Springs is one of the most non-sexist people I have ever run into. The counselors are very easy to work with ... [and] everyone is pulling their own weight in their own area.' Jerry, too, praised the group, and during one discussion described his feeling about Marjorie: 'Marjorie and I get along perfectly. We complement each other. She is a hard worker, she has a lot of initiative, she takes problems and works with them. She does things just to relieve the burden off of me, which really helps and I appreciate it.' The feeling of mutual respect that the administrators and counselors shared is clearly echoed in Thomas' remarks: 'One thing that I think ... is our strongest point is that there is a mutual respect professionally within the group. Every one's opinions or suggestions are listened to and [we] try to work out collectively the best solution.'

Most of the members of this group did recognize that despite their good working relationship, their not finding time to sit down and discuss school operations together was becoming more and more a major concern. Jerry often voiced his feeling about this growing problem.

> Things are decided and things are done and a lot of times I will hear about them through other sources, sometimes through a teacher, or one of the other members of the team comes and tells me. It's not even when something is decided, or this is the way we are going to go; there's no clear way that that's communicated to everybody on the team, so everybody knows right away what's going on.

Our Analysis of the Administrative Team

The administrative team at Five Bridges saw its mission as more than simply administering the day-to-day operations of a school. Recognizing that the school had a pluralistic student population and a history of poor academic performance, they saw it in their mission to raise the students' academic performance and make the schooling program multicultural.

Let us look more closely at the school's two main objectives. In aspiring to raise students' reading and math scores, the administrators were attempting to bolster the quality of education the students received. Low basic skill levels were correctly seen as a major impediment to substantial academic learning, and were targeted for remediation. Was this an aim toward academic excellence? By itself, we think not. It was insufficient. It was a move toward establishing a minimal level of acceptable academic performance, but was not a move higher than that. Most of the administrators' attention was focused on this minimal level, not beyond it toward excellence.

The administrators were concerned with equity in that they ensured that all students had equal access to the curriculum. There was no tracking or ability grouping. Remedial instruction and special education were abundant for those who needed it. But no student was in a remedial track for academic learning — unless one were to consider the entire school as a remedial track. Viewing the school as a remedial track, its overwhelming concern with basic skills remediation to the exclusion of more complex learning prevented the Five Bridges students from being prepared to compete as equals with their peers from other schools for entry into college and careers. This was a very real problem.

We applaud the administrators for recognizing equity as encompassing more than equal access to school resources, in spite of the limitation just noted. The reports on the state of education that we cited in the opening of this chapter take a very narrow view of what equity means. The administrators at Five Bridges recognized that it meant learning about human diversity in America, and about the barriers that have historically oppressed people of color, women, low income people and the handicapped. They recognized that school knowledge is not culture-free, and believed that it should be expanded to include more than just white middle class perspectives on what is worth knowing. This insight and conviction on their part led them to adopt the multicultural objective for the school's program.

We think they could have carried their conception of this objective further, however. The administrators had varying degrees of understanding of what it entails. Sarah and Marjorie did not talk much about it, and what they said revolved mainly around including contributions of different groups into the standard curriculum. Anthony, on the other hand, would have it include analyses of racism and classism in society as well. As the objective was articulated to the staff, it focused mainly on including men and women of color and white women in the curriculum, materials, classroom displays and teaching students to show respect for cultural differences.

We sensed that in general the administrators felt social justice could be achieved if people interacted fairly with each other in interpersonal relationships, learned to cooperate and became interested in the positive contributions of different groups in society. Judging from their discussions of their own comfort levels around the students, we felt that to varying degrees the administrators were themselves learning to achieve these kinds of relationships with the students.

But to a large extent the students already appreciated their own diversity — especially their racial diversity — and cooperated well with each other. They did lack knowledge about their different cultural heritages, and could benefit from learning in school America's multicultural heritage (including learning about different handicapping conditions and about the history and culture of women and different social classes, as well as that of different racial and ethnic groups). But what the students did not know enough about was their own position in the social structure, and what to do about it. They did not realize the extent to which they as a group were economically and politically oppressed. They did not realize the extent to which people of color are today denied access to resources based on race and racist acts historically which have structured non-whites into disadvantaged social strata. Neither did they realize the extent to which women were and still are today an unequal group. Women, non-whites, members of the lower class, and handicapped people are involved in struggles today to achieve more equitable access to resources. It would be to the Five Bridges students' benefit to know about their status, and the struggles going on to achieve equality. It would also be to their benefit to appraise the success of those struggles and to explore ways to strengthen their success.

We did not see too much of this thinking reflected in the administrators' goals for the school. We do not believe the administrators would have opposed these ideas, but they did not surface when school objectives were discussed. Thomas was the spokesperson for the group, and he himself was attempting to work out an analysis of human diversity in our society. As noted in the introduction at the beginning of this chapter, it is a problem for which he had perhaps more preparation than some people, but still not enough to tackle alone.

Given, then, that the school objectives did not go far enough, how might we assess the administrative team's probable success in achieving the objectives they did set? Based on their expressed attitudes about human diversity, we might give them a good chance at success. Overall, they scored very well on the attitude assessment scale. Even though individual members of the team agreed with some biased or stereotypic quesions on the scale, no biased statement was accepted by the majority of the team and each individual team member displayed an overall non-biased attitude on each of the subscales.

However, interviews with the team revealed some differences between stating attitudes in the abstract and applying those attitudes in concrete situations. For example, on the class subscale only Sarah agreed with several stereotypic statements about lower class people, and all five team members including Sarah rejected the notion that middle class students are better learners than lower class students, and that people on welfare are lazy. But when they talked about the students and the community, both Jerry and Sarah on several occasions put some blame for the students' poor academic performance on the home and the parents' social class.

As another example, on the attitude assessment scale the team agreed that the curriculum should include attention to different racial groups, both sexes, all age groups, all social classes, and the handicapped. But when discussing the curriculum at Five Bridges, they often 'forgot' about attending to sexism, classism and handicapism in the curriculum. Neither of these examples suggests that attitudes espoused in the abstract do *not* reflect a person's thinking. But they do suggest that a person's thinking often contains inconsistent ideas, and on a day-to-day, 'real-life' basis ideas may predominate that are not the same as those one professes, especially when one is in the process of learning to deal with forms of human diversity with which he or she has had little experience (such as Jerry with handicap, and Marjorie with race).

Therefore, we must question whether this administrative team had the knowledge or experience that would help them act on their ideals in real situations. For example, based on their backgrounds we know that none of them had skill in developing a multicultural curriculum, although they were leading the school doing this. None had experience rebuilding the academic program in a lower class or desegregated school, yet this is what they were aspiring to do at Five Bridges. None had much experience working with handicapped students, yet they were attempting to lead academic development in a mainstreamed setting.

Let us now turn our attention specifically to the leadership team's strategy for achieving the school objectives. Based on a review of studies of principal behavior, Leithwood and Montgomery (1982) have outlined factors that distinguish effective from typical principals' strategies in implementing change in the school. They report that effective principals establish strong leadership for change in the form of either carefully selected influential staff members or themselves. Effective principals acquire a strong knowledge base in the proposed changes early on, and take regular steps to provide their staff with knowledge and skill that will enable them to implement the change. New teachers are selected for their potential for helping implement change, and are given in-service help to orient them to the school's program. Teachers are provided with planning time on a regular basis, and with materials; resources are secured from government agencies or other external sources and from district sources. Effective principals regularly monitor both student progress and staff instructional practices, and regularly provide staff with feedback about their progress. While they try to build positive relationships with staff, they are primarily task-oriented and willing to sacrifice relationships if necessary to keep teachers on task. Effective principals also facilitate school-community communication, centering much of this around their goals for the school. Finally, effective principals organize their own time well, and do not allow themselves to get bogged down by administrative trivia.

At Five Bridges, the school objectives had been set at the administrative level and approved by the staff. The administrators were genuinely committed to them. The staff was not overtly opposed to them, or else the administration would not have adopted them (we will examine the staff's feelings about the objectives in the next chapter). But how committed can one expect the staff to be to objectives they themselves have not had a major role in generating and selecting?

Thomas used two somewhat different strategies for leading the school. For daily operations, he delegated areas of responsibility to the other four members of the team, and counted on their professional competence and interpersonal congeniality to get things done. This seemed to work quite well. Each member of the team was clear about his or her role regarding daily operations, performed it well, and had worked out ways to coordinate efforts informally with other team members as needed.

Thomas' strategy for long-term goals included assessing needs and setting a direction, procuring resources, providing some in-service, communicating with the community, establishing good teacher-principal relations, and encouraging staff involvement. Let us consider each of these. Thomas successfully obtained a variety of resources for the school. We have pointed out earlier that it housed a number of special programs; along with these programs came money for resources and staff, which Thomas actively let the rest of the staff know was available. Thomas also arranged for workshops which he encouraged staff members to attend, providing them with release time to do so. In addition, he used external funding to provide a day of staff planning time during a vacation, which was attended by more than half the staff.

We wonder, however, why Thomas persisted in attempting to 'go with the goers' on the staff, given what he knew about their professional history. While on some occasions he praised them, on other occasions he clearly saw problems in their willingness to perform, their teaching skills and so forth. It seemed odd that he waited for leadership to emerge from the staff, rather than delegating someone on the administrative team (or himself) to take active charge of implementing each of the school objectives. We would have expected a reduction in administrative time for handling discipline to provide time for implementing these objectives, since the administrators agreed that discipline was not a major problem in the school and that teachers did not handle discipline problems themselves as much as they could have.

Given the leadership team's ambivalent feelings about the professional capabilities of the staff, we wondered why the staff's daily teaching practices were not more closely scrutinized and supervised. We wondered why the administrators were hesitant to make the staff really 'put out', especially since they saw the staff as having low expectations for the students. We suspect that Thomas' concern for human relations and lack of experience in carrying out the specific changes he was attempting to institute impeded his progress. He believed that people perform when they are comfortable and trusted and when their personal needs have been met, so he provided psychological support to staff members. In the process, he did not give staff specific instructions about what they should be doing in the classroom nor did he monitor their teaching behavior closely fearing he might alienate the staff.

Two of Thomas' co-workers were critical of the human relations emphasis, pointing out specific actions that should be taken, such as observing teachers in the classroom on a regular basis, assigning specific tasks, requiring that they be carried out and so forth. But, there was no procedure used by the team for mapping out new strategies. Daily operations in the school ran smoothly, so they did not meet as a team very often to discuss what they were doing. They all saw the Principal as the official school leader, so they all did what they were told to do and did not see it as their place to do more than make suggestions to him. And, since they all liked each other personally, it is likely that no-one wanted to risk personal friendship or professional compatibility by stepping too far outside his or her role to critique Thomas' leadership strategy openly.

In sum, we found the school objectives to be necessary but insufficient for providing the Five Bridges students with both excellence and equity. The objectives took account of students' academic weaknesses and diverse backgrounds, but did not sufficiently take account of what the students would need in order to succeed in a society that is biased against them. We found the leadership strategy to have some strengths, but also two serious weaknesses: overreliance on a staff perceived as unwilling to work hard, and insufficient administrative time for long-range planning and monitoring instruction.

Now let us turn to the teachers to see what they actually did about the school objectives, and become acquainted with their teaching.

Chapter 5

The Teachers

Teachers constitute a core group of those who make schooling what it is. Teachers are the final arbiters of what is taught in classrooms, how it is taught and what actions and interactions can legitimately occur.

We studied the teachers at Five Bridges, examining them against a backdrop of knowledge about teachers in schools throughout the United States.[1] If we examine the research on teachers in American schools similar to Five Bridges, what attitudes and behaviors might we expect of a 'typical' faculty of teachers? How typical were the Five Bridges teachers?

Research tells us that teachers in desegregated schools typically have low expectations of minority students; they blame students' home backgrounds for the problems they see. Control of student behavior is a frequent and central concern. Racial diversity is seen as irrelevant to academic content, and teachers often believe that students should deal with their own racial differences. Believing this, teachers try to overlook race when dealing with students (for example, Cusick and Ayling, 1974; Gerard and Miller, 1975; Willie, 1978; Carew and Lightfoot, 1979; Clement, Eisenhart and Harding, 1979; Scherer and Slawski, 1979; Rist, 1978; Schofield, 1983).

Teachers see themselves as middle class, and prefer to teach middle class students. They tend to see lower class students as low achievers and behavior problems (McPherson, 1972; Ogbu, 1974; Rist, 1970; Sennett and Cobb, 1973). In mainstreamed schools, regular teachers are apprehensive about working with handicapped students because they have not been prepared to teach them. They are more comfortable with students classified as mildly handicapped and most comfortable with non-handicapped students (Boyle and Sleeter, 1981; Garrett and

Crump, 1980; Shotel, Iano and McGettigan, 1972). Finally, teachers have different behavioral and academic expectations for boys and girls, expecting boys to be more active and assertive than girls, and sometimes expecting boys to be more able than girls in math and science (for example, Serbin, *et al.*, 1973).

Based on research findings, how would we expect these 'typical' teachers to teach in a school like Five Bridges? We would expect their room displays to omit people of color and students' experiences (Leacock, 1969; Rist, 1978). Their teaching materials would contain racial, sex and social class stereotypes, and omit entirely, or include in a token-position, the perspectives and contributions of people of color, women, handicapped people and lower class people (Butterfield, *et al.*, 1979; Frazier and Sadker, 1973; Sapon-Shevin, 1982). They would also drill students using worksheets, while they would use more varied forms of resources with middle-class white students (Metz, 1978).

Research has not examined the extent to which classroom content apart from materials would include women, handicapped and lower class people, but it suggests that the typical teacher (especially if he/she is white) would rarely refer to race, or include the perspectives or contributions of people of color (Gerard and Miller, 1975; Rist, 1978; Willie, 1978; Clement, Eisenhart and Harding, 1979; Scherer and Slawski, 1979; Schofield, 1983). In addition, we would expect the content to be shallow and focused on basic skills, and homework to be rarely given (Leacock, 1969; Ogbu, 1974).

We would expect the 'typical' teacher in a school like Five Bridges to instruct students by giving them specific material to learn and reproduce on tests, dominate classroom interaction, restrict talking and movement by students, tolerate some student inattention, and quite possibly spend more time walking around helping students complete written work than providing them with new information or involving them in activities (Leacock, 1969; Metz, 1978; Noblit, 1979; Cusick and Ayling, 1974). Students would not be expected to think analytically about the world or create their own interpretations of it, rather they would be expected to learn someone else's interpretation (Everhart, 1983). At the same time, we might expect teachers to negotiate with students, offering them time to talk with friends in class in exchange for good behavior (Metz, 1978; Scherer and Slawski, 1979). This is a profile of the 'typical' staff in US schools. What was the staff at Five Bridges like? We will begin by giving an overview of the composition of the staff.

Staff Composition

We analyzed the composition of the staff during school year 1979–80; although there was some yearly staff turnover, composition patterns changed little during the course of this study. Table 5 depicts staff composition by sex, race, and handicap. As this table shows, the great majority of the teachers and aides were white. Furthermore, none of the non-white teachers were teaching core subject areas (i.e., English, social studies, math, science). One black teacher taught Title I reading and the other taught home economics; one Hispanic teacher taught music, and the others (predictably) taught Spanish and bilingual education.

Table 5: Staff composition

	Sex		Race					Handicap
	Male	Female	Asian	Black	Hispanic	Native American	White	Physically impaired
Certificated teachers	24	22	—	2	3	—	41	1
Non-certificated aides	—	—	—	—	2	—	13	1

The sex composition of the staff was better balanced than the racial composition: twenty-four teachers were male and twenty-two were female. Although both sexes taught math and science, women taught home-economic courses and men taught industrial arts. There were two physically impaired staff members, both in wheelchairs. The physically impaired teacher taught math; the aide assisted in the multiply handicapped program. Almost half of the staff was between the ages of 40 and 50; a few staff members were nearing retirement. Only about one-fifth of the staff was below the age of 30.

Staff Backgrounds

We looked briefly into the personal and professional backgrounds of the staff, focusing most of our attention on their preparation to work with a diversified student population. First, we assessed the regional diversity of their backgrounds: one-half of the staff had been born and raised within fifteen miles of Five Bridges. Most of the others were raised in neighboring states, although a few had come from more distant parts of the country. About 60 per cent came from white collar homes, in which the father was, for example, a lawyer, a manager, a banker or a business owner. The remaining 40 per cent came from blue collar homes in which the father held a job such as janitor, meat packer or laborer. About two-thirds of the staff came from homes in which the father held a job and the mother stayed at home. Most of those mothers who had worked outside the home held jobs such as teacher, secretary, or nurse.

The great majority of the staff members had received their bachelors' degrees from colleges and universities within the state (many from small private colleges). One-third of the teachers had also completed master's degrees; most of these had been completed at either a large state university or a small private university in the city.

We asked twenty staff members in interviews what kinds of informal experiences they had that would prepare them to work in a multiracial and mainstreamed school. Many of these staff members stated that their first personal contact with a non-white person had not occurred until high school or college, although one had attended a multiracial public school as a child. Prior to teaching, most had little contact with non-whites or handicapped people. The few who did have some contact mentioned instances such as a family member marrying a non-white, having a black roommate in college or the service, serving as a Vista or Peace Corps volunteer, and having a handicapped family member. For five teachers, their main experiential preparation for teaching the Five Bridges students was prior teaching experience in another multiracial school.[2]

We asked the same twenty staff members about their formal preparation for working in a multiracial, mainstreamed school. Ten said that they had none. Of the ten who had some such training, the most common form it took was a human relations workshop (five staff members) or a human relations class at the university (four staff members). A course in mainstreaming, careers for women and black literature had also each been taken by one staff member. In addition, one or two staff members each had attended a workshop on Mexican culture, American Indian culture and learning styles. Finally, one staff member had attended Teacher Corps' Corps Member Training Institute, which helps participants develop skills in working together, providing school leadership, and curriculum building, for the purpose of improving schooling for students from low income homes.

In an effort to prepare the staff better for teaching at Five Bridges, the administration had made arrangements for a two-week institute to be held prior to the opening of school in August 1978. This institute was designed to raise teachers' level of awareness about age, race, sex, social class and handicap diversity, provide them information about different groups, and help them begin to assess and modify their curriculum to make it more responsive to diversity. This institute was attended by about thirty staff members — the administrators and counselors, most of the special education and remedial teachers and aides, and teachers of special classes (for example, affective education, multicultural education) and the Teacher Corps interns, but few core area teachers.

In summary, most of the staff had grown up in the geographical region in which the city was located, and many had grown up geographically close to Five Bridges. Over a third were from working class backgrounds, but few had grown up in racially diverse neighborhoods, and few had extended contact with people from different racial backgrounds before they were adults. Also, few had much experience with handicapped people in their personal backgrounds. Although their formal education had prepared them to teach in their subject areas, little in their formal education had prepared them for a pluralistic student population, with the exception of the special education teachers' training and experience with handicapped students. For the most part, the staff's knowledge about non-white and handicapped students — especially that of the core subject area staff — had been acquired on the job at Five Bridges or at a previous school.

Teachers' Perceptions of Human Diversity

In Chapter 4 we described the attitude assessment scale we used to measure the teachers' and administrators' attitudes about age, class, handicap, race and sex. In the next few pages we will describe the teachers' attitudes about each of these areas, then describe their overall awareness and beliefs about human diversity. We analyzed responses to questions about each 'ism' by identifying questions that elicited virtually unanimous agreement, those for which there was a high level of agreement but one to four staff members disagreed, and those questions which elicited a considerable amount of disagreement.

Handicap

The staff agreed to a large extent on many items related to the intent of PL94–142. They agreed unanimously that handicapped children have the same rights as other children, and that handicapped children should have equal access to community programs. They also agreed unanimously that the school curriculum should contain information that would alleviate the curiosity and anxiety people feel when dealing with handicapped people, and all but a few staff members believed that students should be introduced to devices used by handicapped people for this purpose. In addition, all but a few staff members rejected the idea that it is in the best interests of the handicapped to be left alone.

A few questions provoked some disagreement or lack of certainty on the part of some staff members. For example, about a quarter believed that money rather than attitudes of people hindered mainstreaming, and a few more were unsure about this. A third of the staff accepted the stereotype that mentally retarded boys are sexually promiscuous; and a third was unaware that research has not found special education classes better than regular classes for the mildly handicapped. But overall, attitudes toward the handicapped related to public and school policy and to curriculum were quite positive.

We compared the responses of special education teachers plus one handicapped staff member with those of the rest of the staff. Although the average scores of the special education teachers and handicapped staff member were higher than the average of the other teachers, the difference between the two groups was not large. In fact, the five staff members scoring the highest on this sub-scale were regular education teachers.

Sex

The majority of the staff agreed with most non-sexist viewpoints represented in the questions. They agreed unanimously that sexism is learned behavior, and that parents should encourage independence in children of both sexes equally. All but one to four staff members rejected stereotypes such as: men are better administrators than women, men are more ambitious than women, and boys innately have better math aptitude than girls. All but one believed men should be willing to work for women supervisors, and all but four believed women with children should be able to hold jobs even if they don't have to for financial reasons.

A few questions received a variety of responses. Only half the staff rejected the idea that men should be given preference over women in being hired or promoted in some jobs; a few more were not sure. Over a quarter agreed that using language like 'chairperson' for 'chairman' is nonsense. Also, one-fifth of the staff agreed that it is only natural for women to have less freedom of action than men, and a few more were not sure about this. When shown a lesson containing various kinds of stereotypes, a few staff members picked out the sex stereotypes first, although about half of the staff did not pick out any stereotypes.

But by and large, responses reflected a large amount of acceptance of non-sexist ideas. Furthermore, on the average there was no difference in scores on questions related to sex between male and female staff members.

Age

The staff was in virtually unanimous agreement on only one statement related to age: American society should adopt a policy of education for life, including preparation for retirement and use of leisure time.

There was a high level of agreement on eight questions on the age sub-scale. Three were related to curriculum, and the teachers' answers suggested that elderly persons should serve as classroom aides, volunteers, etc.; curriculum material at all levels of school should deal with life from conception to death; and the elderly should be invited to the school to help with curriculum implementation at appropriate times. There was also a high level of agreement that there is a crucial need for a guaranteed adequate income, free public transportation and adequate and sufficient housing for the elderly. Additionally, most of the staff did not believe that intelligence normally declines as one ages.

Although the staff agreed on many questions related to age, they also disagreed or were uncertain about some other questions. One-third of the staff believed that elderly persons in this country are made to feel unproductive or unwanted, although the other two-thirds rejected that idea. One of the staff believed that people should retire at age sixty-five, and almost one-half believed that respect for an individual declines with age.

Class

Virtual unanimous agreement did not occur on any questions on the class sub-scale. However, there was a high level of agreement in rejecting the ideas that children from middle class homes are inherently better learners than children from lower class homes, and that lower class students lack desire to work. Most of the staff supported policies such as schools in low socio-economic areas being provided with additional funds to expose children to a broader range of social and academic experiences, and requiring that a part of the student teaching experience be in such a school. Most of the staff also believed that stories in textbooks should feature a balance of middle-class and lower-class families.

The staff was evenly split over whether middle class families prize education more than lower-class families. There was also considerable disagreement concerning such policy issues as continuation of the free lunch program, the appropriation of monies for in-service training for working with low income students and whether classrooms should reflect middle class values. The staff was also in disagreement concerning class stereotypes such as: most people on welfare are lazy, students from lower class families are culturally deprived, and lower class students cause more behavior problems in school than do middle-class students.

Race

Although the staff did not express unanimous agreement about any of the questions related to race, there was a high level of agreement on several items. For example, all but two to five staff members agreed that neither the observance of special ethnic events such as Black History Week or Puerto Rican Independence Day, nor 'ethnic awareness experiences' such as taking trips to Chinatown or eating soul food, in and of themselves, are sufficient means of exposing students to our multicultural society. All but a few rejected the notion that there are few stories about minority group members in textbooks because either they are inappropriate for textbook use or minority groups have few stories.

But on other questions related to policy, curriculum and general knowledge, there was much more disagreement and greater acceptance of racist viewpoints. For instance one-third agreed that, if people want to live in the US, they must learn in the language of American English, and one-fifth agreed that non-English speaking students should be treated as handicapped learners. Two-fifths accepted the idea that students should be taught that Columbus discovered America even though history tells us Indians were here when he arrived. A little less than half of the staff considered it disrespectful to the Cherokee Indians to nickname a school the 'Cherokees'. Finally, less than half agreed that multicultural education should be taught in a monocultural setting.

The attitude scale contained some sections which tested sensitivity to racial stereotypes. On one section respondents were asked to circle words describing members of specific ethnic groups; a little over half the staff did this, thus stereotyping these ethnic groups. Another section asked respondents to comment on a passage from a history book glorifying white 'progress' at the expense of Native Americans. Half the staff clearly recognized that this was biased, one-quarter stated that it was correct, and the rest were not sure. In other sections of the instrument in which racial stereotypes were present, less than half the staff commented on them.

We compared minority group staff members' scores on the race sub-scale with those of the white staff members. Although on the average the minority group members' scores wre higher, the difference between the two groups was very small.

Human Diversity Overall

Overall, the staff displayed the most knowledge and acceptance of human diversity based on handicap, sex and age (in that order) and the least toward human diversity based on class and race (in that order). In fact, one-third to one-half of the staff expressed agreement with several racial and class stereotypes.

We examined individual profiles of staff members to find out if there were any obvious differences between high and low scorers and to note any patterns in how individuals scored across sub-scales. One pattern was that the two Teacher Corps interns were among the highest overall scorers on the staff, and one was the highest scorer. We think this speaks well for the training these interns received and the kind of people Teacher Corps attracted. We also discovered that the minority teachers were scattered throughout the list in an almost random fashion. They had scored on the average slightly higher than the white staff members on the race sub-scale, but did not stand out as a group on other sub-scales. This indicates racial minority people are not necessarily any more accepting of human diversity than white people. The special education teachers, however, tended to score above average on all sub-scales; three out of four of them were above the overall average score. Like the Teacher Corps interns, this probably reflects on their training and the nature of person who is attracted to special education.

In examining individual profiles we noticed two patterns: many teachers had similar scores across sub-scales, scoring equally high or low, for example, on the sex and class sub-scales; we also found several teachers who scored much higher or lower on one or two sub-scales than on the rest. Most striking were the two lowest overall scorers: both were near retirement age; while their responses consistently showed little appreciation of diversity based on race, sex, handicap and gender, they showed great awareness and appreciation of diversity based on age. Another low scorer on most sub-scales scored high on the handicap sub-scale, while a high scorer overall scored somewhat low on the age sub-scale. This suggests that one cannot be certain how a person feels about various dimensions of human diversity by knowing how that person feels about one or two dimensions.

Taken as a whole, we were not as optimistic about the teachers' responses to the questionnaire as we were about the administrators'. The teachers' responses ranged greatly from very positive attitudes about all five forms of human difference to very stereotypic and unaccepting attitudes, especially related to race and class. Given the teachers' backgrounds, this should not be surprising. But given the kinds of students they were teaching, it was disheartening and could be described as unprofessional.

Teachers' Cultural Knowledge about Students

In order to understand the Five Bridges teaching staff's cultural knowledge about the students, the school and their work there, we interviewed most of the teachers who were responsible for the core subjects, three special education teachers, a remedial reading teacher and her aide, the affective education teacher, a home economics teacher, a graphic arts teacher, the multicultural education teacher, and both music teachers. Many interviews were conducted with these teachers over the duration of this study; the cultural knowledge described here represents a distillation of many hours worth of taped interviews and conversations.

Understanding how teachers see students is crucial to understanding what they do in the classroom and why. We asked many different questions about the students over the course of this study. As we examined the responses, we found that most remarks could be grouped into one of three categories: students' academic abilities, students' value orientations and students' social behavior. Some teachers focused almost exclusively on one category; others talked equally as much about two or all three.

Most teachers discussed the students partly or wholly in terms of their academic abilities. The special education and remedial teachers described academic problems their students were having and classwork they were giving these students to build their academic skills. They tended to talk about the students as individuals with different academic needs that were being met in their classrooms. For example:

> In special education we have the individual education plan and we have to teach what the child needs. That is outlined on the IEP and what I have is individual reading levels and skills and tutoring.

The special education teachers did not lament their students' academic abilities, but instead matter-of-factly told us what they were doing to build them.

Many of the core area teachers talked in some detail about the students' poor reading skills and how this made teaching difficult. These teachers tended to generalize about all students, suggesting that the majority had reading problems, or that the students lacked academic strengths in other areas. They made comments such as these:

> *Tim:* I think reading skills is the biggest [problem], being able to communicate. And they usually, if they can do that, those students that are able to read seem to be able to handle themselves pretty well. At least you can give them some things to do self-directed and they are able to handle it.
>
> *R:* How would you describe the students here at Five Bridges? Say, if I was a new teacher coming in and you were orienting me.
> *Jo:* I would say be careful because a lot of kids have reading problems. I guess I would say spend some time on prepping them vocabulary-wise.

The English teachers clearly distinguished among the students in terms of academic ability. These teachers talked about three different kinds of students, differentiated by reading ability: remedial or special education students, average students and smart students. One of these teachers explained that when she first came to Five Bridges she saw the whole student body as below average in reading ability, but had since changed her perception recognizing that their academic abilities were not uniformly poor:

> For a school like this, you have programs that deal with kids who are having reading difficulties. So if you decide that you want them to do more difficult work, and these kids cannot do it, they can be given opportunities to improve their reading, maybe in a specialized reading program. But you have nothing for the really bright kids, the average and brighter. And so I kind of shifted my teaching expectations from the lower to the average, from the average to the higher. Throughout the year, because I began to see more and more that maybe these kids are better than we think they are.... The reputation the school has for being low on reading is district-wide. And I hate to admit that I really allowed that to influence me. At first, in September, I thought gee, if they can't read above a third grade level, what am I going to do? I mean, now, I'm beginning to see that those aren't the kids I've got in my classroom necessarily.

Finally, two social studies teachers and one home economics teacher talked about the students' academic abilities in terms of strengths. These teachers described students as strong in problem-solving and thinking, and they noted that student thinking skills were not always reflected well in their written work because many had poor writing skills. Of the teachers we talked to it is noteworthy that only this small minority looked beyond the students' reading and writing skills to see what else they could do intellectually. Most judged the students as having low academic potential — as being hard to teach — because they did not bring to school the knowledge and skills the teachers thought they should have in order to learn.

A few of the teachers talked about the students in terms of their value orientations. Some compared the value orientation of students in this community with those in communities they lived in, noting how these students were different from middle class students. They made comments such as the following:

> *Betty:* I see them as less interested in the education types of things than in the social or family related things.
>
> *R:* When you say family related, what do you mean?
>
> *Betty:* I always find that if I can pull discussions around to something which can have examples elicited about family situations or how they see people and family and things like that. I get a lot more discussion than if I don't.

R: How would you rate Five Bridges academically, as compared to other schools perhaps that you've been in?

Natalie: Well, the only one I have to compare it to is probably the one that my daughter goes to and that is rated very high in the state, so it's like taking there and here and trying to compare them and it wouldn't be a fair comparison anyway. The backgrounds of the children there are entirely different. The importance of an education is stressed so much more by home. You know, I'm talking about the home situation, what their feelings of importance are.

Nell: It bothers me to think of them as lower class, I don't like that. But I guess that's as good a label as any. And believe me, I know class. I have an education, and motivation. I have different ideas than they do. I see them with low motivation, I don't see them with long range goals, but I think that might really be more with age than their immediate life here in this community. I think there are just so many things that discourage them to have any motivation and all these things that the middle class can have.

Others, clearly in the minority, discussed the values students brought from home as a strength. They talked about students' positive feelings about their community and neighborhood and their positive self-concepts about their own identities. To these teachers, the students' background did not limit them by providing them with anti-academic values, as several teachers thought, but strengthened them by providing them with a stable self-identity. One additional teacher pointed out that a teacher cannot really teach kids without understanding their background and what beliefs and customs they bring that can be built upon in school.

Most teachers discussed the students' social behavior, for the most part making positive comments such as the following:

They're nice kids and for the most part I think they're working hard.

I think they're really nice kids. They're optimistic. They're cheerful, usually. They're friendly, usually.

Most of the kids are caring kids. I see youngsters who are very willing to help other youngsters.

> I see them as friendlier than other kids I have taught. They seem
> to talk with teachers as adult friends rather than as someone
> who is far off and standoffish.

Since the administrators had told us that they spent a lot of time on
discipline, we asked a sample of fifteen teachers to describe the extent to
which they saw student behavior as a problem. Nine thought the
behavior of the students was quite good; it was not perfect, but good.
Five more saw it as reasonably good, although they were disturbed by
troublemakers and the tendency of many students to follow the lead of
these troublemakers. Only two teachers saw student social behavior at
Five Bridges as being poor; they talked about problems with vandalism
and student attacks on one another, indicating that they saw these
problems as characterizing a large proportion of the student body. We
asked the thirteen teachers who did not see student behavior as a large
problem what the nature of the problems were. Two sources were
cited: a small group of troublemakers (who did not represent any
particular racial group), and silly, fidgety behavior these teachers
believed was typical of junior high students. Thus, most teachers saw
the students as having good social behavior, marred largely by what
they saw as a natural tendency of junior high students to act silly and
squirm about.

When talking about student behavior, the teachers did not mention
special education students, so we asked several of them if they saw
students in special classes being teased or put down by other students.
The regular education teachers said they had not seen this, with the
exception of a few physically impaired students being teased by others.
One said that the physically impaired students were being teased less
and less because:

> *Don:* The physically handicapped kids are much more assertive.
> They've been here for three years. They'll go up to other kids
> and demand attention from the other kids or get in with other
> kids and won't back down at all.

Two of the special education teachers pointed out that there was a
pecking order among handicap groups, and how much students put
down a handicapped student depended on the nature of the handicap.

> *Carlotta:* Those who can walk or talk are way ahead, even if
> they're cerebral palsy and they have braces or anything like
> that.... Fannie [multiply handicapped] refuses to sing with my
> kids [multiply handicapped]. And I'm sure it's because she really

doesn't want to be associated with them. She's in the class and she's really a part of this group, but she doesn't want to be associated with them because she's so much more socially aware. . . .

R: Do EMR kids consider themselves handicapped at all?

Carlotta: Oh, no. Especially at the senior high. We would talk about birth defects and children who are born with cerebral palsy or who are born mentally retarded. And they never connected themselves with that.

In our discussions with the teachers, we became curious as to what they thought the students did when they were not in school. The majority of the teachers said they did not know for sure, but imagined the students did such things as watch television, play sports, visit the local recreation center and do odd jobs like delivering the newspaper or babysitting. We then asked the teachers if this knowledge influenced what they taught students. Some of the teachers skirted around answering the question. Others said that they used examples related to students' activities outside school to help explain concepts they were teaching. Still others said this knowledge did not influence their teaching, and could see no reason why it should.

In sum, the teachers were most positive about the friendly attitude and compliant behavior of their students. Most saw them as deficient academically; some blamed this on the deficient value orientations they assumed the students were learning at home. They seemed to equate ability to think with proficiency in reading, and lamented students' reading levels because that made it more difficult to transmit academic knowledge to them. We found it interesting that most teachers did not seek alternative reasons for low reading levels of their students, such as poor prior teaching or seeing little point or interest in reading skills instruction. The teachers assumed this problem stemmed from lack of motivation, impoverished home experiences or general lack of ability. We also found it interesting that the teachers rarely brought up the students' diversity when talking about them. It almost seemed that they were trying not to attend to the students' membership in race, sex and handicap groups.

Based on the students' academic abilities and home background, the teachers formulated expectations for the Five Bridges students. We asked fifteen teachers what they expected to see the Five Bridges students doing after high school. Seven said they expected less than 25 per cent of them to go to college and one of these said he would be surprised if 5 per cent went to college. The rest would go to vocational school or take jobs right after high school. These teachers made remarks such as the following:

Betty: They are not really interested in a career that will take a long time to prepare for. That seems to be quite an overriding thing. I think that many of them feel that once they get through twelve years of school they will have accomplished something. There are some of them who will even doubt that they will make it that far. Not that they wouldn't like to, but that there are circumstances and how they are doing in school, they would maybe like to leave. That isn't to say there aren't some kids who are college bound, but I don't think there are too many of them that are.

Sam: Well, sometimes I think my expectations run a little low; because I see where the kids are at now. And I get the idea maybe they're not going to make a whole lot of progress. Sometimes I think that's something I have to remind myself of frequently; that they could come a long way.

Bernice: I would see them as probably staying in this community and not having very high aspirations for some of the things that you and I would want to do. In talking with my students about trips they've taken and places they've been, it's very limited. So I think if you're brought up with staying pretty much at home all the time and being with your family, you're not going to have those ideas unless you meet someone or are influenced by someone that does.

Four teachers did not know what the students would do, commenting that they had not thought about it, or that the students were too young to know yet. One added that she hoped what they do is not the same as what their parents did.

Only four gave somewhat positive, hopeful responses. One of these said that some will become leaders and all will become involved in the democratic process if they are prepared in school for this. The other three said that what the students do depends on how hard they are pushed in school, but added that the school tends not to push the students very hard.

Claudio: I think if we started building our expectations and trying to help them along, I think they would improve also.

One of the teachers who had offered a hopeful response was a special education teacher, who refused to let the students' special education status discourage her from attempting to build their aspirations.

> *Marilyn:* I push the kids that I know have the ability and tell them not to set their goals short. I want them to think about going to a vocational school, or go to college. . . . What is happening is, a lot of these kids are getting out and if they go to vocational school, that is where they go. Otherwise, they go out in the work field and they are taking semi-skilled jobs.

Thus most of the teachers looked at the students' low reading skills and home background and the values they thought were being learned there, and projected that relatively few students would go to college, and most would follow much the same occupational path as their parents. Only a few viewed the students' abilities and background as strengths to succeed in life, and only a few saw themselves or the faculty as a major factor determining student success. What strikes us is the inaccuracy of the teachers' expectations. Just as most knew little about student activities outside school, most were equally unaware of student aspirations.

School Objectives

All teachers who described the students in terms of their poor reading abilities supported the school objective of raising reading scores, echoing that reading opens doors and that content area learning is impaired by poor reading skills. They looked to the English department and the remedial classes to do the bulk of the work toward this goal. Most did not consider it their job to help improve student performance in reading.

When this study began we found students in remedial reading programs getting a daily diet of reading skills instruction, but the rest of the students did not necessarily receive regular work in reading. Annette, who was new to the school in 1978 as an English teacher, was given charge of developing the school's reading program after she had been there a few months. She told us that there was no coordinated plan to develop the reading of students who were not in special programs, despite the fact that reading was a school objective that teachers supported.

> *Annette:* [The reading program] was a hodgepodge. They got a little of this and a little of that, and sometimes the 7th and 8th graders had a whole year of grammar but hadn't any literature and had no creative writing, or else they had reading all the time but they had real big gaps. They don't have skills. They lack skills — they don't know how to study, they don't know how to use a dictionary, they don't know how to use the library well.

Seeing these and other problems, expressing a commitment to developing students' reading abilities, and having a background in reading, this teacher voluntarily took leadership in furthering this school objective. For example she instituted a developmental reading program for students who were a little bit behind grade level (those she saw as average students), a Great Books program for top readers ('bright students'), and a schoolwide reading time in which everyone read for a 45-minute period once a week. It is interesting that Annette's assessment of the reading program in the school when she arrived did not cause other teachers to reassess the reasons they attributed for the students' poor reading skills.

The objective of implementing education that is multicultural was received by the teachers somewhat differently. Most said that they thought it was a good idea. The following comment is illustrative of their views on this objective:

> *Bernice:* I guess I can see that it's very necessary for these students in particular.
>
> *R:* Why for these students in particular?
>
> *Bernice:* Because I think that very often we ignore their culture and it's very easy to do that, without intentionally doing it. I can see that with just a little bit of interest shown towards something, they do light up, it really does make a difference.

Several teachers indicated that they thought they understood the objective well enough to implement it, although several also said that this objective should be implemented slowly. For example:

> *Robert:* I am well aware of what's going on and I'm well aware of the things that we need to progress to, we're heading in one direction, and that is to make everything multicultural. It doesn't happen overnight and it won't happen with any specific or particular thing, I don't think. I think it has to come a little at a time, and everybody being aware of it and that's the big interest we seem to have.

Bernice: I think that when you start a new idea going that it doesn't just, zip, bang, here-it-is, I'm doing it. I think that maybe you have to do things, kind of ease in a bit, and then think for a while.

We wondered how the teachers actually perceived the 'flesh and blood' of this objective, so we asked them what they thought an ideal multicultural classroom look like. Responses such as the following were typical:

Jo: I guess I'd start out by saying first of all any classroom we have is bound to have a mixture of groups and some sort of appreciation for one another.

Paula: I think one thing is when the kids come in they feel good about coming in, they feel good, they feel comfortable with you as the teacher, they know if they're minority or Anglo or whatever, that doesn't make any difference, everybody gets a fair shake.

Joan: There's a classroom at Five Bridges that is an ideal classroom all the way around, and it's the Spanish classroom. And it's got lots of posters up with kids on it, with little drawings of people, and they're all different colors and hairstyles.

Only one teacher mentioned teaching content from a multicultural perspective, and only a few emphasized the importance of materials reflecting different groups. For the most part, teacher definitions of the objective centered around students getting along and feeling good about being in class, teachers treating them fairly, and room decorations reflecting different racial groups.

In contrast to the reading objective, no teacher stepped forward to take leadership in implementing this objective. Thomas delegated some leadership responsibility to a staff Intercultural Committee, but Claudio, chair of this Committee, was never certain what his leadership role should be. At the end of the first year of the study he told us:

It wasn't real clear to me what my role was, the Intercultural Committee and multicultural education.... Thomas was still saying, multicultural education really still falls within the area of the Intercultural Committee. That just gives it a broader base. What's confusing to me is the involvement that I've been asked to take. When there's a meeting, when the proposal was being written for the upcoming [Teacher Corps] proposal, when there were meetings on this mini-grant or whatever it is for next year, on education that is multicultural, I've never been involved in those or asked to be, so I'm kind of wondering. I'm here, and yeah, that falls within the Intercultural Committee, but yet I'm never really involved with education that is multicultural in the sense of being a part of the group that talks about and plans regarding EMC.

We could say, then, that the teachers liked the idea they believed each objective represented, but few saw themselves as actively instrumental in working toward the objectives. It is even questionable how well they understood the objectives or the work each would entail. While they could recognize an improvement in reading after the fact, they did not talk about how to initiate improvement. And their understanding of the multicultural objective was rather limited, focusing mainly on room decorations and affective factors, neglecting the curriculum, teaching strategies, teacher goals for students, parent-school relationship and so forth. Thomas did provide some in-service for them and in Chapter 7 we will discuss the impact of this in-service as one determinant of the teachers' cultural knowledge.

Teaching at Five Bridges

The heart of any examination of teachers is their work in the classroom. We wanted to find out what the Five Bridges teachers did there, and how they thought about teaching. We were particularly interested in examining what they did in relation to their students and the school objectives. We focused on several dimensions of teaching: classroom and hall environments, instructional materials, content of lessons, teaching strategies and social organization of classrooms. We gathered data by observing twenty-three classrooms and by regularly interviewing the sample of teachers described earlier.

Environment

The hall environment in a school, especially the bulletin boards and display cases, are often used by teachers to announce some theme such as Career Day or Thanksgiving or to display classroom work. Hall walls are also often used to display posters or signs that tell of forthcoming school events. We took note of the hall environment and recorded how it was used, its messages and the extent to which it related to the school objectives of reading and education that is multicultural.

During the course of our observations the display cases and bulletin boards portrayed human relations messages, often intended to promote a positive student self-image. Titles such as 'Look in the Mirror Every Day and Tell Yourself that You're Okay' and 'We Were Made to Help Each Other, We are Here to Make Each Other Happy' were used. Teachers also periodically used the display cases to exhibit certain themes, such as careers and sea shells. Such exhibits included pictures and books. One display case showed different handicapping conditions along with books about handicapped people. On occasion, a hall bulletin board was connected directly to a classroom project. For example, one display asked students to match pictures to the names of famous Americans and another challenged students to match phrases from several languages with their English meanings. Reading as a theme was rarely addressed in hall displays.

For the most part, the work on the bulletin boards and in display cases was a combination of magazine clippings and letters and cutouts from colored construction paper, which were choreographed by teachers and students. Most of this material included people of different races and ages and of both sexes.

Sitting in the classrooms, we noted several aspects of the room environments, including their neatness, the extent to which they were decorated, what constituted the displays and how they were used and the arrangement of furniture. The neatness of the rooms varied: in a few, all furniture, materials, and displays were consistently neat and orderly and the floor was never littered; another few rooms consistently had a cluttered, unkempt appearance. However, most rooms fell somewhere in between, leaning in the direction of neat and clean.

We itemized the displays in twenty-one classrooms (two teachers we observed did not have their own rooms). Nine of these had few decorations or displays at all. Seven consistently had a few things on the bulletin boards and two or three posters on the walls. Four rooms were alive with displays — these rooms sported such a variety that only small patches of bare wall remained. Most commonly displayed were posters (nature posters were popular); seasonal themes; subject area themes (for example, the periodic table in science rooms, maps in the geography class); calendars; lists of classroom rules; in some classrooms, student work. Of the twelve teachers we observed who regularly decorated their rooms, eight used the decorations for display only and four used the displays as teaching tools. For example, the English teachers put up posters, calendars, seasonal displays and samples of student work; these were always attractively done and changed periodically, but were rarely used as lesson materials. One social studies teacher, on the other hand, placed charts and diagrams around the room that depicted procedures for doing projects, broadcasted student activities, or delineated student responsibility for various parts of a current project. This teacher frequently referred to these displays and sometimes created them during the course of a lesson; and he changed displays as he moved the class from one project to another.

A few teachers consistently tried to include a diversity of people in displays using human relations posters and posters that included people of different colors. These posters were often commercially made and provided information about an ethnic group, as for example 'Famous Mexican-Americans', or they illustrated human relations slogans. There were also a few posters about famous women and sexism. Some special education teachers displayed pictures of newspaper articles about handicapped people: one article reported the results of the Special Olympics. In addition, a few teachers displayed 'multicultural calendars'. Teachers who used their bulletin boards to represent diversity tended to erect displays and leave them without necessarily using them.

On the whole, displays in classrooms provided factual information and decoration. There was little attempt to construct displays that would provoke critical thought. Conceivably one could display news articles providing varying interpretations of an event of interest to the students, thereby challenging students to identify sources of bias in the media. Or, one could depict the development of devices such as electric wheelchairs that have helped free physically impaired peopled, and invite students to suggest additional devices that could be produced, or to critique the effectiveness of the devices that already exist. But this sort of thing was rarely done with displays.

In core subject areas, the seats were almost always arranged in rows. In remedial, special education and home economics classes, seats were arranged around tables. In industrial arts classes, seats were arranged either around work tables or in rows at one end of the classroom, depending on the preference of the teacher. Rooms were built to accommodate wheelchairs, but that did not guarantee that furniture arrangements would be accessible to all students. The teachers who had not taught physically impaired students before had to rethink room arrangements in some cases to make their rooms accessible to all their students. The following quotation illustrates the concern and frustration this problem evoked in some teachers:

> *Tim:* I got to thinking about the two kids who come in in wheelchairs, and it's impossible for them to get their equipment. We have it stored in those drawers now, each student has his own drawer and they store their equipment there ... I realized that would be a problem for them because someone would have to get everything out for them and put it away for them and also that they leave a little early and they are often a little late, so the time that they are actually here is being cut down more and more. That was a problem and I had never dealt with that before. I arranged it as I thought it would be best for the entire class and then after I did that I got to thinking now what about those kids? So, I moved this table right over by the door so when they come in they only have a couple feet to go, and after I did that I said, 'Well, now I made it easier for them, but that's not going to be natural because maybe they should have to fight the drawers, just for experience'.

We found it curious that Tim did not simply ask the students what furniture arrangement would be most convenient for them, since he obviously did not know. Teachers did not often ask students such questions.

Curriculum

During the in-service institute described earlier, two short activities were administered to gain some understanding of the teachers' approaches to curriculum and instruction. We will examine what the teachers did with these activities first, since they shed some light on their approach to teaching.

The first activity asked teachers to comment on a traditional lesson plan in which students were to write a library research paper about the Vietnam War, choosing from several topics that focused on the US political role and on military aspects of the war. One-third of the staff at the institute did not change the lesson. All except one of the remaining two-thirds made minor changes, adding interviews as a means of collecting data in addition to reading, and/or expanding the list of topics to include South Vietnamese experiences with the war.

One teacher — Carlotta, a special education teacher — added a panel discussion and a debate, and specified that this lesson should be adapted to various learning styles.

The second activity asked the teachers to design a lesson or unit that would motivate students to do 'a thoughtful piece of work'. All but two teachers took one of the following approaches: several wrote sketchy, didactic or skills-oriented lessons within their own subject areas (such as a lesson for practicing math facts); a few wrote lessons about prejudice or about an ethnic group, taught in a didactic manner, with students absorbing information from the teacher, from books or from films; a few wrote lessons about self concept in which the students' feelings were the focus of the lesson and active student participation was encouraged. Two teachers — Carlotta and a Teacher Corps intern — wrote plans that put students in an active role collecting data about an academic topic, synthesizing their findings, and relating their findings to information in other source material.

From these two activities we drew several tentative conclusions. First, since the great majority of the teachers accepted a traditional library-research approach to teaching about a controversial recent historical event, and since most wrote didactic plans in their attempt to motivate thoughtful student work, we suspected that they viewed learning as a process of gaining information directly from the teacher, or from print material in the library (perhaps supplemented with an oral account) for a paper to hand in to the teacher. But, when the focus of a lesson was on self concept, feelings or interpersonal relationships, the mode of instruction was completely changed to promote sharing of personal feelings, with almost no input from the teacher. Second, since no teacher completely rewrote the Vietnam lesson to substantially include diverse perspectives on the war, and only a few teachers thought to add one or two topics that would offer at least one additional viewpoint, we suspected that the teachers would take for granted a white middle class male perspective on America's culture. Most teachers had shown themselves able to recognize blatant stereotypes when they were expecting to have to identify them, but seemed unable to detect bias in the portrayal of the Vietnam War. The teachers who dealt with human diversity in their lesson plans did it by proposing a separate lesson about a group, rather than by bringing perspectives and contributions of several groups to bear on a topic.

Now let us step into the classrooms at Five Bridges to see how the teachers actually thought about and proceeded with their own teaching.

The content that was taught in most classes could best be described as having a basic skills and basic concepts emphasis. For example, the science classes taught basic concepts related to life science, physical science, and chemistry. The English classes taught spelling, grammar and literature selections, for example, *A Light in the Forest*, that are commonly found in junior high English classes. In band class students learned to play marches and simple classical or popular pieces commonly heard in school concerts; in home economics class students learned about basic foods such as beef and eggs, and 'standard' recipes such as muffins and cakes.

In some departments, particularly science, content was planned by the department to coordinate teaching in different classes and with the senior high. In other departments, such as social studies, content in part revolved around the interests of individual teachers. Courses such as money and banking and futures, were viewed more as self-contained experiences rather than part of a spiraling curriculum.

Regardless of planning source, the great majority of content was selected to meet at least one of three needs. The first was to remediate students' basic skills, which guided much of the instruction in English and math classes.

The second was to provide students with practical knowledge of use outside school, which might be combined with remedial work depending on the teacher's view of skill levels and academic needs of the students.

> *Nell (math):* [In general math] the boys were supposed to have done a worksheet on auto parts, and pricing and percentages, so this is an area now that I'm getting into, things they can use out in the real world. I think tomorrow we'll make change, I'll give them a price that I buy something for, and they're going to have to count back the change for me.

> *Betty (social studies):* One of the things I am trying to tell them is the things I am trying to teach you are things that you are going to need in the real world.... In order for these kids to get along in the world I think it is important that they learn that same stuff so they don't have to sit back and say, 'Oh yeah, that guy is talking about Franklin Roosevelt, who is he?' and not be sure who he is.... I want them to know practical things. How to write a budget, how to write a check, how to balance your checkbook.

The special education teachers also tended to focus on skills students would need for survival in school and daily life situations, especially after they leave school.

> *Marilyn:* There's three things I think are important. One is good behavior management type techniques where you teach kids how to get along. I call it survival. Secondly, I think they have to learn their academics, which is your math and reading.... And the third thing that I think is really important is this language component....
>
> *R:* What's your overall goal for them?
>
> *Marilyn:* Getting them ready for the job market. Getting them so that they can survive in another teacher's classroom. Getting them so that they can survive out in that regular world.

The third need, mentioned by a few teachers, was to provide students with academic skills and concepts for further academic learning in high school. For example, in science students were taught very basic academic concepts such as the periodic table; students who took further science courses would be expected to have this basic foundation (but many students did not take more advanced academic classes in some subject areas). The same was true in other subject areas such as math and English, for example:

> *Don:* I teach grammar so when they get next door [high school] they will have heard it. I don't get all uptight if you don't know what a predicate nominative is, but you should know that one exists. That is the only reason I go into grammar, because it's expected of you.

Student interest rarely played a significant role in decisions about what to teach. Although teachers might at times select, for example, one story to read rather than another because students generally like one better, they rarely used the interests of the particular students in their classes as a starting point for deciding what to teach. Rather, students were usually 'plugged into' content that had been planned before the teacher had gotten to know a particular class of students. Then the content was modified as needed to fit the students' skill level or level of prerequisite knowledge, but rarely to build on the students' interest. For example:

> *Don (English, social studies):* What I try to base my teaching around is to find out where the kids are, what they need to know, and try to give them some tools.

R: How do you go about deciding what they need to know and where they are?

Don: Sometimes I pretest them to see where they are in various classes. Sometimes I start teaching something and I start asking questions and see what type of answers I get and then find out if they have the prerequisite knowledge for what I'm talking about. If they don't have the prerequisite knowledge then I don't bother to muddle ahead, I go backwards and fill in whatever prerequisite knowledge needs to be there instead of saying. 'Well, you should have had this'.

The teachers did not seem to see the importance of providing content that would stimulate student interest or intellectual inquisitiveness. We found it disheartening that teachers did not seize upon student interest and activities they enjoyed outside school to stimulate their motivation to practice basic skills work. There seemed to be the feeling that if you can't read well you cannot think. And if you cannot learn to read in the way you are being taught, then there is very little hope for your learning to read.

Over half of the teachers we observed — fifteen out of twenty-three teachers — relied mostly on printed materials for instruction. Four teachers by and large depended on one text; these teachers taught English and math. The two science teachers used a text, films, and lab equipment. Nine additional teachers used several kinds of print materials such as textbooks, dittoes, reading books and magazines; these teachers taught English, remedial reading, and social studies. The remaining eight teachers used materials in various forms, including a variety of non-print materials, such as films, speakers, 'hands-on' equipment, and items the students would have brought to class. These included the industrial arts, home economics, music and affective education teachers, plus two social studies teachers. We found it interesting that so many teachers — especially in core subject areas — relied heavily on print materials, especially given their awareness that most students were not strong in reading. We might have expected teachers to use a greater variety of materials to capture the interest of students, teach reading in different ways (for example, language experience), or respond to the students' strongest learning modalities. We might also have expected them to use more high interest reading materials in place of textbook materials to promote interest in reading and in academic learning.

The majority of the materials used had a basic skills orientation, and their activities or questions are found on the lower level of Bloom's taxonomy. For example:

> During a visit to the zoo, what do Henry and Janet observe about the snake eating habits?

We often had general discussions with the teachers about instructional materials. From these discussions we discovered that several strongly believed that resources, especially materials, limit what a teacher can do. A social studies teacher explained it in the following way:

> *Betty:*   I guess I use whatever I have and whatever I find, you know, and if I don't, if I can't, if I've got a good idea and I can't find something, then I'll just shelve it until I can come across something.

The teachers' feelings about the importance of materials could be plotted along a continuum. A language arts teacher and a graphic arts teacher would be at one end with the view that they were greatly aided or hindered by availability of materials. At the other end of the continuum would be a language arts teacher and social studies teacher who were not limited by the availability of materials but continually found or created alternative materials. Subject matter that the teachers taught did not seem to be important in influencing how they felt about materials. Note the difference in response between two language arts teachers:

> *Jo:*   I guess I go by whatever books we have. I check them against those to see if they are ready for them or not, and I have worksheets, or whatever else I need, to plug them [students] in.

> *Don:*   The kids that I've had in previous classes, the Future studies classes, will come up . . . and say, 'Hey, I'm watching this good thing on TV called *COSMOS*, and it would work real nice with that future stuff you were doing last year. . . .' I took the video cassette recorder home [to record *COSMOS*]. I buy all my cassettes . . . I got *Tora, Tora, Tora*, the whole movie one night, I blanked every commercial out so I have the whole film if I ever want it.

In other words, available materials dictated what some teachers taught, while others were resourceful in locating materials they needed to teach what they believed was worth teaching.

We examined the teaching content and classroom materials to determine the extent to which they reflected human diversity. Table 6 depicts curricular inclusion of human diversity and the number of observed classrooms in which that form of inclusion occurred.

Table 6:   *Attention to human diversity in classroom content*

Number of classrooms	Description of attention
2	No attention to diversity in daily content or materials
5	No attention to diversity in daily content but materials included both sexes and three or more or more racial groups
5	Teacher tried to teach one or two 'multicultural lessons'; otherwise, no attention to human diversity
3	Teacher periodically brought up spontaneous discussions about diversity that related to topic being studied and teacher's own interest; most materials included both sexes and three or more racial groups
2	Teacher regularly integrated content with interests and concerns of students and community
3	Teacher regularly planned lessons and discussions about racism, sexism, handicappism; selected materials to include both sexes, different races and handicapped
3	Teacher taught course about a racial group or several racial groups

As shown in this table, fifteen of the twenty-three classrooms paid little attention to diversity in the course content. What was taught was predominantly the white, middle-class experience taught in most schools. For example, in these classrooms most authors of stories or books that were read were white; the great majority of the scientists mentioned were white males; most interpretations of history and social issues were those of the white middle class. These interpretations also did not invite the students to critique social events as much as to accept them. In five of these classrooms, the materials reflected some attention to diversity, but the teachers did not attempt to include diversity in daily content. For example, two of these were science classes; the science texts adopted by the science department were fairly well racially balanced and included women as well as men in active roles; but there were no class discussions of science as it developed in non-white cultural contexts, of non-white scientists, or of reasons why scientists are still disproportionately white men. Four teachers tried teaching one or two lessons that incorporated some attention to diversity; for example, a math teacher taught a lesson using Chinese tangrams, and the band director taught an isolated lesson about the history of jazz and also taught Latino music to be played during Mexican American week.

Aside from these sporadic attempts, attention to human diversity in these classrooms was minimal. Three teachers, who had selected books such that different racial groups and both sexes would be represented, occasionally had discussions related to human diversity. For example, a female geography teacher sometimes discussed women's rights and mentioned the ethnic makeup of geographic areas being studied. Another female social studies teacher discussed sex discrimination in the job market while teaching a course on careers.

Eight of the twenty-three classrooms systematically included the perspectives and contributions of at least one group that has historically been omitted in school curricula. Two of these classes were taught by teachers who were very sensitive to the interests of the students. One, an Hispanic music teacher, included music by contemporary black and Hispanic composers (for example, Stevie Wonder, Freddie Fender), teaching students to sing popular music. The other, a white male social studies teacher, regularly taught an oral history class in which students interviewed community residents about the history of the community. Two special education teachers and one remedial reading teacher regularly had classwork and discussions about different groups. Examples of such classwork were reading stories by non-white authors; discussing non-white contemporary figures; reading newspaper articles about the handicapped; discussing physical impairments; discussing sexism. Finally, three teachers taught classes about race and racial groups. Of these, two taught multicultural education (one during 1978/79, and the other during 1979/81), which was a class about non-white racial groups, prejudice and racism. The third taught an extensive unit on the Ojibwe Indians in her state history course and also taught cultural foods.

In no course was content regularly planned and taught to include the perspectives and experiences of many racial groups, both sexes, different social classes and the handicapped. For example, literature was not deliberately selected and taught to include works by and about all racial groups, both sexes, different social class and age groups, and handicapped people on an ongoing basis. As the lesson plans teachers wrote during the in-service institute suggested, what the students were taught when there was an attempt to modify the curriculum was usually information about members of specific racial groups (mainly Mexicans), about sexism (largely in the work place), and about handicapped people (in special education classes).

A Mexican American week was celebrated each year in May at Five Bridges. The celebration often consisted of essay writing and art contests, fashion shows, Mexican dancing and the school was decorated with Mexican American artifacts and regalia. The activities to highlight the event were, for the most part, orchestrated by the Chicano committee.

During this week, we asked the teachers to discuss the celebration with us. We found that the majority of the teachers did not actively participate in it, nor integrate the theme into class activities or regular schoolwide events.

R: Did you participate in the Mexican-American Week?
Sam: Not really.
R: Any special reason why?
Sam: Well, for one thing, this is my student council spring week. I've been busy with that.

R: Have you participated in any activities for the Mexican American Week?
Tim: Only in that I encouraged the students to take part.

Bernice: Well, I went to the assembly, yesterday. I really haven't done anything.

Most of the teachers, however, believed that the Mexican American Week celebration was important and a big success.

Bernice: I think there's been a lot more this year than last year at this time, so the kids really seemed to like the assembly, which probably shows that there should be more for the kids to do like this.

Annette: I felt a lot of kids became aware of their heritage, of what heritage was about. Some of them brought pictures to school for me to see.

We found it interesting that, although the teachers reported it to be very socially and academically rewarding, they had not participated much in the celebration, and follow-up activities or 'lesson learned' were not integrated into daily plans and instructional procedures.

As you recall, approximately 2 per cent of the student population was black, and there was only one black staff member. In many schools across the nation, black history is celebrated during the month of February. At Five Bridges, daily announcements during February commemorated famous black men and women and acknowledged the contributions of blacks to society. In our observations we saw little attention to black history, so we asked the teachers about their teaching of black history in the classroom and discovered that the majority had not addressed it in their teaching.

> *Kay:* Yeah, the announcements featured various people, important Black people, their history, they told what they did and why. I didn't do anything in my class.

> *Nell:* I have not really paid attention to that [black history], because I am a first-year teacher, and I am just struggling to maintain my immediate material which is science facts. I am anticipating when I settle down in my second year, then I can start looking at extra things.

Although most of the teachers did not include black history in their lessons, they did say it was important. Observe the continuation of our discussion with Nell and Kay.

> *Kay:* It's our feeling here that we should have black history all year, and Chicano history all year, and Asian-American history all year, and Ameican Indian all year. And I, myself, personally think it's good because it makes you think a little bit harder than you might normally, but we should be thinking all the time along those lines and make it just integrated. It seems more natural that way, too. It seems unnatural when it's just one month.

> *Nell:* I think that it is great [black history]. It should be — the curriculum to begin with. My curriculum isn't conducive, but I hope the social sciences are doing something. The only area that I could integrate would be through black scientists. Do you know anything about them? I desperately need some of that material. I do not have it, and I don't have time to look for it.

Thus, attention to black history was more in thought than deed on the part of the teachers. When teachers' perspectives about Mexican American Week and Black History Month are viewed together it is readily obvious that the teachers at Five Bridges did not seriously address human diversity — even on special occasions.

We asked teachers why they were teaching so little from a multicultural perspective, especially given the fact that this was a school objective and they had attended workshops designed to help them modify their curriculum to make it multicultural. Many of the teachers said that they saw multicultural concerns as separate from the content they were supposed to teach and either did not know how to integrate it into their curriculum, or saw it as 'off the subject' from their curriculum. For example:

> *Science teacher:* I really want to be careful that I just don't do something just to be doing it, that I don't just take something from social studies and do it in my room, just to say that maybe it would be good for me to do because I would become involved in it, but that really isn't what I think is a useful idea.

> *Affective education teacher:* If it's a class where you try to get some information like math or literature, it might work real well. In peer counseling it works really well.... I guess I think that the junior high age can bring up all kinds of things that are off the wall that really shouldn't be discussed in class if you try to teach them something that is not connected with that.... If it's a putdown kind of thing [for example, namecalling], I have to address that. That kind of thing could take 15 or 20 minutes out of a class. It's like getting off the topic.

> *English teacher:* I'll tell you this, it isn't the foremost thing in my mind. When I'm planning a lesson, I'm planning it in terms of what do the kids need to learn about this. How can I explain it to them in a way that they'll understand it. How does this fit in with the curriculum that this school has written up and that I really am bound to follow. Now, whether it's multicultural or not will only come in where it fits naturally and accidentally, okay?

> *Science teacher:* I know it's how I treat my kids, I can call from all different groups for answers or for help. But as far as making an overt attempt in what I am saying, I haven't given it any thought. I was teaching a section in there called 'Technology', which is chemistry and physics put together, and they wanted to use one of my labs and actually talk about different cultures. I didn't feel that it was really science and I felt uncomfortable working with it.

Seeing multicultural content as consisting of lessons about getting along or as lessons about cultures, then, many teachers did not see it as relevant to what they taught.

However, a few teachers in special education, as well as the multicultural education teachers, struggled with the concept and gradually infused their teaching with a multicultural perspective. One teacher who did this most consistently described the process of her growth over time.

> It went from almost nothing to almost daily. It's just grown in terms of quality. I try to give it quality and as I learn more, I know what quality is. First, I just sort of bombarded my students and now I'm starting to sort and pick up what's really quality.

> (Later):

> I'm the only teacher in the building who pushes all five 'isms' on a regular basis. If I were to give people a pattern, I'd give them my pattern, and that is one day you teach sexism, and one day racism, and so forth. The reason I would do this is because you become comfortable with it. Otherwise, you're going to say, 'I don't want to talk about classism today, that's the hardest one,' and you ignore it. How can you learn about it unless you work your way through it? It's sort of a fighting, working situation. You fight your way through it. All of a sudden, one day you come through and you say, "Hey, I know something." Suddenly, you're not uncomfortable with it.'

To the few teachers who wrestled with multiculturalism, a shortage of time, knowledge, or resources did not present potential barriers to their progress. They were barriers that could be hurdled by persevering and trying. And as barriers were gradually crossed, teachers like the one above believed the effort was worth it.

To what extent did teachers deliberately select and use materials that would promote recognition that there are diverse interpretations of events, and that knowledge can be problematic? Most teachers did not — they relied on one text from which students were to learn right answers, or delivered one interpretation in the form of a lecture. However, two social studies teachers and a multicultural education teacher tried to teach students to analyze different points of view. They used several different resources and regularly drew students' attention to viewpoints and biases in different interpretations of the same event. They also reported having difficulty teaching students to think analytically because the students were not asked to do this in most of their classes.

In addition to attending to what teachers taught and what kinds of materials they used, we also examined the way teachers were teaching and why they taught as they did. To understand how the teachers viewed instruction, we asked many of them what kind of classwork they thought the students found most and least interesting. Although the teachers' answers to these questions were not identical, they were quite similar. The teachers told us that students were most interested in group activities, hands-on activities, work that involved them, work they had some choice in planning, and variety. The following responses are illustrative:

Home economics teacher: Activities. In my section they like to be doing something, cooking something, something active. They like contests, testing what they know against each other. But they also like working together. That sometimes turns into more a social session than a productive session.

English teacher: They like to read plays, like to take parts. They don't care much about standing up in front of the room and doing an individual thing but they like to do group things. They like to do something with somebody.... They like to discuss if it's something that really pertains to them. They don't like to discuss something that I think is important necessarily.

Special education teacher: Things that they can be involved in themselves. Hands on, too. I find that my sixth-hour class where they are doing some kind of job, whether it's passing parts or transplanting things, my students seem to like that the best.

Remedial reading teacher: They like to have explained to them why they need something. They like to have some voice in what they're doing, a few choices, but not too many choices I guess. That's frustrating, too. Generally, they like some sense of humor. They like it not to be too serious all the time, which I can certainly appreciate. But sometimes I think we forget and get carried away with facts they need to know, and don't remember the fun.

> *Science teacher:* Variety. I think they get tired of doing the same thing, regardless of what it is, in junior high. They get tired of activities, they get tired of sitting in one place, they get tired of moving around.

The things teachers said that the students liked least included lectures, note-taking, sitting and listening, reading and activities they could see no reason for.

Based on these responses, one would expect classroom instruction at Five Bridges to include a lot of group work, active projects, activities that would draw on students' backgrounds, discussion that included topics of interest to students, choicemaking, and general variety. To what extent did teachers teach in ways they believed students were most interested?

In fourteen of the twenty-three classrooms we observed, the prevailing instructional pattern consisted of a large-group lesson followed by individual seatwork. When seatwork was being done, the teacher usually circulated through the class, offering help to individual students. There were several versions to this pattern. In six classrooms (English, social studies and math) a large-group lecture by the teacher or a recitation session usually occupied the first part of the period, then students worked independently at their seats on dittoes or exercises from the textbook. In two social studies classrooms this same pattern prevailed but was occasionally varied through the use of projects or simulation activities. Four more classrooms (science and home economics) followed this basic pattern about three days per week, but about two days per week students did hands-on lab work in pairs or small groups. In two music classes, the great majority of instruction was in large groups.

Independent seatwork was used virtually all period in three remedial classes (reading, math). In one social studies classroom there was a combination of large-group lecture or discussion and small-group discussion.

In only five classrooms were multiple kinds of class activities used. Three of these were special education classes, in which there was a combination of small group discussion and small group hands-on activities, individual tutorial work and independent seatwork. The other two (social studies and affective education) used activities such as small group projects, simulations and role playing, small- and large-group discussion, and independent work. In addition, two of the special education teachers and the one social studies teacher in this group were the only teachers who consistently varied their teaching strategies to teach the same concept to students whose learning styles differed.

Cooperation was common, to some degree, in most classrooms. Teachers often allowed students to help each other with assignments, although expected each student to turn in his or her own individual work. In addition, teachers were usually very pleasant toward students, and willing to offer them help. But, in only a few classrooms were students expected to complete a common group project, and was the process of cooperating discussed and consciously developed. Competition among students was rarely seen in classrooms. Most often, if a teacher used competition, it was in the form of a game such as Scrabble during free time.

Why did so much of the instruction use activities that the teachers said students did not find interesting? We talked with teachers after our observations about their instructional strategies, asking them why they taught lessons as they did. One common large-group teaching strategy was lecturing, with the students usually taking notes. Sometimes students copied notes from the board or a transparency; other times they took down what the teacher dictated to them. The following two quotations illustrate reasons why teachers often felt lecturing and giving notes was appropriate:

> *Don:* I wanted to make sure that the ideas I was talking about yesterday on the weather got into their notes. They hadn't taken notes. This is the stuff that is important on this particular thing — the cause and effect relationship, if we have this much ice what are some of the other effects. I wanted to make sure that they got that stuff noted down in their books.

> *R:* We talked a little bit about notetaking but I wondered why you used that particular method of lecturing. You have the notes on the overhead transparency and you kind of go step-by-step and they take the notes and then you show them some more notes and you wait for them to write it down.

> *Kay:* There's two reasons. One is that I think there is a connection between writing something out and thinking about it and memory. The other reason is that I give them tests from the work-sheets and from the notes. I want them to learn some things and do well on tests and on their report card and so if they write these things out, they have a better chance than if I just say them. When people say things, you don't remember them. . . .

> *R:* It helps them on the test?
>
> *Kay:* Yes, and it helps their attention. They pay attention a lot more if you've got something there that they have to copy than if you are just talking to them. I guess if you're just talking to them they don't have to listen.

Thus, it seems that many teachers saw it important to deliver information to students to commit to memory and reproduce on tests, and found lecturing and giving notes to be an effective way to accomplish this. Mainstreamed physically impaired and learning disabled students were often unable to keep up with writing notes, so most teachers who lectured allowed other students to write notes using carbon paper so those who could not write fast enough would still have complete sets of class notes.

Individual seatwork was common in many classrooms, and we wondered why, given that the teachers believed students preferred group work. Teachers believed individual seatwork was appropriate because it gave them an index of what each student had accomplished and who needed help in what. It was also the form of work they were personally most used to, as the following comment illustrates:

> *R:* They were working on individual tasks. Do you ever have them work together where they are working on some sort of a group task?
>
> *Kay:* Just the labs when we go to the kitchens and cook. Then they're doing group work. I guess being a teacher, I worked individually all my life on projects and I guess just because of who I am and where I come from, I guess I think others are just like you are. I know they aren't, intellectually. I know that, but I guess unconsciously I still teach like they are. I always think that if I did a lot of work I want it, I want to take it home and treasure it and keep it. I guess I kind of think that's how kids are.

Mainstreamed students who could not complete seatwork by themselves or in the alotted time were allowed by some teachers either to complete the work at home or with a resource teacher, to work with another student on it, or, if an aide was present in the classroom, to work with that aide.

In remedial classes, students usually worked by themselves all period. Teachers usually had separate schedules of work for each student, designed to remediate the skills each individual student was having difficulty with.

> *Carlotta:* I think you should really be concerned about the individual differences in each of the students. Whether they learn best by listening, or seeing if they need to use the typewriter — just really being aware of the diversity of learning styles and then getting the adaptations that they need.

To this teacher, individualizing meant adapting instruction to the modalities as well as the skill levels of each student; other remedial teachers targeted instruction toward individual skill levels but most of the work consisted of reading and writing only. Sometimes teachers did all of the deciding about what work each individual student should do, but in some cases they gave students a chance to have some input.

> *Bernice:* Well, I do have specific things they must do in the week, and sometimes there's more than one way to work on that same thing, so if there's one way that they really don't want to do, then I wouldn't let them not do what they need to do, but I would give them a little choice in what it is that they're doing.

One teacher, as noted earlier, used mostly large-group discussion and small-group discussion or projects. She talked to us about why she taught that way, as well as commenting on the fact that her teaching style was unique at Five Bridges.

> *Tina:* [The students] just don't understand where this off-the-wall person came from who wants them to divide into groups or talk to each other, or shake hands and look each other in the eye, or maybe gets to be called by her first name. . . . I like to let the kids know that the teacher's a person and a human, and when I make a mistake I tell them. And when I'm wrong I say I'm sorry. . . . When I give an assignment I do it with them, you know, if it's a group thing I divide myself into the group. Just sort of normal, things that I've been doing all my life that I always saw as normal teaching procedures. Like, if I say, 'Get up and talk about your family', at the end, now all the kids will shout to me, 'What about yours?' and I have to say it. And they realize that that's part of it. And I know that doesn't go on. I can feel that doesn't go on. Participating with them, not having them do anything I wouldn't do myself.

Five of the twenty-three teachers we observed regularly offered the students a variety of kinds of class activities. By variety of activities, they meant individual as well as group work, participatory as well as written work. They explained that they did this because different students learned in different ways, and varying how they taught ensured the success of more students. For example:

> *Shelby:* I try to offer to all students a variety of activities. I don't try to seek an activity that one student finds comfortable and then allow that student to continue in that activity. I think that's been done before and when you're talking about low expectations, that's certainly a way to fulfill one's prophecy. But, I'd like to see that the students are successful in any event. And in a variety of events, there's a higher chance of finding something that would be considered successful. Also, I like to have students challenge themselves and if you try a variety of things, you figure there's a possibility that we'd find something that would challenge a student.

Shelby had a schoolwide reputation for teaching in ways that actively involved the students. He did this for reasons beyond keeping student interest and adapting to different learning styles, although these reasons were by no means unimportant. Below he explains his rationale behind the way he taught government:

> We talk about not only learning about the government but also practicing government. If we are going to be citizens in a democracy then we either ought to be able to practice that democracy as 11, 12, 13 or 14 year olds or experiment with other modes of government which might be interesting. If we had a choice to choose a government for this class, which one would it be, based on the information that was gained through four or five weeks of class. First of all that encourages discussion. The discussion is not only, is democracy better than monarchy, or is it better than an authoritarian decision. It's how it will work in this class, so that the discussion generates itself. . . . It is my job of course to see as discussion develops to know the materials available, the texts that are available, whatever it is to emphasize a point. . . . Let's say that the choice was a representative democracy . . . and they begin to write legislation, we deal with the legislation like a committee at the state legislature. There are legislative hearings and then there are moments when there are caucuses, the girls in the class may caucus or whatever. We try to use the vocabulary and a piece of legislation will be developed, there will be some lobby in-

volved, there will be legislative hearings involved, there will be discussions between executives and other individuals. . . .

He also explained that this sort of instruction lent itself well to the inclusion of mainstreamed students: students could team up to complete projects, they did not have to sit still for long periods, and successful learning did not depend on reading.

Shelby's class was the only core area class in which classwork was regularly structured in a variety of ways. For the most part, the other classes which regularly used a variety of teaching strategies were special education classes. Since Five Bridges was a mainstreamed school, we wondered why there was not more variety to accommodate the learning styles of its varied student population. Therefore, we asked several teachers how they modified their instruction to include handicapped students. Earlier we described how they modified note-giving and individual seatwork. Teachers who were favorable to having special education students in their classrooms (not all teachers were) also said they allowed students to take tests in a special education room at their own pace simplified tests (for example, from essay to true-false), and contacted the special education teachers if problems developed. They did not change their style of teaching, but added on these modifications as they were needed.

We looked to see whether teachers treated members of different racial groups or of each sex differently in the course of their instruction. We observed no such differences in most classrooms. On the whole, the teachers did not discriminate against students on the basis of race and sex. They gave everyone the same worksheets, texts and assignments. Teachers dominated the talk in classrooms, directing most of it toward the class as a whole rather than to individual students (see Chapter 6 for a description of time spent on different teaching strategies). When teacher-student interaction did occur, it frequently involved the asking and answering of recall-type questions. Higher order questions were not asked by teachers very frequently to anyone. In other areas of teacher-student interaction, teachers responded to students in much the same way regardless of race or sex.

In the great majority of the core area classes, then, the teachers taught by providing the students with information through lecture, recitation, or reading, and by giving them work such as note-taking or seatwork that would help the students commit this information to memory. Different learning styles were accommodated by making small modifications to these forms of teaching. The nature of the information being taught, as pointed out earlier, did not promote critical enquiry or a veiw of learning as problematic. Thus, instructional strategies promoted simple recall of information and not analytical thought. In a very few classes, teachers believed that what students learned from each other was important enough to include as part of the curriculum, so these teachers built group work into their instruction on a regular basis. But, as the lesson plans from the in-service institute suggested, when students interacted and instructed each other in class, it was in relation to self concept and personal feelings rather than academic learning in at least half of the cases. Finally, a few teachers took seriously the idea that different students learned at different rates and in different ways, and attempted (some more so than others) to provide a variety of modes for their students to learn and succeed.

Preparing Students for the Future

Most of the teachers said they were helping the students to prepare for the future by doing one or more of the following: teaching basic skills, giving practical information, and developing appropriate behaviors in students. The following comment illustrates the teachers who promoted basic skills to contribute to the students' futures:

> *Kay:* I think my whole thing is preparing for the future. I think communication skills are improtant. Problem solving, if it's not important now, it will be.

Several teachers believed that the students needed to understand information with direct practical use in order to be prepared for the future.

> *Joan:* Home Economics is really geared to the more practical sides of their future, so I'm teaching child development, and we are studying 3 through 5 year olds, and how they develop and we are talking about discipline and what works and what doesn't, and how to analyze children's stories so later in life they'll be able to make some intelligent choices of what their own kids will read.

> *Nell:* I use the kind of math they would use when adding up a checkbook, when ordering draperies; things that a housewife would use everyday.

There were also the teachers who believed that the students needed to learn how to act, because having appropriate behavior related to their future goals.

> *Don:* I make them behave themselves. And treat each other like they are supposed to, as much as I can. I don't tolerate any kind of rudeness, or disrespect. I try to make them behave, and I try to be a model of what I want them to be.

What is interesting is not what the teachers discussed, but what they did not discuss. It is understandable that the teachers were concerned with basics because the students *did* need work in the basics, but the teachers seemed to be seeing the students' futures as dead ends. Students were not seen to need to know more than the basics — and the attention to practical information suggested that these students needed 'how-to' knowledge instead of 'analytical and evaluative' knowledge.

Most teachers also did not include discussions of the students' futures in their curricula. One teacher shared with us her reason for this:

> *Kay:* Someone told me that our students are not future oriented and to stay away from that. So for a long time I did. . . .

The students had an opportunity to take a course entitled careers to help them look more objectively at their future. When we talked to the instructor about the goal of this class, she described it as follows:

> *Betty:* Basically, what we are really talking about is the kind of future training that they [students] might want to have and high school courses that might prepare them one way or the other, ways to explore career areas. You know the vocationally-oriented and the academic courses that are college preparatory courses. We talk about the dangers of going into those because you like them, not because you are thinking about your future so that when you are making a decision about taking this course, what do you have in mind? What kind of training are you thinking about?

Several of the women teachers also discussed sexism in careers with their students. They tried to encourage the students, especially the females, to be aware of salary discrepencies based upon gender and sexrole stereotyping of job choices. Additionally, the careers teacher said she usually told her class that it is very likely that most girls will work and discussed with them what that means for both sexes.

When asked, the majority of teachers at Five Bridges were empathetic about the students' futures and careers. Even if they actually expected few students to go on to college, they wanted them to live productive and relatively satisfying lives. However, it would be interesting to know how much thought they actually gave to the students' futures or evaluated their thinking of 'where', 'how', and 'why' they saw the students in the future, and how effectively they were helping students get there.

Two staff members (plus Anthony Ruiz) who were Hispanic and had grown up in Rivercrest were not as ready to proclaim the curriculum as relevant to the students' futures. Both were concerned about the lack of college emphasis in the curriculum. For example:

> *Renaldo:* I graduated from here, not ready for anything. I joined the Marine Corps. Then I met a girl and she said, 'Go to school'. No one here had ever told me to go on to school. Same with everyone else on my block. College was someone else's world. Kids today probably know they can go to college. People in Rivercrest have gone to college. How much pushing they get from us — that's another thing. I don't know. There should be more stress on college education.

Thus, it seems that what one teacher saw as relevant for the students depended on his or her view of the students' futures and ability to identify with the students. Those who wished to prepare the students for college were concerned that the curriculum was not geared as it should be to helping the students consider and prepare for that future goal.

Classroom Social Organization

When organizing a classroom, one factor to consider is seating arrangement of students. This requires consideration of both the configuration of the seats and the students that will occupy them. In a desegregated and mainstreamed school, which students sit where often becomes a problem for teachers who are concerned with integrating students across racial and handicap groups.

In all core area classes at Five Bridges, the desks were usually arranged in rows facing forward. Sometimes desks were rearranged into groups in some social studies classes and in science classes students regularly left the desks to work in labs; otherwise desks were rarely arranged into a different pattern. We asked why this pattern was chosen.

> *Don:* It's easier to see the kids. I use the board in front.
> *R:* Have you ever tried or have you thought about trying alternative desk arrangements?
> *Don:* Yeah, for different things I do that. But normally I'll have like thirty kids in there and so there are 32 desks.

Since most core area teachers used lecture and recitation as main instructional strategies, as Don pointed out, it made sense to seat all students facing forward.

As noted earlier, students were seated around tables in special education classes, home economics classes, and industrial arts classes. In remedial classes, they were either at tables or at desks that were not arranged in any particular pattern since the class size was under ten students. This seating arrangement facilitated the form instruction usually took in these classes — small-group work, individual tutorial work or hands-on projects (for example, woodwork).

How did teachers go about deciding who should sit where? The most common ways at Five Bridges were seating students alphabetically or letting students choose their own seats. Kay explained her thinking behind using alphabetical seating:

> I assign them alphabetically so that they know I'm fair, I'm not giving anybody special seats or letting some people sit by their friends. Then I put the end of the alphabet closest to me. I figure that all of their lives the beginning of the alphabet sat in front of the teacher and so they've learned some good study habits and it's time that the end of the alphabet did the same.

Don talked about his thinking related to allowing students to choose their own seats:

> *Don:* They seat themselves first of all and then I break up the groups that I don't like in certain positions because I know some kids talk constantly to each other and so I separate them. I do that on the first couple of days. I let them sit basically where they want to sit and then I move around sort of in the area that they sit. I like to put girls in the back row. They don't lean back on their chairs on the wall.
> *R:* Do you notice kids self-segregating themselves by sex?
> *Don:* Oh, sure, they always do.

> *R:*   Do you switch them at all?
>
> *Don:*   I switch them but I don't like kids to feel uncomfortable.

At Five Bridges the students usually mixed themselves by race in the classroom in the same way that they mixed themselves by race in their friendship groups. Therefore, in classrooms racial segregation did not occur, so teachers did not have to deal with it. Sex segregation often occurred, and most teachers responded to it in the same way Don did — they viewed it as natural and sometimes they rearranged a few students, but they did not see it as enough of a problem to make the students uncomfortable by dealing with it.

The band director dealt with sex segregation of seating and instrument choice a little bit, by encouraging some girls to take up instruments traditionally played by boys.

> *Robert:*   I've got one girl on the tuba for the first time. Now, to me that's something different because girls have always been taught to be feminine, play the flute or the clarinet. But I got one girl on tuba, and two girls on trombone, that's something new here for this group... Usually every semester I have beginners come in and I let them choose what they want, and 90 per cent of the girls want flute or clarinet. Maybe 5 per cent want saxophone, that's bigger instrument. Almost never do they want a tuba. In fact, I jokingly said, 'How about a tuba?'. Especially if they're a larger girl, 'cause it's so hard to get tuba players, even boys. And this one girl said, 'Sure, I'll play tuba,' and she's doing quite well.

Teachers were concerned about social segregation of handicapped students. Most noticed that there was a certain amount of segregation in classrooms, but did not know what to do about it without making it an uncomfortable issue. For example:

> *R:*   I know in one class you have a kid that is in a wheelchair. What happened to her?
>
> *Jo:*   She ended up working on her own. She's fairly bright, but I think in a way she would like to be on her own.
>
> *R:*   I noticed while I was in there a bunch of [students] came up to the little girl and helped her fix her legs back in the —
>
> *Jo:*   They're really good about that.
>
> *R:*   Is that kind of a special person thing, does one or two people do that?
>
> *Jo:*   Usually whoever is around.

R: Does she usually ask or do they just know?

Jo: She'll ask me or she'll ask them.

R: Is she the only handicapped kid you have in your class?

Jo: That hour. I actually have four now.

R: Do they all fit in?

Jo: The only thing I would like to see is more interaction.

One of the special education teachers team taught a health and science class with a regular teacher. The students in this class consisted of regular, LD, EMR and multiply handicapped students. Instruction purposely made use of heterogeneous small groups in order to build interaction across handicap groups.

Marilyn: We have regular kids working with [multiply handicapped students], sometimes it's a school service kid who is normal or LD. We have other kids just volunteering to help them. We never put the same kids together all the time. We do a little bit of the cooperative learning theory. One day when we worked in teams, I had them count off to five so nobody would know who would be with who. And we're mixing EMRs. We're really mixing kids very well in there. We never let anybody get away with putting anybody down.

This classroom was the only one observed in which groups were specifically designed to mix handicapped students. In other classrooms, such as science, teachers encouraged handicapped and non-handicapped students to work together, but left much of it up to the students to follow through on, and tended to be perplexed about what to do when the handicapped students ended up working alone.

Before proceeding to a discussion of major points in this chapter, let us first summarize how the teachers thought about and dealt with curriculum and instruction at Five Bridges. When planning the curriculum, their main objectives were remediating basic skills, providing students with practical knowledge, and, to some extent, preparing students for classes in high school. By this emphasis, the teachers thought they were preparing their students for the future. The teachers rarely considered student interests; activities that promoted critical and analytical thinking; experiences and perspectives of different racial groups, social classes, and handicap groups, and of both sexes. Most teachers relied on print materials and employed such teaching methods as large group recitation and lecture, or individual seatwork. These methods predominated core area classes. Teachers organized seating to facilitate large group and individual work, and did not attempt to develop students' social relationship through their teaching processes. Also, modifications they made for different learning styles were minimal. In contrast, some teachers, particularly those in special education, remedial and elective classes, used a variety of instructional materials and teaching strategies. Some of these teachers also attempted to develop student social relationships through group work, although few consciously and consistently worked on reducing handicap segregation and none worked on reducing sex segregation.

Our Thoughts About the Teachers

Earlier we noted that studies in desegregated schools have found teachers to be preoccupied with student behavior and interracial tension. The need to control behavior becomes an excuse for failing to present a challenging curriculum or incorporating attention to diversity into the curriculum. How would teachers view teaching in a desegregated school in which student behavior was good? At Five Bridges the students were relatively well behaved and displayed little tension among themselves. Yet, teachers continued to focus attention on their behavior, as demonstrated by their answers to broad questions asking them to describe the students at Five Bridges. When probed about the seriousness of discipline problems, teachers described them as being relatively minor — but they still talked about discipline as if it was something they expected to have problems with or were supposed to be preoccupied with. We wonder if it is characteristic of they way teachers see teaching generally, to be strongly concerned about student discipline. Given that discipline has been rated the number one school problem by the public for several years (Phi Delta Kappa Inc, 1980), it may be that this concern permeates our thinking about schools. Especially in desegregated settings, it may be that teachers believe they will be faced with problems of student behavior, even if student behavior is not actually a problem at that school.

The literature, as we commented, suggests that teachers in desegregated schools have a mixture of negative and neutral feelings about race, blaming students' homes for what they see as student deficiencies, but attempting to adopt a 'colorblind' perspective in their approach to teaching. The Five Bridges teachers exemplified neutral thinking about race. While not saying negative things about the students' racial backgrounds, neither did the teachers attempt to build on this racial diversity of their students. They tried very successfully to treat students equally regardless of race, but tended to see race and its manifestations as concerns that were only remotely related to course content. Therefore, they did very little to integrate a multiracial orientation into their teaching. The same can be said of gender and handicap — teachers tried to treat all students as equals, but rarely attended to sexist and handicappist biases in what they were teaching. One could characterize this as a passive or neutral response to human diversity rather than an active response that prizes diversity.

Teacher-student interaction was not an important way sexism was reproduced. Teachers treated both boys and girls the same in the classroom, and few were heard making sexist statements. We believe that teacher behavior is not one of the major ways in which sexism is institutionalized. It is institutionalized by practices such as omitting concerns and viewpoints of women from the standard curriculum, and segregating sports and electives. We will discuss institutionalized sexism in more detail in Chapter 9.

We did find, however, that teachers saw sex segregation as natural in junior high. For example, when students seated themselves in sex segregated groups, teachers rarely felt they should do something to counteract this. Had the students seated themselves in racially segregated groups, the teachers would most likely have been uncomfortable and responded to reduce some of the segregation. Several teachers were, in fact, uncomfortable by the tendency of handicapped and non-handicapped students not to interact as much as non-handicapped students interacted with each other, although they often did not feel like they knew what to do about this. But they did not seem to see a need to foster integration of or communication across sex groups; in this way, teacher behavior was sexist.

The reader will recall from Chapter 3 that, when asked to describe the students at Five Bridges, most of the students first noted that they were racially diverse and got along with each other. The teachers, on the other hand, rarely mentioned the students' racial diversity, concentrating most of their remarks on the students' academic abilities (especially their reading problems) and classroom behavior. One teacher talked to us about this, saying that she had been taught to ignore racial differences and treat everyone alike. She had grown accustomed to adopting a colorblind perspective, and became very uncomfortable if she thought there was a reason to ask a student about his or her racial or cultural background. Since teachers and students are in close contact with each other every day, and should have a common goal of successful student learning, we wonder how much more productive their interaction would be if each group gave attention to the things of most concern to the other. If the students prized their own racial diversity, it is likely that they would welcome classroom instruction that attended to it. It is also likely that they would 'tune in' to content that built from and extended the domain 'what to do and who to do it with' that composed much of their cultural knowledge. We are not suggesting that schooling be trivialized, but we are suggesting that bridges need to be built between students' cultural knowledge and academic knowledge, and we are suggesting that this may not have been happening much at Five Bridges.

How did these teachers view the acts of teaching and learning at Five Bridges? Most of them viewed teaching as the process of transmitting a body of knowledge and skills to the young, and learning as a process of memorizing that knowledge and being able to perform those skills. Like the teachers Cusick (1973) studied, these teachers saw themselves as subject matter specialists whose job was to impart knowledge to students, modifying that knowledge to make it the right level of difficulty for the students and, where possible, making it practical to what they saw the students' needs to be. Content was defined as what traditionally falls within a discipline (or, in the case of social studies, what interests the teacher within that discipline), not as what interests the students. Instructional processes that were used were those that could most efficiently get this knowledge transmitted to a classroom of students in ways that would not be *too* unpleasant for teacher and students.

Only a few teachers, most notably Shelby, saw learning as a process of growth that comes from within and is enhanced by an environment that is structured to stimulate interests defined by the student. To Shelby, teaching meant developing students' thinking processes. He did not see it as passing on any definable body of knowledge — he allowed the students to help define what they would learn, guiding them toward learning to think critically about the political process. Both Shelby and the special education teachers saw the students as people with legitimate interests — interests worth pursuing in school — and with legitimate, varied approaches to learning. What and how to teach evolved as teachers got to know students; it was not planned out in absence of any knowledge about the students, or planned in an attempt to catch the students up to a certain level of knowledge in a predefined area. We wonder if the special education teachers differed as a group from their regular education peers because of their training, or because child-centered people are attracted into special education.

Thus, in most classrooms, students were being taught to recall information, which is similar to how teachers have taught in other desegregated, working class schools. The process of learning to think critically and pursuing knowledge the student defines as worthwhile — or even of evaluating what makes anything worth knowing — was conspicuously absent at Five Bridges, as it has been found absent in the teaching in other similar schools.

Students were also being taught to exchange their time on routine tasks for certain rewards — grades and interaction with friends. The hidden curriculum in classrooms at Five Bridges was similar to that described by Cusick (1973). Teachers expected students to come to class on time and follow orders, but in exchange for routine work, usually attempted to make the classroom atmosphere a pleasant one. Students were allowed to help each other complete individual assignments and to talk quietly when their work was done. Also, they were given credit for having completed a class. Later, if the students move into factory or bureaucratic work situations, these work patterns will be quite functional. Students will be well trained for carrying out dull, routine orders in a setting that has positive interpersonal relationships, and in exchange for which they are given a regular paycheck and not hassled.

Since the teachers saw themselves as transmitters of knowledge, it makes sense that they would support the school objective of improving reading, but have mixed emotions about the objective of implementing education that is multicultural. To them, reading was a proper school objective since the students' reading skills interferred with their ability to learn what the teachers were trying to teach. The students' level of multicultural understanding did not interfere. Racial conflict among students was not a problem, nor was teacher-student tension over differences in racial background. Seeing the world from a multicultural perspective was not a prerequisite to learning what the teachers had selected to teach, since what they taught by and large reflected the white, middle-class experience. Learning style differences were not seen as important, since the blame for poor learning was placed on the students' reading skills. Seeing no practical use for education that is multicultural in the classroom, but at the same time feeling that education that is multicultural was a democratic ideal, the teachers paid this objective lip service, but did little to work toward implementing it.

While we are discussing the subject of instruction, we would like to share some thoughts with people involved in secondary schools. The nature of teaching we have described here is not atypical of teaching in many — even most — secondary schools. Secondary teachers frequently see themselves as transmitters of a body of knowledge, rather than as human developers. Secondary teachers, therefore, often rely principally on printed material or lecture to transmit their knowledge, and do not explore in much depth alternative modes of teaching, nor do they use the room environment as a dynamic teaching tool. Too often, they are busy teaching information as factual rather than helping students work through the reasoning undergirding concepts and the social context in which they are embedded. In addition, content is usually dictated by subject matter specialists and rarely by student interest. This is quite different from how much teaching occurs in elementary schools, where teachers often see themselves as developers of individual children. We believe that human development should be seriously considered as a legitimate aim of secondary education, and that teachers in secondary schools should learn more diverse approaches to teaching, and to teaching potentially diverse classrooms of students.

Changing how teachers teach is not easy, however. The teachers at Five Bridges were challenged to change their teaching radically by the administrators who adopted the objective of implementing education that is multicultural. In response to this objective, rather than reorienting their thinking about teaching, most of the teachers incorporated bits and pieces of it into what they were already doing. For instance, they put up a multiracial bulletin board, or selected a racially nonbiased textbook. Some even redefined education that is multicultural to simply mean treating all students equally, and then declared that they had already reached this objective. Only one struggled continually with the concept, slowly reorienting her entire approach to teaching to make it affirmative of human diversity.

One final observation about the teachers is that they did not discuss professional concerns with one another extensively, and therefore tended not to learn much about teaching and schooling from each other. Departments met to plan curriculum, and some teachers exchanged ideas, but they tended to let each person do his or her own thing without exploring in depth what their different experiences and outlooks might have to offer their own individual thinking. As one example, while several teachers said they admired the way Shelby taught, none made a conscious attempt to learn about teaching from him. As another example, most had mainstreamed students in their classrooms, and had access to special education teachers who were trained in the teaching of these students. But, rather than 'pumping' their special education colleagues for thoughts about teaching and mainstreaming, the regular teachers asked the special education teachers for a few specific techniques that would enable the main-streamed students to 'survive' in their classrooms, and that was that. Only one regular teacher attempted to reexamine and redefine her approach to teaching by teaming with a special education teacher. This suggests that these teachers viewed teaching as something one does and learns about alone, in the isolation of one's own classroom.

Let us now turn to the students again. How did they react to the school experience they were offered by the teachers? To find out, we will rejoin the students as they go to their classes.

Notes

1 For an excellent review of research on teachers see Marilynne Boyle (1982) *Teaching in a Desegregated and Mainstreamed School: A Study of the Affirmation of Human Diversity*, unpublished PhD dissertation, University of Wisconsin-Madison.
2 We consider the experience of these five teachers as more on-the-job-training — akin to an apprenticeship — than professional training where there is an organized body of knowledge and a professional of the area to carry out the instruction.

Chapter 6

The Students and Classroom Life

When the school bell rings signaling the end of a period, you can observe the excitement, actions and interactions of the students as they pass between classes. Their behavior seems typical of that found in most junior high schools visited and the activity evokes personal memories — memories like shouting to one another as you dash down the hall to the next class; balling up a quiz paper and throwing it into the trash because you are annoyed with the grade you received; 'setting the locker' of a friend so books and other articles fall from it when opened. Although adolescence can be a frustrating period of life, it has many, many pleasurable moments.

As the second bell rings students are entering their next period classrooms and taking their seats. We have observed the teachers' thoughts and actions as they step to the front of the room and call for order. What of the students? As they stop chattering and open their books, as they dutifully complete their assignments, whisper to their friends, take lecture notes or answer questions asked of them by the teacher, what are they thinking? What sense are they making of the classroom experience?

Several of our student interviews began with the question, 'Pretend I'm Mork[1] and I just came to Five Bridges and came up to you and said, "Tell me about this school. Tell me what a typical day is like"'. We chose to ask the students broad questions about school to determine what they found important enough to talk about. More specific questions were asked in subsequent interviews to probe their opinions on topics viewed important by us but not raised spontaneously by them. We then analyzed these interviews, first to determine the categories students used to structure their thinking about school, and second to examine student perceptions about a range of issues related to school.

The categories that representative students used to organize their cultural knowledge about school are depicted in Figure 2. While students did not organize their thinking about school in exactly the same way, there was considerable overlap in categories. Most of the students talked about teachers and classes/classwork. About half talked about kids, and about half talked about rules/getting in trouble. Activities and grades were categories a few students discussed. We will now examine each category of student cultural knowledge. (We have already described the students' cultural knowledge of other students in Chapter 3.) We draw not only on the topics spontaneously mentioned by students but also on their responses to questions posed by us. Finally, an analysis of our observations of students in classrooms is presented here.

Teachers

Students talked quite openly about their teachers. As they talked, they usually classified teachers into two distinct categories: those they viewed in a positive light, and those they viewed in a negative light. Although all students did not emphasize the same criteria, most categorized teachers into bipolar categories based on their own criteria. We examined the students' descriptions and evaluations of teachers to discern what criteria they used in their evaluations. We found them to include how well a teacher explained classwork, how fair a teacher was, and whether a teacher had a sense of humor.

A third of the students who talked about teachers in relation to school evaluated them on the basis of their ability to explain classwork and their willingness to help students with it. Comments such as these were made about teachers they liked:

Sue: Miss Jones is nice.
R: What makes Miss Jones nice?
Sue: She just explains things in class and if you need help she always helps you.

R: How do you describe a good teacher?
Carlos: One that would sit down with you and be there to help you all the time. One that wants to teach you. One that thinks you got something going...
R: What's your favorite class?
Carlos: Probably math.

Figure 2: *Students' cultural knowledge about school.*

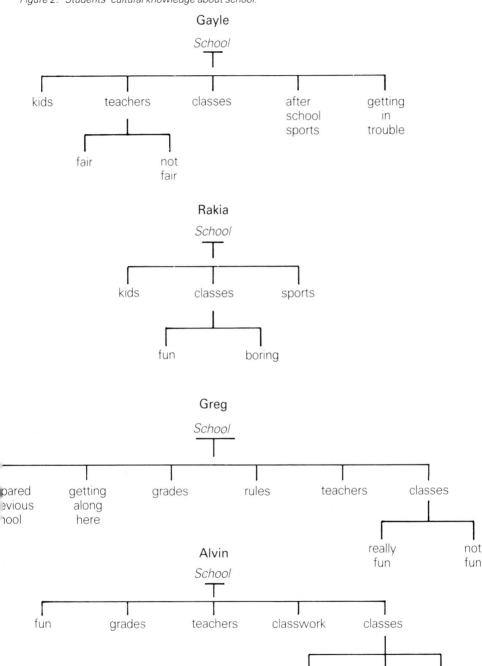

> *R:* Why is that your favorite class?
> *Carlos:* The math teacher is there all the time, sitting right by me helping me out. Always talks about interesting stuff.

And about teachers they did not like:

> *Kristen:* [Mr. Morey] gives you a weekly assignment; every single week it's the same thing. He doesn't tell you how to do nothing, he just gives the assignment and he's so strict.
> *Carmen:* It's so quiet in there, you can't even talk or anything. If you need help and you feel embarrassed to go up and ask the teacher and you ask one of your friends he'll usually yell at you.

One-quarter of the students evaluated their teachers on fairness. The students judged fairness on related but not identical teacher behavior. For example:

> *Pam:* She gives you what grade you deserve and all that. You know she's really fair.

> *Yvonne:* [Teachers] treat everybody equally and they don't have their picks in class. They don't mistreat anybody.

If a teacher did show favoritism in class, students complained about lack of fairness.

> *R:* What are the teachers like here?
> *Greg:* I'd say they pick their favorites. Like last trimester I didn't get along with this one and he gave me a bad grade in both of my classes that I had him.

Half of the students explicitly evaluated teachers based on how 'nice' they were and how much concern and understanding they showed to students. Teachers who empathized with students and showed personal concern for their welfare were rated positively. For example:

> *R:* What is a good teacher like?
> *Ricky:* To understand the kids, to help them out as much as they need the help, to be nice to them, don't put them down if they can't do nothing.

Teachers who seemed more concerned about maintaining control than they were about the students' welfare were called 'mean' and seen negatively. For example:

R: Mrs. Weisman, you didn't get along with her at all and I wondered why.

Carmen: I don't know. I guess she just didn't like me. She was really nervous all the time and she didn't control the kids or anything.

R: I sat in her class a few times and she was a new teacher and she was trying to learn how to handle kids and the kids were really mean to her.

Carmen: I guess the kids didn't really like her because she was always mean, like if you didn't get your work done she would call home or go to the office or something like that. She would pick on kids for any little thing.

The one thing 'mean' teachers were most consistently described as doing was yelling. 'Yelling' meant a teacher being critical of a student's behavior without necessarily raising his/her voice, or a teacher raising his or her voice (shouting) at the student. For example, when asked to describe a good or bad teacher, some students specifically mentioned this:

Frances: [A good teacher is] one who's patient, who understands when you have problems with your work, who won't holler at you when you make mistakes.

R: What don't you like [about teachers]?

Grace: Like, if you are going down the hall and you have a pass and they say, 'Let me see your pass' and you show it to them, they still yell at you. They say, 'You should be in class, you shouldn't be going here'. This is the way some teachers are, even if you have a pass. That is one thing that makes me mad.

A few of the students used a teacher's sense of humor as an important criterion for evaluation. For example, when asked why he liked a particular teacher, Ricky said, 'He likes us, he helps us out and cracks jokes and stuff'.

Half of the students evaluated teachers on their strictness. Teachers were criticized for being either too strict or too lenient; they were favorably evaluated if they struck a middle balance. For instance:

R: What are some things you admire most about Mrs. Smith?

Hugh: The way she teaches. She almost lets you do anything you want but you have to go by the rules.

R: And why do you think Mr. Lopez is a nice teacher?

> *Sue:* Because we have to work for him and that, but then when we work for him then we can do things on our own too.

> *R:* What's teaching right?
> *Hal:* Well, you gotta be strict enough to have the kids learn, where they won't be goofing around a lot, and you gotta be easy enough on them so that they will learn. So that they'll be happy enough about it to learn about what's happening.

As we examine these students' remarks about teachers, it is striking to note the relative absence of criteria related to academics. The students tended to judge their teachers based on the social atmosphere they created rather than on their success in stimulating learning and thinking or in preparing the students for their future lives. It seems as though the students had faith that their teachers were doing right by them academically, and were critical only if teachers were unpleasant socially. You will recall that Anthony, reflecting on his own experience as a student at Five Bridges, pointed out that this had been true of him, and regretted the naive faith the students had in their teachers.

Classwork

The great majority of the students talked about classes and classwork when asked about school, although most seemed reluctant to go into much detail about this. Students talked about their typical class periods in an almost monotonously similar fashion. Several devoted their most elaborate descriptions to the first few minutes of a class period, such as in the following statement:

> *Carlos:* [I] walk in, put my notebook on my desk, get our book, and sit down and wait for the teacher to call role and maybe crack a few jokes. Then we get our work.

This work was described as remarkably similar from one class to the next; in fact, several students told us that this repetition was very boring. For example:

> *Jody:* I got science first hour, and you know you're gonna be doing an experiment or taking notes or something. It's one of three things: you take notes, you read, or you do an experiment, and that's it. And you know what's coming up and it's not no fun, it's better if you get surprised.

In some classes there was a weekly routine that the students described in much the same way:

Shirley: We always do a certain thing through the week [in English]. Like the first day we do these little things, we read and then we have to answer questions about it. And the second day, he's got it planned day through day so if you miss Tuesday you know what you did Tuesday because you always do the same thing. Tuesday we have to work out of a workbook. And Wednesday we finish up the workbook, turn in the assignment, and start on our spelling test. Like, we write down words and get their meanings and stuff. And it goes on like that. It's boring in his class.

Did the students consider all classes a boring routine? Carrie's response to the question about a typical day is representative of all our students' responses in its singling out of one class, if any, that differed significantly from the routine:

Carrie: In my first hour I have government and we pretend like we are a city council and everything, so we get involved in that class. Then, in math we just sit there and listen to the teacher and then at the end we get an assignment. And in English we do the work in class and then we go over it and then we have to do book reports on our own. And in science we do labs and stuff.

The students classified classes into two categories: those that were 'good' or 'fun', and those that were 'boring'. Boring classes signified a daily routine absent of variation or surprise. In these classes students played a passive role, as the following comments indicate:

R: Why was [social studies] boring for you?
Robin: Because I just sat there. We just sat down and listened to him and that gets boring.

Anna: With him you watch TV, and with her you watch films.
R: You mean you are just sitting and listening, it doesn't matter if it is social studies or science?
Anna: Yup.

Not all classes were seen as boring, and most students were quite specific about the things that made a class good. We asked which classes they liked best and why. Several thought certain classes were good because they were interested in the content; others named student participation as a major characteristic of a good class; a few students named both criteria:

> *Kristen:* Multicultural [education] I like because it's different and publications because it's fun.
>
> *R:* What makes publications fun?
>
> *Kristen:* You get to go out and report and interview people, write stories to put in the [school newspaper].
>
> *R:* Why do you like multicultural education?
>
> Kristen: You get to study all the different people and stuff you never knew before — things that people say about people that are in books and stuff that you think is true, and we learn the truth about it. Like how the whites treated the Indians a long time ago.

A few students said that teachers made classes good:

> *Sam:* It's the way he gives you the work, you know, the way he talks, you can understand him better than you can understand other teachers.

A few listed the teacher plus the content:

> *Carmen:* I took multicultural education before, and I learned a lot about it because we had a really tough teacher. She really digs into your mind and tells you that whatever color you are it really doesn't matter as long as you are a person and you're just like everybody else. I really learned a lot in that class and I wanted to take it again.

Finally, one student said that friends in class made it good:

> *Yvonne:* When you have friends in a class and the teacher is nice and they let you talk to your friends sometimes that makes it fun.

It is interesting to note that this was the only student who clearly evaluated a class as good because her friends were in it; the rest of the students used academic criteria to describe good classes.

We asked the students how well they liked and learned from various specific classroom activities. We categorized responses to uncover those activities that received nearly unanimously favorable remarks, neutral or mixed remarks, and unfavorable remarks. Table 7 summarises the students' appraisal of thirteen class activities.

Those activities rated favorably by students involved a high degree

Table 7: Students' appraisal of classroom activities

Like, learn from this activity	Neutral or mixed appraisals	Don't like or learn from this activity
Small group projects	Independent projects	Listen to lecture without taking notes
Whole class discussions in which kids do most of the talking	Recitation: teacher asks questions and kids respond	Films (especially science films)
Speakers	Taking lecture notes	
Interview people	Doing dittoes	
Labs, experiments	Read then do questions	
	Read but no questions	

of student-student interaction. We asked students why they preferred working together. They gave us several reasons:

Elaine: If you don't know how to do it [the lesson] you can ask them.

Sue: I like working with people, then you are all thinking of things and can all share it with each other.

Linda: We get it done fast. If you don't know the answer, they might.

Hal: I think it's easier for a student to teach a student than a teacher to teach a student because the kids can understand each other better than the kids can understand the teacher.

Only one student did not prefer group classwork for this reason:

Larry: Usually when I do it with somebody else, I don't get it done.
R: Do you talk?
Larry: Just fool around.

The activities the students preferred also involved a high level of active participation. Less popular class activities placed students in a passive role and involved working alone.

During the course of a typical week, how much time did students spend engaged in activities they preferred? To estimate this, we tracked time students spent on different kinds of activities in their classes. Active discovery lessons and simulation activities, which usually took the form of small group projects, occupied on the average only 5 per cent of a student's day. (Actually, this meant that on many days students were never engaged in this sort of work, but sometimes they were for one of their six periods.) Listening to speakers and interviewing people occupied less than 1 per cent of their time. Labs and experiments (including home economics and industrial arts projects) occupied about 17 per cent of their time.

Nineteen per cent of the day was occupied in large group discussions of some sort, but usually large group discussions were dominated by the teacher, with students being called upon to answer questions. In other words, such discussions were actually recitation sessions, not true discussions. Commonly, teachers asked students to recall information, as the following example from a science class illustrates:

> T: What did you use this object for?
> S: To see the colors.
> T: OK. It's a tool you use to see the colors. What did you do with it?
> S: Used it to see colors.
> T: The colors you saw were incandescent. Do you remember what they were, Frankie?
> S: Red, yellow, green, blue, orange.
> T: What else?
> S: Violet?
> T: Red, orange, yellow, green, blue — what is between red and blue?
> S: Purple!
> T: Purple.

Discussions of this sort were used to make sure the students had the correct information and understood it well enough to recall it. Much less frequently did discussions challenge student thinking or did student ideas form the core of the exchange. In the following example, notice how the teacher allows student-suggested ideas to direct the discussion:

> T: How many of you heard Jeff on the PA today? He was really good. Jeff's announcement was pretty important.
> S: It's the last day for registration for student council.
> T: Why is that important?

S: If you don't register·you can't vote.

S: Same as out there [in the community].

T: Right. Remember the day we went down to the polls?

S: If you were running, you'd want people who like you to register.

T: That's really an important idea. You'd want your supporters to register. Your suggestion to remind people to register is very good; but teachers don't like interruptions in class, so we have to hope kids remember.

S: What about reminding them during lunch?

T: Good idea. How about a loudspeaker in the lunchroom? What do you think? Would that be too big of an interruption?

S: The kids are so loud they might not be able to hear.

Small group discussions occupied about 11 per cent of a student's day; these might be either open-ended discussions or group completion of a worksheet. Often student talk in small group discussions strayed away from the lesson. In some observed instances, students discussed their assigned work with each other, but in many others they discussed social things while completing their assignments. For example, the following conversation was overheard while students were supposed to be helping each other find information in social studies books:

Carmen: Shut up, Lupe!

Lupe: I don't wanna use a pencil. (Carmen goes to teacher's desk.)

Lupe: Can I use this [pen]?

(to a third student)

Student: It don't work.

Lupe: Yes, it does. Give it to me. C'mon, Carmen, get to work.

Carmen: (Inaudible)

Lupe: No, because there was a little thing on there.

This type of student-student interaction during small group work was frequently recorded in our observation notes, as the following example describes:

Students get out of seats — go to groups — noisy — I'm not sure if students are discussing projects — I went to check — Social talk between students and some talk of projects — [classwork] not organised in any way to ensure that this type of conversation is taking place.

As we will see later in this chapter, students did not 'stick to the topic' when they worked in groups because the topics were often not interesting to them. As long as the required work was completed, teachers made little effort to keep the discussion related to the work.

Students spent an average of 10 per cent of their day listening to lectures and taking notes. We found 28 per cent of class time taken up with independent seat work, and drill and practice exercises (for example, math problems, answering questions from the book, reading silently, completing worksheets). During much of this time students did not talk to anyone; they sat and obediently worked on their assignments. Teacher-student interaction was friendly and work-related. Student interaction was quiet and sometimes minimal. Students spent about 4 per cent of their class time watching films. About 5 per cent was spent taking tests.

Thus, students participated in those classroom activities they reportedly liked or learned from about one-third of their time. The rest of the time they were occupied with class activities they did not like but from which they felt they learned adequately, or routine activities they were unenthusiastic about. These activities put students in a very passive role, rather than involving them actively in learning and thinking. It is no wonder they described much of their classwork as boring, as we saw earlier.

Perhaps student tolerance for the class activities (note-taking and independent work) that they disliked was a result of their belief that these activities helped them prepare for tests.

Pam: In science we have notes about one or two times a week and in money and banking we have a notebook to write notes in.

R: How much do you learn from that?

Pam: A lot because if she says we're going to have a test you can go back and study your notes instead.

Kristen: Usually we read out of books and sometimes they have speakers come in and we do worksheets and we usually have to save them and then we have a test at the end of a certain period to see how much you learned.

We observed the students taking tests and quizzes fairly regularly. Few tests and quizzes we saw were above the recognition and recall levels of Bloom's taxonomy (Bloom, 1971). We often saw students asked to write spelling words, insert punctuation into sentences, fill in blanks recalling cooking or social studies concepts, and mark answers true or false. We also saw students apply math concepts to solve problems on quizzes. On only one occasion we observed a test in which students were asked to analyze and evaluate; one of our sample students pointed out that this test was a clear exception:

> *R:* What do you think about those kinds of tests that you got today? You had to write definitions and then answer questions on the last part. They weren't really questions that you could answer by giving one or two words. It looked like they were questions you really had to think about.
>
> *Grace:* Yeah. We had to write long definitions for them and then you had to write what you thought on the last ones.
>
> *R:* Would you rather have a test like that where you write down what you think or where you write down answers?
>
> *Grace:* What I think.
>
> *R:* In other classes are you asked to write down what you think like you were in this one?
>
> *Grace:* No, in most of the classes they give you notes and you have to study those notes and then what is in those notes you have to write on the test.
>
> *R:* What is different about the class you were just in?
>
> *Grace:* I guess it's harder.

Homework assignments were rarely noticed in classroom observations, so we asked thirty students, ranging from top students to special education students, how much homework they got. Of the thirty, eighteen replied that they never or rarely had homework. The only homework they had was make-up work from an absence, or finishing an assignment they did not finish in class. Nine students replied that they got a little bit of homework. Only three of the thirty students reported having homework regularly — at least twice a week, requiring at least an hour on each assignment. Most of the homework students got was from algebra, math, or foreign language.

In Chapter 5 we described what the students were being taught in their classes. What sense did the students make of this content, and how hard were they applying themselves to learn it? We asked the students if what they were being taught related to their lives in any way. Almost half said that none of it related; almost half said that one or two classes related somewhat; the rest named two or three classes that related to their lives quite a bit. In general, when the students said they found the content relevant, what they meant was that it had some practical use to them, either at the present or in the future. For example:

Pam: Money and Banking, you're going to use that when you grow up. Or, [publications], if you wanted to be a reporter, that is just starting you out a little.

Sue: I use math a lot. I like it.
R: What do you feel you use your math for?
Sue: Anything. Try to figure something out.

Lupe: I think a lot about my multicultural class.
R: What are some of the things you learn in there that you think about?
Lupe: About how I was prejudiced, things I do.

Hal: Science [relates] once in a while. If you want to know about the octane in gas and stuff like that. Math, you hardly ever use, government and all that junk.

The most relevant classes named were government because current events that one hears on the news were discussed there; oral history because the content was about the students' own neighborhood; money and banking because the students will use it later; math because it helps in counting change; and English because it teaches words students need to know. But no student said that most or even as much as half of what they were being taught had any relevance to them.

On rare occasions, students were invited to participate in the selection of content. When students could exercise some choice over what they learned, they felt positive about the experience for the most part. For example:

R: So you feel like interviewing is a good way to learn?
Hal: Yeah, because you're asking questions that you want to know and they're giving you answers that are interesting about what you're asking and stuff.
R: How about listening to speakers in class?
Hal: Yeah, because again you're asking questions that you want to know. One of my friends' dad came here and he was from Lebanon and we got to ask questions about it. It's easier to remember than learning from a book because they're telling us stuff that you really don't care about. This way you're asking what you want to know.

Lupe: In our government class we have to take a vote and the whole class is all together in it. We make up our own tests and take votes and stuff. That was only in one class. We only did it one time.

R: What did you think about that?

Lupe: I like it because that way you get more ideas.

Considering much of the content irrelevant, students often reported being bored in class, and sometimes said they forgot what they learned once they had been tested on it. One student made the following comment:

Phil: A lot of the reason why the kids screw up in class is because they can see no practical use for what they are learning.

In addition to seeing much of the content as irrelevant, most of the students did not see it as particularly difficult. Fifteen students talked about the difficulty of their classwork. Seven said it was easy, five said it was about right, and only three said it was hard. Several students specifically stated that they would like more of a challenge than they were being offered. For example:

Sam: I've got reading right now.

R: What do you think about it?

Sam: I don't like the class.

R: Why is that?

Sam: The teacher, I don't like the teacher. I've had her for two trimesters before this and I don't like her.

R: You don't like the work or you don't like her?

Sam: It's the same old kind of work, it's just boring.

R: What kind of work would you like?

Sam: Stuff that gives me a challenge.

R: That work doesn't challenge you?

Sam: Hardly at all.

R: Do you get most of it right?

Sam: Yes.

R: If you could tell a bunch of teachers what you thought would be the best way to teach, what would you tell them?

Ricky: To give me some homework. They talk all day, and so give us some homework.

R: Do you have homework?

Ricky: No.

R: And you think you should?

Ricky: Yes.

Others said that they did not want harder work or homework because they preferred spending their time and energy on other things that interested them more. The students saw little point in learning the content they were being taught, beyond memorizing it to pass tests in their classes. Furthermore, many did not see it as especially difficult, and most students found the manner in which it was taught boring. Therefore, they learned what enabled them to pass their classes, but most did not engage in schoolwork beyond that minium level. In this manner, they slowly worked their way through basic skills and concepts, but were rarely ready (or seen to be ready) to go beyond that, to develop complex thinking skills or acquire the high status knowledge that is tested on achievement and intelligence tests.[2]

We examined class content to determine the extent to which it enriched the students' cultural capital and provided them with high status knowledge. First, we looked at the course offerings, and found them to be strongly weighted toward the remedial end of the spectrum. For example, during winter trimester of one year, 28 per cent of the course offerings were remedial (Title I, ESAA, special education), while only 2 per cent were academically advanced (algebra and physics).

Second, we looked for the inclusion of high status knowledge within the courses that were taught, and found little. We found, for example, very few references to classic works of literature (let alone study of the classics); few complex concepts in science classes, and few analyses in social studies of, for example, the causes and outcomes of major wars or historic technological changes. The knowledge students were being taught would lay a foundation for acquiring high status knowledge (assuming the students retained this basic knowledge and were later offered an opportunity to learn high status knowledge), but did not in itself constitute high status knowledge.

We asked students if there was attention paid to non-whites, women and the handicapped in their classes. Their responses corroborated our observations reported in Chapter 5. A few students said there was not; about half said that there was none outside of multicultural education, cultural foods, Spanish and special education. A few students replied that they learned about different countries in geography or that a social studies teacher sometimes talked about equal rights for women and/or blacks, or that they had to do a report about a minority person, or that they had teachers who mentioned something about handicapping conditions.

By attending very little to diversity in class lessons, the school was not broadening the students' knowledge about human diversity. Furthermore, by presenting knowledge by and about oppressed groups in separated lessons and separate classes, the school was teaching the students to see 'ethnic' knowledge as separate from 'regular' knowledge. In the following discussion with Alvin, this separation is clearly indicated:

> R: Do they talk about [different cultural groups] in the classroom?
>
> Alvin: Probably in the race class, Spanish or something probably they talk about it, 'cause otherwise I ain't had no teacher who's talked about it.
>
> R: Which classes do you take?
>
> Alvin: I only take regular classes, working classes you know. The other classes like Spanish and all that — just regular classes.
>
> R: Well, what are your regular classes?
>
> Alvin: Reading, Math and English
>
> R: And they don't talk about it in those classes?
>
> Alvin: No.

Although they did not talk much about the absence of attention to diversity in their schoolwork, the students were not completely unaware that it was being left out, and several of them mentioned things they would like to be taught. For example:

> R: Do you think it's important for the other kids here to know about what the blacks do, who the heros are, the contributions made?
>
> Alvin (black):   Yeah, because some people think that blacks are troublemakers. They don't know what they do or nothing.

> R: What do you like least about [school]?
>
> Mark (Native American):   Well, they teach you everything almost that you know, but I think, like the Little Red Schoolhouse, the Indian school, they teach you about the Indians, their culture and stuff, here they don't.
>
> R: And you would like to know about your culture?
>
> Mark: Yep.
>
> R: Do you ever say anything to them about that?
>
> Mark: There's mostly Mexicans in this school and that's what this stuff is. That usually happens, like on announcements they have Manuela saying announcements in Spanish, they don't teach Indian languages here and stuff like that.

R: Have you gotten to know more about handicapped kids since they go to school here?

Carlos: Not really.

R: Are you interested in finding out how they think or how they feel about their handicap, or how they see things?

Carlos: Yeah, I would like to learn about them and see how they feel.

R: Do teachers in class ever explain or try to help the kids learn anything about what you can do or what you can't do?

Ruth (physically impaired): No, they don't have anything like that.

R: Do you think they should?

Elaine (physically impaired): For the mean kids, yes. If it was explained to them maybe they wouldn't have that attitude.

Ruth: They don't have anything like that.

While most students accepted what they were being taught, then, many were aware of things related to their different backgrounds that they were not being taught, and some students believed more content about the students' diversity should be included in school learning.[3]

Students talked little about the social organization of their classrooms; they talked about their friends in class but tended to take the social system for granted. By observing the students in class, however, we noticed some patterns in the way they structured themselves socially in classrooms.

You will recall from Chapter 5 that students mixed themselves

Figure 3: *Seating patterns: clustering by Sex*

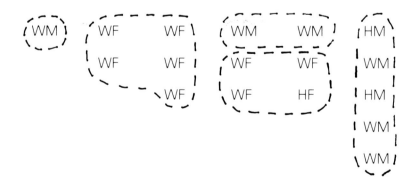

interracially in classrooms. Seating was usually mixed by sex when teachers assigned seats, but there was some sex segregation when students chose seats. Most commonly, students clustered by sex, illustrated, for example, in Figure 3. Sometimes the entire room was roughly divided by sex, as in Figure 4.

Figure 4: Seating patterns: segregation by sex

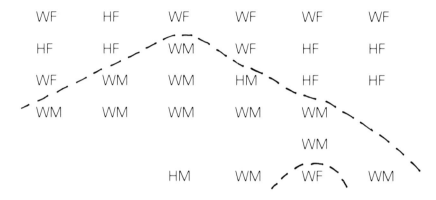

Physically impaired students usually ended up sitting at the periphery of the classroom. For example, the seating pattern illustrated in Figure 5 was common because in most classrooms seats were close together in rows; the fewer desks the student in the wheelchair had to dodge, the easier the process of coming and going. But, being seated on the periphery of the classroom decreased opportunity for interacting with other students. For example, the student in the wheelchair in Figure 5 has only one or two students easily available to talk to, while most other students have three or four.

Figure 5: Seating patterns: position of wheelchair

WM	HM	WM	WF	HF	WM (Wheelchair)
WM	HM	WM	WM	WF	
WM	WM	HM		WM	
		WM			

What interaction patterns occurred within these seating arrangements? In the rooms in which the least amount of student-student interaction took place, seats were often assigned and students were mixed by sex. In rooms in which student-student interaction was allowed, seats were usually student-selected and about two-thirds of the interaction remained with members of the same sex, as illustrated in Figure 6, which superimposes observed interaction patterns over the seating pattern illustrated in Figure 4.

Figure 6: Student interaction patterns

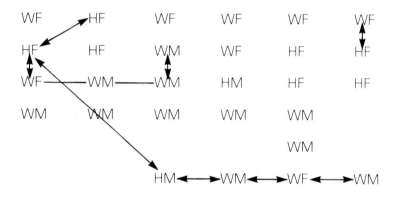

In science and cooking, labwork was done in pairs or small groups, which were almost always student selected. These groups were usually racially mixed but not sex mixed. For example, Figure 7 illustrates the groups observed in a sceince lab.

Figure 7: Student pairs in a science lab

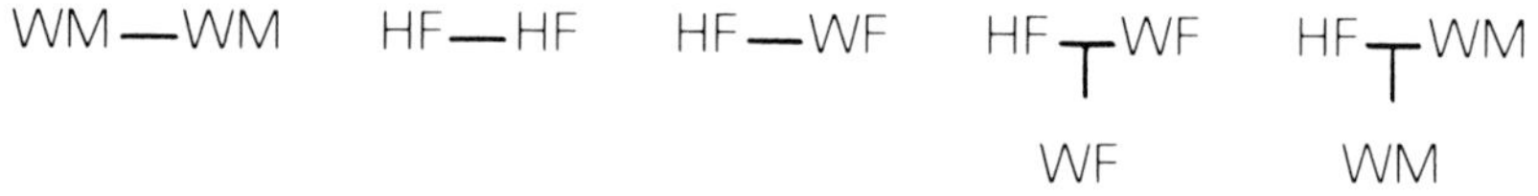

Is there any evidence that social divisions based on sex or handicap could have been weakened by manipulating seating and providing for interaction? Some students said that they got to know physically impaired classmates by being allowed to help each other with classwork. When asked if they ever talked to handicapped kids, several gave responses such as the following:

Rakia: I have a handicapped kid in first hour and he helps me with my math.

Alvin: I have Phil first hour for biology. He sometimes helps me out in the lab.

Pam: Anita's in my math class. She asks for help to get her books and stuff. She's nice.

Thus, students did cross handicap and sex barriers to talk to other peers, and thereby sometimes got to know students they did not usually socialise with. But, left to chance, this interaction did not occur nearly as much as interaction within sex and handicap groups. In fact, when classrooms were observed, there were a few instances in which few if any words passed between a handicapped student and another student throughout an entire class period.

We looked at the relative amount of time students interacted with each other and found that interaction was dominated about 54 per cent of the time by the teacher, by way of lecture or teacher-directed discussion. About 8 per cent of the time there was confusion, little interaction (for example, music classes), or no interaction (independent study). The remaining 38 per cent of class time involved some student-student interaction in the form of a large group discussion led by the teacher, small group work, or individual work with help from peers. But even during this time, interaction among students was not often sustained or academic in emphasis. It consisted instead of social chatter while work was being completed, or contributions by a few students to large group discussion.

Seating patterns are important in affecting student social organization if students are required to remain in their seats. Two-thirds of classroom time was spent sitting without permission or motivation to move. Teachers circulated to offer help, while students stayed seated. During about a fourth of their classroom time students were allowed to move to get materials or to comply with a teacher request. In only about one-twelfth of their class time (excluding physical education classes, which we observed infrequently) could students move freely about the room to form groups, ask questions or use materials in different parts of the room. Therefore, since students stayed in their seats most of the time and interacted with peers near them, sex segregated seating and seating that excluded students in wheelchairs reinforced these social divisions among students.

Did students see teachers giving preferential treatment to any particular group of students? Based on students' reports (as well as our own observations), there was no evidence of staff members differentiating among students on the basis of race. Also, many students agreed that teachers treated both sexes equally, but a few commented that girls tended to get easier treatment than boys by some teachers for similar offenses. We did not observe this happening, although occasionally it may have occurred. Students often did complain that handicapped students received preferential treatment. However, as teachers gained more experience with them and as students became more knowledgeable about their needs, this complaint decreased somewhat.

What kind of leadership did students exhibit or develop in class? We saw very few instances of leadership or influence. A group leader sometimes emerged when students worked in small groups but just as often did not. In a very few instances individual students were observed leading the direction of class discussions, with other students following their lead. More often, individual students exerted influence over their peers by distracting them from classwork. This lack of student leadership in class seemed to result directly from the passive role they occupied in most classes, and the amount of time they spent being clearly directed by the teacher. The respect for authority learned at home may also have contributed to this — students were taught to follow the teacher's lead, and therefore rarely looked to their peers in the classroom for leadership as long as the teacher did not encourage it.

Rules and Discipline

The students at Five Bridges did not volunteer comments on classroom discipline during our discussions. When asked, their responses were typically grouped as follows: teachers are not strict; detention; discipline is not a problem.

> *Carrie:* Some teachers can't handle it, you know, they … they put up with it but they don't do nothing to them [misbehaving students].

Marsi: There's not much authority, the kids get to do a lot. They get away with a lot.

Detention took place after school. It usually lasted for half of an hour depending upon the punishment handed down by the Vice Principal or the Administrative Assistant. In detention, the punishment was often writing lines. Many of the students believed that detention was often given for dumb reasons, and it was not worthwhile.

Hal: Everybody ditches [skips] it [detention] because they get it for a stupid reason. When you get it for a stupid reason, they'll ditch it anyway. I know I did.

A number of students reported that they did not see discipline problems occurring in the classroom. As Gina stated, 'It's not really a problem'. During the three years of the study, we did not observe any serious classroom discipline problems. The nature of the discipline problems we observed were students talking when assigned to do work, chewing gum, talking back and throwing paper.

Outside of the classroom, infractions of school rules took place when a student did not attend a class, was in the hall without a pass, smoked on school grounds or was in a fight. Students did not often fight or get caught wandering in the hall or smoking. Not attending class, therefore, was the rule infraction that the students usually discussed when describing discipline problems outside of the classroom. Many students believed others did not attend class because they found the work boring or did not like the teacher.

Lisa: I don't think it's right for kids to come to school and then not to go to class.

R: Why do you think it is that kids don't go to class?

Lisa: Maybe they don't like their teachers or they think it's cool or they don't want to do their work.

Harriet: I just stopped ditching because I got two 'Ds' in my classes and I wanted to do better, so I just stopped.

R: What did you do when you ditched?

Harriet: Just walked around, sometimes I went home.

R: Why did you ditch?

Harriet: I didn't want to go to class because it was boring.

R: Had it [class] not been boring, would you have come? Do you want to learn?

Harriet: Yeah, but they don't teach you nothing. . . .

Discipline, it is reasonable to summarize, was not a major problem at Five Bridges. When the students talked about discipline and rules — which was not often — they talked mainly about teachers controlling student behavior, and students acting out and ditching classes because they were bored. Also, disciplinary procedures were most often involved with student physical actions (acting out) as opposed to student academic learning.

Grades

Several students brought up the subject of grades, and we asked most of our sample students how they saw and felt about their grades. A third specified that it was important to them to get passing grades, but that it did not matter if grades were above passing. These students talked about grades in the following way:

> *R:* How important is getting good grades to you?
> *Hugh:* Very important.
> *R:* How come?
> *Hugh:* If I fail two classes I have to make them up in summer school and it's about the hottest time of the year.

> *R:* How important are grades around here?
> *Richard:* Well, if you don't get good grades you stay in that grade.
> *R:* So it's important to get passing grades?
> *Richard:* Yes.
> *R:* Does it make any difference if you get an A, or a B, or a C?
> *Richard:* To me, not really.

One third of the students associated good grades with pleased parents. The following kinds of response was common:

> *R:* Is it important to you to get good grades?
> *Sue:* Yeah.
> *R:* How come?
> *Sue:* So my mom and dad don't get mad and so they'll trust me and let me do more things and take more classes if they know I can do good.

When asked about the importance of grades, few students saw a relationship between junior high grades or academic achievement and college entrance. Only one student said she valued her grades because they would help her get into college. A few students connected grades in high school with college entry, but said they would worry about their grades later. For example:

R: Are grades important to you?

Hal: Just as long as I pass. I'll have to start next year because I want to go to college and you have to have good grades to go to college so next year I'll have to worry about my grades.

One student connected academic competence with specific careers rather than with college entrance requirements:

R: Do you ever think about the fact that you want to go to college but you're flunking classes?

Lupe: I never think about that. Like if you're going to be a lawyer or something you have to think about it. You don't really have to think to be a coach.

In general, then, to most students junior high grades meant little or nothing in relationship to their future ambitions. Most often, good grades meant happy parents and passing to the next grade level.

Extracurricular Activities

Five Bridges offered a variety of sports and a student council as extracurricular activities. Most of the students participated in at least one activity and many talked frequently about the activities in which they were involved. We asked twenty-four students about participation in extracurricular activities; only four of these did not participate.

Two of these four students were physically impaired. Physically impaired students rarely participated in after-school activities because there were no wheelchair sports or non-physical activities available and because they had to catch a bus home.

R: Would you like it if they had more things after school that handicapped kids as well as non-handicapped kids could be doing?

Ruth: Yeah, but we can't. Our buses come and we have to go.

Elaine: I live in [suburb] and my mom doesn't like to drive way down here.

Ruth: I live on the East Side and my mom drives a half hour to get here.

If physically impaired students were rarely included in extracurricular activities, it was not because they did not want to participate. When asked to join the swim team in the high school, for example, Phil was elated:

> *Phil:* I recently was asked to be associated with the regular swim team, which is something that handicapped kids aren't often asked to do, and so my house is pretty much in an uproar.

Girls had about as many sports available as boys (there was an effort to keep the number equal but sometimes one sex had more as one additional sport was getting underway). However, after school sports were sex segregated and girls and boys did not have exactly the same sports. For example, in school year 1978/79, the following sports were available:

Girls	*Boys*
track	track
basketball	basketball
softball	baseball
gymnastics	wrestling
volleyball	

A few students said that they felt boys' sports were taken more seriously by the school than girls. For example:

> *Gina:* Well, like for the girls' sports they always get ladies, you know, I mean lady coaches, and for the guys they always get like Ted Smith, he's a really good basketball coach, and we asked him if he would coach us, and he said no, because he doesn't like girls' basketball, and we're just as equal as the boys, I think.

> *Linda:* Their [the boys'] coach works them a lot harder than ours.

> *Jody:* Something happened yesterday. We were supposed to have a gymnastics meet here, and the gymnastic team from Garfield was supposed to come over here to have a meet with us. And the boys basketball team was supposed to go over there. And they cancelled the gymnastics meet because of bad weather, but they didn't cancel the basketball team, and we really thought that was terrible. We thought that was sexism.

But, not all students shared this perception: several others commented that they thought boys' and girls' sports received equal attention by the school.

We asked the students why they signed up for the activities they did. Only one said she chose an activity to be with her friends. Three-quarters said they signed up for activities because they enjoyed the activity itself, and they often made friends with other students as a result of being on the same team together. The rest said they considered both the activity and who else was joining when deciding whether to participate. One student explained that the activities were important to students because 'It's something to do after school'.

Sports was by far the main kind of activity at Five Bridges, and it was the only extracurricular activity many students considered possible. We asked several students what additional activities they would like to see, if any, and they all replied in terms of sports. For example:

> *R:* Do you feel like there should be after school activities besides sports?
>
> *Gayle:* Yeah, I think they should have like Open Gym and shoot baskets or go to the other gym and have gymnastics or whatever. Today, like from 1 to 3, there is going to be a dance.

In other words, extracurricular activities such as science, chess, and 4-H clubs that are often a part of the program in other junior high schools were not a part of the thinking of the Five Bridges students.

The Purpose of Classroom Life

Does school exist primarily to benefit all young people by helping them develop intellectually, or does it exist primarily to sort and select them for different kinds of futures? While most Americans like to believe that school exist for the former reason, the evidence at Five Bridges strongly suggests the latter.

The students at Five Bridges thought school existed for their benefit, so they complied with its demands. But they also realized that it was irrelevant to their interests and boring — it did not seem to be seriously helping them to develop their minds. During the interviews the students talked much more fluidly and enthusiastically about their friends and social activities than they talked about school. When asked about their classwork, for example, several like Carlos, whom we cited earlier, devoted most of their description to what happens between the time they enter class and the time they get their work. Some of the students flatly told us that they did not think about school, nor did they talk about it with their friends. We had the impression that they spent much of their time going through the motions of classwork, and rarely becoming actively engaged in it.

The students seemed very unaware that the school might be sorting them into working class futures by failing to prepare them to compete successfully for anything else. Earlier we cited the findings of Bourdieu (1977), that students are channeled through school and into different futures, based largely on their competence with white middle class cultural capital. The students at Five Bridges, by and large, were not being exposed to high-status cultural capital either inside or outside of school, and plans or funds to ensure that they would acquire enough knowledge to compete successfully were lacking. Student exposure to status culture outside school through means such as attending museums, reading or traveling widely was very limited. In school they were taught the most basic academic knowledge with an orientation toward practical application rather than further academic learning. Although the Five Bridges students were rarely placed in competition with each other (apart from sports), they would be in competition with their peers city-wide, statewide and nationwide for college entry, scholarships and jobs. We believe their chances for success are poor.

What is ironic is that the students were unaware of this. They believed that if they attended school, passed their classes and cooperated with teachers, they would be well prepared for the future. Quite likely their families were under the same impression. Because they were unaware of how the system works, the students had no basis for critiquing their preparation for it. It is important to note their lack of knowledge about the importance of grades. This could indicate that the students were not being told or allowed to discover the important role that grades can play for enabling life's opportunities: the differences in opportunities available to an 'A' student as opposed to a 'C' student can be significant. Although the students knew an A is higher than a C, they did not seem to understand what difference one has over the other, and school and home were not working cooperatively to help the students understand the importance of grades in our credentialed society.

The students evaluated course content on its perceived practical relevance and on its appeal to their interests. This is not radically different from the way the teachers selected what to teach since they too considered practical application of knowledge as well as basic skills.

What the students did not know was that knowledge can be practical in that it opens doors. For example, one may never need to know about Mozart to get by in everyday life, but Mozart may be the subject of an item on the college entrance exam. Unaware of this practical use of knowledge, students did not demand status knowledge or make a tremendous effort to learn its fundamentals.

We found it particularly ironic that the teachers felt they were working most of the students to their capacity, but the students did not feel the work they were given was particularly hard. Quite likely the students' class performances did not shine because they were bored, which led the teachers to assume the students were learning as much as they could. Assuming this, the teachers did not challenge most students, thereby reinforcing their boredom with school.

It is important to note that most of the teachers' assumptions concerning the academic ability of the students were to a large extent derived from hearsay or from the expectations the teachers had of the students based on their home backgrounds and reading scores. For the most part, their 'inability to perform' was accepted without investigation and without an alternative plan to spark the students. If the teachers had been told the students were smart, we wonder how their teaching and the students' consequent academic performance would differ.

If the students did not see school as an arena of competition for different kinds of futures, even less so did they see it as a place where one could learn to fashion a more just society. Students occasionally said that they thought classes should pay more attention to human diversity, but this was not a major point they made when telling us what they liked and did not like about school. This strongly suggests to us that most of them took it for granted that school knowledge does not deal with human diversity. They rarely questioned the fact that, for example, most stories they read were about whites, and the handicapped people with whom they shared classes rarely appeared in books. Probably the only school knowledge they had ever experienced had a white middle-class bias, so the students saw this knowledge as standard and thought that was what schools were supposed to teach.

Students also did not criticize the school for not challenging them to think analytically and question their place in an unequal social structure. It did not seem to occur to them that their own perceptions of life — their own ambitions, their notions about reality, their hypotheses about their life conditions — should become central to the curriculum. For example, although some girls were angry about doing most of the housework at home, they did not realize that the woman's place in society could be critically examined in school. Instead, they saw this anger as something to try to submerge while in school so they could concentrate on other things. Similarly, the students' interest in their own racial diversity was viewed as irrelevant in the curriculum. It did not seem to occur to the students that school might be a place where they could learn more about their own diversity, or learn to question and challenge race relations in society as a whole.

It was interesting to find that discipline was not talked about much by the students even though student behavior was a concern of the teachers. The students who mentioned school rules and discipline were those who sometimes got in trouble. When students did talk about discipline, it was often to point out that the teachers did not do enough to control it.

Why did the students and the staff see things as they did? Why did their perceptions converge in some ways and diverge markedly in others? In the next chapter we will address those questions, as we explore determinants of the students', teachers' and administrators' cultural knowledge and actions.

Notes

1 From the television show *Mork and Mindy*, in which Mork was from outer space.
2 Toward the end of this study one of the English teachers noticed both the lack of challenge for more able students and the absence of classic pieces of literature from the curriculum, and began revising the English program to challenge more students in reading and to include extra study of 'Great Books' for the better readers.
3 As the students got older they became much more aware of this lack in the curriculum. During untaped conversations with several of the students later in high school, they told us explicitly that information about groups other than caucasians should be taught in classes and should be required for everyone.

Chapter 7

Why the Students Believed as They Did

Why did the people of Five Bridges School think and act as they did? We began exploring this by asking them and cataloguing the factors cited. We examined their responses to see to what extent the same reasons were given more than once by the same person, or by several different people. We considered our evidence to be especially strong if the same 'why's' were stated by individuals representing different role groups or backgrounds. But we did not stop with what people said, because we recognize that people are not always aware of or willing to share determinants of their thoughts and actions. So, based on our observations and perceptions of Five Bridges, we identified additional determinants to those named. The process that will lead to an understanding of the 'why's' is often very speculative. But, we believe our speculations are reasonable because they are based upon a procedure for triangulating or cross-checking our findings.

In our search for determinants, we looked for both factors in the immediate environment of Five Bridges that supported the actions and beliefs of people and the impact of unequal social relationships in society as a whole. For example we believe it is not coincidental that people learn to think and act in sexist ways in a sexist society. Inequality based on sex supports and feeds situations into which people are born. Sexism as it is concretely manifested daily presents to the child patterns of human relationships and opportunities, and explanations for those patterns, that the child usually apprehends as normal. Sexism also makes it very likely that girls and boys will be exposed to somewhat different worlds as they grow up.

Then what causes people to fight sexism, racism, classism or handicappism? The will to forge a more just society rises out of two different kinds of situations. One is a situation in which social inequality as it is experienced by the child flies in the face of the child's own dignity, wrenching the child from acceptance of the world to rejection of its injustices. The other is a situation permeated by contradicting determinants; for example, the child who is expected to bow to authority in one cultural site but to think and act independently in another may eventually reject the norms supported by determinants in one site in favor of those in the other.

At Five Bridges we found a student population that was not simply reproducing social inequality, but was questioning and to some extent actively rejecting it. What was it about the students' world, for example, that led them to see it as sensible to embrace racial diversity and to see race as irrelevant to the distribution of goods and privileges? What was it about the teachers' world that led them to see race as unimportant and tacitly to accept inequality based on race? What led the administrative team to see racism as something that ought to be fought in school but tacitly to accept much of it nevertheless?

An examination of determinants will help answer these questions about race, and similar questions about gender, handicap, and social class. We begin in this chapter by examining determinants of the students' cultural knowledge about human diversity. In Chapter 8 we examine determinants of the teachers' instructional approaches, the administrators' leadership style, and their responses to human diversity.

Determinants of Students' Cultural Knowledge about Human Diversity

From our interactions with the students, we discovered factors in the school and the community that were the major determinants of their cultural knowledge. We will examine those related to their cultural knowledge about race, handicap, gender and social class.

Race

Students' interracial friendship patterns and cultural knowledge about race were influenced primarily by the racial makeup and distribution of the community, the community's value for getting along, residents' common lifestyle, and the geography. According to the students, as they grew up in this community they grew used to seeing people of different colors living around them, including mixed marriages down the street or even in their own homes. Especially on the lower bluff it was easy to get to know people of different races and racial mixing was not presented in everyday life as a problem or as something unusual. For example, according to Juan:

> [Racial mixing] just comes natural to most of us mainly because we live with them. We probably have someone who is black next door and someone who is Chinese down the street. We grow up with these kids.

Racially mixed housing does not, however, produce integrated friendships by itself. In Rivercrest, there was also a strong cultural belief in getting along with others. In the interviews, the students consistently talked about how important it was to get along with each other. Although there was no specific interview question about 'getting along', two-thirds of the students brought it up. For example:

> *R:* If somebody came from California and asked you about the kids here at Five Bridges, how would you describe them?
> *Carlos (Mexican):* There are white, black and Mexican kids who all get along.

> *Ricky (white):* They get along with each other.
> *Hugh (white):* No matter what color they are they get along.
> *Ricky:* They don't put you down because you are white and you're black or nothing because you can't change yourself.

Residents of Rivercrest shared a similar income level, leisure activities, and dress and shared a common pride about the community. In addition, all students who had grown up in Rivercrest spoke English fluently even though some spoke an additional language at home. Students said that from visiting each other's houses they learned that they all shared a common life style regardless of race. Almost half of the students described Rivercresters as being all 'the same' except for color. On the basis of this knowledge they rejected racial stereotypes they were exposed to that contradicted their experience.

> *R:* Do you feel you learn anything about different racial groups from hanging around with kids who are different?
> *Maria (Puerto Rican):* You get to know them and not what you hear.
> *Kristen (white):* You hear that black people are wild and crazy and they aren't.

> Carmen *(Puerto Rican):* Like Kristen, she slept over at Maria's house before and she was eating dinner and stuff, and she had rice and beans and chicken and all that.
>
> *Kristen:* . . . my mom thinks that Mexican people have you for a friend and then they just do tricks on you and they don't want you for a friend.
>
> *Maria:* You hear they walk around in sombreros —
>
> *Carmen:* And all they eat is tacos and stuff and enchiladas and all that.
>
> *Maria:* They don't. They are the same as us.

As described earlier, the students were not very knowledgeable about race relations outside of Rivercrest. Rivercrest was bounded on three sides by a river which discouraged people from venturing out. Most students said they spent little time outside of Rivercrest. They learned about race relations through their experience in their own community. When they did encounter racial prejudice, for example when they had gymnastic meets with all-white schools, many interpreted this as the attitudes of a few individuals rather than as a characteristic of society at large. One Mexican student said she had gone to an all-white school with some white friends and students had commented that they were having an 'invasion' of Mexicans. This annoyed her but did not cause her to wonder if it was typical of the world in general.

One would expect parents to be a significant determinant of the students' cultural knowledge about race, especially since several studies have found beliefs of the young to be closely aligned to those of their parents (for example, Elkin and Westley, 1955; Hollingshead, 1949; Kandel and Lesser, 1972). Students reported that their parents' views ran the gamut from full acceptance of racial mixing to refusal to allow a member of another racial group into the house. According to students, parents accepted racial integration up to a point: usually interracial dating or mixing with members of a particular group. For example:

> Carmen *(Puerto Rican):* My mom, she's kind of weird. She says she don't want me to marry no Mexicans or stuff. 'I want you to marry a nice Puerto Rican like your dad'.

> Lupe *(Mexican):* I want to learn about [prejudice]. My dad is prejudiced. My brother is very prejudiced. He started to get me thinking like that. He doesn't like white people.

Gayle (white): My dad doesn't like us dating Mexicans, neither does my mom.... My dad don't like it because he thinks that just because some Mexicans get into trouble they all do....

Almost without exception, the students rejected their parents' racial prejudice. They made comments like the following about their responses to their parents' beliefs:

Carmen: I said, 'well, you never know. I could fall in love with somebody that is not even Puerto Rican'. I mean, I really don't care about color, it's just if I like them.

R: How did you learn to view people differently from the way your mom does?
Jo Ella (white): Well, because I've seen the way my parents felt towards people, and I felt that you judge people by what they are and not their color.

R: How come your views are different from you dad's?
Hal (white): I have no reason to be prejudiced against [blacks and Mexicans]. They don't bother me. Either I'm friends with them or they don't bother me and I don't bother them.

Many parents did attempt to transmit their own cultural knowledge about race relations to the young, telling them negative things about other racial groups and encouraging them to limit the extent of their racial mixing. The young rejected messages that conflicted with their experience, and interpreted their parents' beliefs as products of a by-gone era.

In the school, several structures facilitated interrracial contact, allowing students to develop the positive perceptions about race that they brought from their neighborhood experiences. The desegregation plan was one structure. Before desegregation students from the upper and lower bluffs did not mix as well. They attended separate schools until high school and tended to draw friends from their own immediate neighborhoods. After desegregation, neighborhood and therefore race played a less important part in friendship selection. Students said that racially mixed friendships among students from different areas of Rivercrest did not always develop immediately, but evolved over a period of time as students attended school together year after year. For example, Greg entered Five Bridges as a seventh grader with strong reservations against racial mixing. By ninth grade, he said that being in a desegregated school had changed his attitude:

> *Greg:* Right now I play football, hockey and baseball and I hang around with a lot of the kids here and I've really changed a lot.
> *R:* What do you think caused your change?
> *Greg:* Probably a little bit of everything.... Probably sports or just being around.

Housing students under one roof was not the only thing the school did to mix the students by race. Students were assigned to core classes by a computer which was programmed to randomize students by race and sex. In algebra (the most academically advanced class), electives, remedial classes and special education classes, students were not randomly assigned but racial composition still usually approximated that of the student body. Thus, students could interact with members of other racial groups in almost all of their classes. Within classes, as noted earlier, seating was always racially mixed, whether seats were selected by students or assigned by the teacher.

Extracurricular activities were all racially mixed, roughly in proportion to the racial distribution of the school. This interracial mixing was accomplished by the students themselves, however; by offering the activities the school merely provided a common ground in which the students could mix. In general, students said they joined activities because they were interested in the activity itself, although some said they joined to be with friends. In any case, the activity often promoted interracial friendships. For example, Yvonne (black), who joined a racially mixed badminton team along with three friends (two Asian and one white), commented:

> I don't feel bad that I'm the only black girl on our team. I like that. Well, I don't *like* it, but I don't mind it at all. I like to meet Mexicans, whites, and Japanese.

Thus, the school brought all Rivercrest junior high students together under one roof, mixed them by race in assigning them to classrooms and provided an opportunity to mix interracially within classrooms and in extracurricular activities. This allowed the students to get to know peers from different racial backgrounds — to form friendships and to base their cultural knowledge about racial diversity on these friendships.

The curriculum, however, acted as a determinant by segregating knowledge by and about non-whites from other school knowledge, and by treating it as relatively unimportant. Knowledge contributed by or about non-whites was divided from other school knowledge into separate classes — multicultural education, cultural foods, Spanish and bilingual education — suggesting that there is a difference between 'ethnic' and 'regular' knowledge. One could take for example either social studies or multicultural education. In social studies, one would not learn very much about the experiences of non-whites, women or lower class groups, but one would in multicultural education. As another example, in regular cooking one would learn mainly middle-class Anglo recipes; in cultural foods, one would learn to cook 'ethnic' recipes. Cultural studies classes were few and were elective, suggesting that 'ethnic' knowledge has less status than 'regular' knowledge. This pattern in the course schedule did not affect how the students saw racial diversity. But we wonder whether, as they grow older and have more contact with the outside world, this pattern will support their accepting white middle class culture as having greater status and legitimacy than that of other groups.

The attention teachers gave to racial diversity in the regular curriculum was sparse and sporadic. Although the hall displays were usually multiracial, room displays were not. The content and materials in most classrooms tended to omit people of color. When they were included, it was usually in the form of separate lessons about specific ethnic or racial groups. The most enthusiastic attention the school gave to teaching about a racial group was its yearly celebration of Mexican-American week, which focused on Mexican culture, but also included displays and performances representing a plurality of cultures. By not including people of color in the curriculum with much regularity, the school was limiting students' opportunity for learning about other cultural groups and about race relations in society.

Many students were fluent in both Spanish and English, some were much more proficient in Spanish than English, and some were bilingual in other languages such as Arabic or Japanese. But outside the foreign language classes and the bilingual program, these languages were not used much in the school. Periodically, however, there were attempts to increase the school's use of Spanish, such as when announcements were read over the loudspeaker in both Spanish and English for a few months. What were the students' beliefs about languages other than English? Aside from commenting favorably on the bilingual announcements, most students did not offer evaluative comments about language. However, two Puerto Rican students said they felt the Spanish classes favored Mexican over non-Mexican

Spanish usage, and a Filipino student complained about not under-standing class discussions because they were all in English, and being teased by peers when she did not speak English.

It is little wonder, then, that most students were not very knowledgeable about different cultural traditions. In their classrooms, they were exposed to relatively little that was rooted outside the white middle-class experience, unless it was on an elective basis. If they believed that cultural diversity is valuable on the basis of their experience at home, in school they were being taught that it is not as valuable as the culture of the white middle class.

But the school conscientiously taught the students that individuals were equal regardless of race, through the staff's success in treating students as equals. This equal treatment probably reinforced the students' belief that the races should be equal in status, as well as their belief that racism is not a major problem. It may also have sown seeds for action in the future against a steady diet of white interpretations of the world. If the students were to grow up believing that different racial groups are or should be equal in status, quite possibly they would begin to challenge institutional dominance of white culture. (Conversely, of course, they could resolve this contradiction in messages by rejecting the notion of racial equality and believing in white supremacy, although we sensed it was unlikely that many of them would take that position.)

Handicap

None of the physically impaired students lived in Rivercrest. There was a residential home for handicapped people in the community but none of the sample students mentioned having had any contact with people there. A few students had handicapped relatives; for example, Hugh's uncle was an amputee. But aside from them, most students reported having had no contact with handicapped people before main-streaming.

The presence of physically impaired students in the school in-fluenced most students' perceptions of the handicapped and led to many becoming more accepting of, or at least 'used to', having handicapped people around. For example:

> *Anna:* Handicapped kids are just like other kids. I'm used to them. They've been here for a couple of years.

> *Phil (physically impaired):* Being handicapped doesn't matter so much here because able-bodied kids are used to the presence of a handicapped kid.

However, there was an important difference between desegregation at Five Bridges and mainstreaming. Five Bridges, as a desegregated school, drew students from adjoining neighborhoods in the same community. This meant students could see friends very easily after school. Physically impaired students, on the other hand, were bused to Five Bridges from across town. This made it much more difficult to sustain contact beyond school hours. Only Doug managed to sustain close friendships with non-impaired students because his mother was willing to drive him back and forth. In other cases, students said that the distance posed a problem.

To the extent that special education students could benefit academically from regular classes, they were mainstreamed into them, and the only students who spent their entire day in special education classes were the multiply handicapped. Physically impaired students could be assigned to any class, and were sometimes enrolled in algebra, the most advanced course in the school. LD, ED and EMR students could also be mainstreamed into any regular course, but tended to be assigned to teachers who were less demanding than others. Thus, most special education students shared classrooms with regular peers most of the day. But, as noted in Chapter 6, within classrooms students in wheel-chairs often sat at the periphery, and often interacted less than other students with their peers. Thus, the school facilitated students' acceptance of handicapped people by putting regular and handicapped students under the same roof and in the same classrooms, but allowed some segregation to remain through the seating and interaction patterns in classrooms.

Physically impaired students rarely participated in extracurricular activities because they had to catch a bus home. Floor hockey during one period was open to both physically impaired and non-impaired students; this provided a good opportunity for some mixing. But after-school activities, which were sports in which many non-impaired students participated, did not include the physically impaired, with the exception of a physically unpaired floor hockey team that competed with similar teams from other schools. This helped to reaffirm a social division between the two groups.

A number of courses were available specifically for special education students. These included math and language separately for LD,

ED, EMR and multiply handicapped students, reading, language skills and life skills for the physically impaired, adaptive physical education, tutoring, work experience and Bliss language. Being in these courses separated special education students from regular peers, but these courses contributed to their status by legitimating their special needs. As Phil pointed out about adaptive physical education: 'It's not so much a fact that I have a gym at all but it seems like when you're willing to give a group a gym it helps them to feel like equals'. By providing courses such as these, the school was helping to equalize the special education students' status within the school.

But many non-impaired students did not see the physically impaired as equal in status, partly because of their inability to participate in after-school activities, and partly because of the deferential treatment teachers gave to physically impaired students. When the physically impaired program was initiated at Five Bridges, teachers and administrators were unsure what to expect from physically impaired students and sometimes made unnecessary allowances for them. Jerry Springs believed that this occured in part because physically impaired students were used to getting extra privileges and manipulated the teachers. Early in this study, many regular students were complaining that physically impaired students got away with too much: they did not have to do some classwork, they got to leave class early, and they did not get in trouble for offenses other students would have been disciplined for. But toward the end of this study, there were far fewer complaints because the staff had learned to make only necessary allowances and non-impaired students understood better why some allowances, such as slightly longer pass times between classes, were necessary. In fact, some staff members were treating all students exactly alike which sometimes put physically impaired students at a disadvantage. For example, a teacher of physically impaired students recalled this incident:

> Two [physically impaired] girls were having a lot of trouble in math because of the way that math was presented, but I think every student in the class was having trouble. They weren't using a book, they were having to copy off the board and here these two girls didn't have writer, they were expected to take these notes and by the time they had the notes done he was on to something else.

The curriculum also helped preserve their secondary status as well as the regular students' misconceptions about handicapped students.

Special education teachers included the handicapped in classroom displays, curriculum and materials, but regular education teachers did not. In this way, the school allowed students to develop their cultural knowledge about handicap without the benefit of much additional information and open discussion.

Actually, the school took a more active role toward promoting equality for handicapped people than it did toward promoting racial equality. The community provided the school with a racially mixed student population, but not with a mix of handicapped students. They had been in a separate institution elsewhere. To include handicapped students in the school, the building was made accessible to wheelchairs and a cadre of special education teachers was brought in to teach special education classes. These teachers did more than that: they also attempted to educate students about handicapping conditions (most of this education was received by handicapped students), and help regular teachers treat the handicapped more fairly. In addition, the counselors made sure that handicapped students were mainstreamed as much as possible. The physically impaired students were still not an accepted group among their peers in school, but their presence, along with the advocacy of the special education staff, was gradually eroding non-impaired students' ignorance about them.

Gender

Students' cultural knowledge about gender was influenced by the local economy, the community lifestyle, community values defining family responsibilities, the media and school-related factors. All of the girls aspired to have jobs probably because many women in the community had jobs. At least three factors supported this: there were enough jobs within the local economy for most adults, families desired the material possessions and activities two incomes could provide, and it had been the practice within the community that many women held jobs. But few women in the community had attended college and over half of the girls in our sample said they planned to attend college. It appears that women working in the community supported girls' aspirations to work but did not define the kind of work to which girls aspired.

How things were done at home was a major determinant of the students' beliefs about domestic work roles. Three-quarters of the sample students' families had children of both sexes living at home. In only a few of these families were chores divided without regard to gender; students from such families reported believing that was a fair system. Students from the great majority of the remaining families, in which chores were divided by gender, accepted that division. An adult who had grown up in the community explained that family sex roles were usually accepted because of community members' belief in the importance of the family and in accepting family responsibility. Young people were taught from childhood their contributions to the care of the family. Traditionally, family responsibilities were divided such that the father provided the major portion of the family income while the mother took care of the children and the house. With women working to supplement the family income, this division was altered somewhat by shifting the mother's chores to other female members of the family. Most students probably accepted the way things were done at home because they had little, if any, exposure to different patterns or definitions of family roles and responsibilities. However, as you recall from Chapter 3, a few girls did consider their share of work unfair. In these families traditional sex roles were placing a burden on older daughters who were picking up after brothers responsible for few domestic chores. Perhaps their anger and questioning of sex roles at home was a result of the girls' quest for the same kind of equal treatment they received at school.

Many students accepted sex roles for boy-girl relationships because they were part of the tradition taught at home and students saw no reason to believe otherwise. For example, Juan said he believed in traditional sex roles on dates because 'that is the way I was brought up'.

Few students mentioned the impact of magazines, television and movies on their cultural knowledge about gender. However, many girls read fashion magazines and boys read sports and motor magazines, and doubtless these media reinforced their beliefs about gender.

Overall, then, dominant patterns in the community portrayed gender as a meaningful human difference defining domestic responsibilities, male-female relationships, and interests, but not necessarily work opportunities. Variations in this pattern from one household to another bred variations among the students in their beliefs about gender.

The school served as a determinant of students' cultural knowledge about gender in several ways. It accorded the sexes equal status in most situations: both sexes attended most classes, both sexes did the same work in classes, and both sexes were provided after-school sports. But the school allowed students to remain segregated socially and to continue to hold sex stereotypes learned outside school. Students chose electives and few elected courses traditionally the domain of the opposite sex, with the exception of cooking. No boys were observed in Self Improvement (a course that dealt with topics such as facial makeup and hair care) or Sewing, and few in child development. Cooking classes were more popular with the boys, but were still dominated by girls. Few girls enrolled in shop classes. After sitting with the only two girls in Marquetry for a period, we asked why more students did not sign up for traditionally cross-sex electives.

> *Kristen:* Like when you're at home and you're growing up you never do anything really until you get into junior high and then the boys think it's sissy to sew and the girls think it's funny to be in woodshop.

In other words, the students came to school with ideas about which sex should do what. When presented with a slate of electives, most chose the classes that related to what they previously had learned girls and boys should know how to do. Thus, perceptions brought from home about the kind of work girls and boys should do were being reaffirmed at school.

Staffing patterns further supported a sex-based division of labor. Although equal numbers of men and women were teachers, the Principal and Assistant Principal were both men. Although part of the math and science teaching was done by women, men taught industrial arts courses and women taught home-economics courses. These staffing patterns reflected patterns most students saw at home, reinforcing their cultural knowledge about both sexes working, but following a division of labor based on gender.

As we pointed out earlier, when students chose seats within classrooms they usually segregated themselves by sex. Also, most interaction in classrooms was sex segregated. Therefore, although there were equal numbers of boys and girls in most classes (aside from electives) the school acted as a determinant by allowing students to maintain sex segregated social systems to the extent that teachers did not actively encourage seating and interaction mixed by sex. Extracurricular activities were mostly sex segregated, which further reinforced sex segregation among the students.

As described in Chapter 4, most hall displays included both sexes, and teachers tried to avoid depicting males and females in stereotypic roles. However, curriculum and materials tended to overlook women and sexism, and rarely showed men in nurturing roles. A few teachers mentioned the issues of unequal pay and voting rights, but these discussions were sporadic and usually brief. In these ways, the school fostered student lack of knowledge about sexism and their beliefs about stereotypes.

Taken together, the school and the community often presented the students with contradictory experiences. Equality was reinforced at school in that the sexes received equal treatment most of the time and had equal access to most courses. It was also reinforced in the community in that both sexes could hold jobs. But sex segregation was reinforced in school, as were sex roles that students brought from home and that are part of a sexist social structure. Furthermore, a sexist social structure was tacitly accepted at school. The school curriculum inculcated the notion of male dominance by its attention to male accomplishments and by its omissions of male-female relationships and challenges to male dominance. The students seemed not to notice this. Those for whom sexism was a problem saw it as an individual rather than as a collective problem, and as a personal rather than an institutional matter.

Social Class

Students' cultural knowledge about social class was influenced by parents' work roles, family income levels and school factors. Most of the parents, as described earlier, held working class jobs. Since these were the work roles students were exposed to, these were the kinds of roles they were most knowledgeable about. Some students reported having an interest in work roles they saw people, especially family members, filling. For example, the following comments were made:

Larry: Two of my brothers went into the marines, one went into the army, and now I have one brother in the navy and I don't know where my next brother is going to go.

R: Where are you going to go?

Larry: Probably the navy.

Delia: I want to be a nurse like my mom.... My sister is a midwife, she's a nurse like my mom.

R: Do you ever go with your mom when she is working?

Delia: Sometimes.

R: Who do you admire the most?

Yvonne: One of my aunts. She has a nice job. She's a supervisor in the Chicago mail service.

However, a few students overtly rejected work roles of family members in favor of higher aspirations. For example:

R: Do you have anybody that you admire that you model yourself after as you're growing up?

Anna: In school my brother but when I get older nobody.

R: Why is that?

Anna: All the kids in our family who have graduated went on to vocational schools and I want to go on to college.

R: What do you want to be?

Anna: A lawyer.

What might have encouraged students to aspire to careers of higher social class position? Parents constituted one factor. We asked a sample of seventeen students how their parents viewed the importance of the school: fifteen replied that their parents wanted them to do well in school, with some parents specifying that children need to do well in order to go to college. Only two students said that their parents did not talk about the importance of doing well in school. But most of the parents had not been to college so quite likely they could have difficulty 'coaching' their children on the specifics of preparing for it. Furthermore, lacking the money for college probably meant that college, while desirable, was not a foregone conclusion in most families.

The media probably influenced some of the boys, by exposing them to sports heroes and to knowledge of the money and status major sports heroes are awarded. While boys aspiring to college football did not directly cite the media as a determinant, they did tell us on numerous occasions that sports magazines were among their favorite reading material.

Students were not very aware of or concerned about social class differences among people. This is probably due to few class differences within the community. For example, in some communities clothes identify differences in social class (for example, designer jeans versus K-Mart jeans). Although a few young people periodically dressed up in Rivercrest, most paid little attention to costly clothes.

The school served as a determinant of students' cultural knowledge about social class in three important ways. First, Rivercrest was homogeneous in terms of social class and by drawing all of its students (with the exception of the physically impaired) from Rivercrest, so was Five Bridges. There was no program to provide a mix of social classes within the building which, quite likely, limited the students' cultural knowledge about social class differences.

Second, there was virtually no attention to classism, or to people or life-styles from different social class backgrounds in the curriculum. Most of the teachers said they did not really know much about classism. so they did not try to make their curricula less classist. For example, they did not teach about working class experiences much, or about the labor movement or historic figures who championed the working class interests. They did not teach the students where their community is in the social class structure and how institutions are biased against people from such communities. They continued to teach the middle class experience. Few teachers even mentioned the concept of social class in their classrooms. Only one teacher reported having tried to attend to classism regularly in her curriculum, which caused her to begin to learn about it herself.

Third, the school saw the students as future members of the working class, and prepared them accordingly. In so doing, the school limited the students' abilities to control their own destinies, regardless of race and sex. Let us examine this in more detail.

Preparing Students to Direct Their Own Destinies

Most Five Bridges students were members of at least one oppressed group in this country. Few were from middle class families. Almost a third were racial minorities. Half were female; and about one-tenth were classified as handicapped, either physically, academically or both. The school can help prepare students to direct their own destinies and change their oppressed status in at least three ways. First, the form in which knowledge is presented influences whether students learn to see the world as unalterable and given, or as capable of being changed and subject to their own influences (Everhart, 1983). Second, the manner in which social issues and political action are treated in the school influences whether students learn to participate actively in the political process and advocate their own interests, passively accept the leadership of others, or reject the political process altogether (Barbagli and Dei, 1977). Third, explicit discussions about their futures and preparation targeted toward obtaining educational credentials influence whether students are challenged to think about and plan for futures in which they have some power and influence. What was Five Bridges doing in each of these areas?

Everhart (1983) has written that students can encounter knowledge in two forms: reified and generative. Reified knowledge presents the world as fixed and unchanging; one learns right answers, one does not challenge or question what one is taught. Generative knowledge, on the other hand, presents a world that is tentative; what one has learned experientially can be as valid as what someone else has written, and one should interpret and question what one learns on the basis of one's own experience. At Five Bridges, most knowledge was presented to students in reified form. Students were expected to learn it and be able to reproduce it on tests. As reported in Chapter 6, students were often bored with classwork of this sort, and sometimes said they did not feel they were learning much. For example, when asked if she learned much by reading from the book and answering questions, one student indicated that she did not even have to understand what she was reading, once she knew the system for finding answers, when she said:

> *Rakia:*   Not really. There's words in heavy print; if you just look there it will give you the answer.

But most students accepted learning reified knowledge as long as it was explained well enough that they could understand it.

Consistently in Shelby's class and occasionally in a few others, students were asked to learn by generating some of their own knowledge. For example in Shelby's oral history class, students interviewed people and observed events in the community, then wrote, published, and sold newspapers about the community. A few other teachers also incorporated some experiential learning or sharing of opinions into their teaching. For example, in a course called Law and Justice students enacted simulations of trials. Students generally reacted favorably to generative knowledge because it involved them. They said they had some say in what they learned and they could learn with and from each other, which they saw as more 'fun' and 'interesting' than working alone. But these experiences were the exception. Most classroom instruction taught the students that other people's interpretations of the world are more valid than their own. Most placed the student in the position of memorizing information about a fixed world 'out there' rather than learning to make sense of the world they knew 'here'.

The treatment of social issues and political action is a second way schools affect students' preparation to control their own destinies. We examined how these were being presented through power relationships in classrooms, content of government classes and student council proceedings. Teacher-student power relationships in classrooms varied somewhat. In 31 per cent of the classrooms, the teacher structured and dominated the entire period through lecture or very controlled seatwork. In 50 per cent of the classrooms, the teacher gave individual seatwork and helped students with it; students had little or no decision-making power over the work itself, but could in some cases help each other, work at their own rates, and move about the room as needed. In 13 per cent of the classrooms, most of the period was taken up with a large-group discussion led by the teacher but contributed to and to a limited degree structured by students. Finally, in 6 per cent of the classrooms, students worked on individual or group projects that they helped design; much of the content and form of these projects was decided by students under the teacher's guidance. Thus, in most classrooms, the teachers held the power and students followed their lead; in a few, students had some influence over what and how they learned.

Students can learn political activism skills and attitudes in government classes, since here the political process is overtly addressed. At Five Bridges two different teachers taught government, and they taught it very differently. Shelby sought to involve his students actively in the political process so that they could make their voices as citizens heard. His students created a government which then governed the class. He also involved his students in community and school elections, teaching them skills for effective political action within a democratic system. He explained his goal for the class as follows:

> If my class works it so that students believe they can actually do something which affects them, then maybe they'll believe that in some other place which was previously as imposing as their school they can also influence what goes on.

The other teacher — Don — did not involve his students in the political process in the way he taught the class. Instead, he presented information about the three branches of government through lectures and readings, and sometimes led a class discussion about various issues, such as voting rights, immigration procedures and the Iran crisis.

Students can learn political skills through student government. But the Student Council at Five Bridges was not used to teaching students about or prepare them for actively participating in the political process. It typically met once or twice a month, usually to plan social activities such as dances for the school. Involvement of the student body as a whole was usually limited to nominating and voting for officers.

A third way in which schools can help students take charge of their own destinies is by encouraging them to think about and plan for their futures, and by preparing them to seek credentials beyond the high school level. This may be done by providing courses and activities that suggest career goals, teaching students the knowledge and skills required for successfully scaling rungs on the educational ladder and having regular, open discussions with students about their futures.

At Five Bridges, some courses and activities attracted students as possible careers. These included, for example, publications, graphic arts and computers. In addition, several male students talked about becoming professional athletes because they were successful in school sports. But missing in options available to students were courses or activities suggesting college or business. For example, algebra was the only college preparatory class. Spanish and French were the only foreign languages available. The principal after-school activities were sports; activities such as Future Business Leaders of America or German Club were not offered. In short, there were fewer courses or activities to suggest to the students that they aspire to college than there were courses suggesting futures in semi-skilled jobs or in sports.

How well were students being prepared to succeed beyond high school? Within core area classes, what was taught was aimed more toward remediation and practical 'real world' use than it was toward further academic learning. Furthermore, as noted in Chapter 6, homework was rarely given in most classes, so students' academic learning hours were limited to the school day.

We asked students the extent to which staff members talked with them about college or post high school graduation plans. Less than 25 per cent named one or two teachers who did. A few said this was discussed in careers class but nowhere else in school. About 17 per cent of the students said that someone in the counseling office had talked with them about college. For example:

> *Carlos:* Anthony, the counselor, that's who brought it up to me. He gave me all hard classes, he gives them to me you know, picks my schedule so I start getting grades up now. Then when I go into the senior high I have a better chance.

Fifty-eight per cent of those who were asked said that no one in the school had talked with them about college or future plans. For example:

> *Maria:* They're just not into talking about college to us. They let the senior high handle all that.
>
> *R:* Have you ever asked anyone why they don't?

> *Kristen:* No, we don't worry about it now. No one ever talks about it around here.

In sum, there was not enough within the curriculum to challenge the students to think about a variety of future alternatives and to inform them about how to prepare for different goals. Most teachers did not mention college or careers. Coupled with the passive role students occupied in most classes, the lack of attention to critical enquiry and the low level of difficulty of most classwork, there was little at school to encourage students to take charge of their own destinies and to aspire to and prepare for positions that carry power and influence. Since the parents, because they had not attended college, would have difficulty giving students guidance in this area, and also since most members of the community worked in semi-skilled jobs, it would be of uppermost importance that the school start very early in the student's education, explaining to them about college and other career opportunities.

Contradictions in the Reproduction of Unequal Social Relationships

The most powerful determinants of students' beliefs about inequality, according to a number of theorists, are unequal social relationships in society as they are presented in specific, local situations in the school and the community. Theorists have discussed unequal relationships based on social class (for example, Willis, 1977; Brake, 1980; Everhart, 1983), gender (for example, Gaskell 1984; Fuller, 1980; Valli, 1983) and race (for example, Ogbu, 1978; Weis, 1985) as determinants. These inequalities perpetuate themselves in two ways: by limiting the access of the young to certain resources, lifestyles and kinds of people, and by defining the cultural beliefs that are transmitted to the young. To what extent do racism, sexism and classism perpetuate themselves in communities such as Rivercrest and do they ever actually contradict themselves in the way they are manifested in local situations?

In Rivercrest, both racism and sexism produced their own contradictions. Racial prejudice in the city's history influenced where immigrants settled. Because they were not welcome in many parts of the city, people of color tended to settle where there were already other people of color (as well as whites), forming racially integrated neighborhoods. Children born in such a neighborhood did not experience the racial prejudice and segregation their parents and grandparents had experienced elsewhere. To the children, it made the most sense to view race as interesting but not very important in forming social relationships. It also made sense to them not to view race relations as a serious problem.

But if the students might have thought to learn more about racial diversity, the teachers did little to help them with it. The students' ability to get along interracially was viewed not as a basis on which to build knowledge and skills for challenging racism, but rather as a nice accomplishment that facilitated harmony in school and needed little further development. The community and the teachers' treatment of the students as equals among themselves provided the basis for an assault on racism; but the students were allowed to be lulled into believing that there was no problem they should be concerned with.

Sexism seems to have produced its own contradictions in homes where chores were divided by sex. Daughters such as Grace had to do what seemed to them more than their share of the work when the mother held a job or there were relatively few females old enough to assume female responsibilities. In fact, the girls may have aspired to higher professional careers than the boys because they had had enough of a taste of the female role to have become disenchanted with it and to desire something else. But again, this is not enough to produce a significant challenge to sexism. When schools treat boys and girls as equals without at the same time helping them to understand that women are oppressed in society at large, girls can interpret sexism in their lives outside of school as individual problems rather than social problems requiring collective action.

One can speculate that classism might have bred its own opposition had the income level of the community been lower and had young people of both sexes felt deeply dissatisfied with the prospect of futures like their parents. It might also have bred its own opposition had more teachers from working class backgrounds remembered the circumstances they had come from. Many Five Bridges teachers were from working class backgrounds, as a sizable proportion of teachers are (Lortie, 1975). But they seemed to have acquired amnesia about classism as they grew older — either that or their successful escape to the ranks of the middle class 'proved' to them that classism is not a problem. But for whatever reason, the teachers did not see fit to help the students become aware of their own social class position so they could challenge inequality based on class.

Handicappism has been perpetuated in the past through the segregation of handicapped people from the rest of society. Non-handicapped people have dealt with the handicapped by providing them with separate facilities, thereby allowing the rest of society to function as if they did not exist. The passage of PL 94–142 seems to be effectively challenging handicappism. At Five Bridges this law was responsible for changes in the school that caused the students to become aware of the handicapped and to begin to question oppression based on handicap.

The students' experiences in school were created and offered to them by the teachers. Let us now turn to determinants of the teachers' beliefs and actions.

Chapter 8

Why The School Operated As It Did

In this chapter we continue our search for 'why'. This chapter focuses on the teachers and administrators: why they performed their jobs as they did and why they responded to human diversity as they did. This chapter begins with the teachers' and administrators' reasons for what they did. We then go beyond that, analyzing determinants of their work that they took for granted or unconsciously responded to.

How Teachers Taught

When teachers talked about why taught as they did, they mentioned determinants that were located mainly within Five Bridges school. The school-related determinants they named included resources, kids, guidelines or mandates from above, colleagues, time and a few organizational variables. The two major determinants were resources and kids.

Many teachers named resources as an important determinant. Available resources dictated most of the content some teachers taught. For example:

> I take a look at the texts at the grade level, where they are, especially grammar. I take a look at all three texts and then I take a look at what is available for me at that particular grade level. I know in government I have these two books available plus some material that I've dragged in. English and social studies, I have a whole pack of English stuff that I used over the years and I keep those together, and I take the basic grammar, then I see what might be appropriate from what else I have in order to fit it in with different programs.

Resources were a strong determinant of how some teachers taught. It was mainly the lack of resources they mentioned as a constraint on what they could do. Lacking hands-on equipment, some teachers said they felt tied to books and worksheets. Lack of resources was also cited as a reason why teachers did not give homework.

> I don't have enough books to give every kid a book to take home and have them read. Right now that is a monetary restraint of the school district.

Kids were named as a determinant almost as much as resources. Some teachers planned lessons in direct response to students' skill and knowledge level. For example, Natalie told us about a unit she had planned to teach for English, which she subsequently replanned to remediate writing skills:

> [At the beginning of the year, as part of a unit on values] I had them each write something about 'The Street Where I Live.' I was so distressed at what came out as far as their ability to express themselves on paper that most of the work that we have been doing has been pretty much geared to that. Not only spelling, which is horrendous, but their ability to put together a simple sentence and recognize it as such.

Several teachers said that students' low skill levels limited how they could teach them. For example, Annette was explaining why she taught a remedial math class using worksheets and helping each student individually:

> With these kids if you aren't just super patient with them, if you get angry, their response is to get angrier. You have to really control their emotions for them because they are really undisciplined. You know, that's part of their problem as being remedial, that they've not disciplined themselves to think and I have to almost stand by them and say, look, you have to learn this. I mean, they can't even see that they need to learn multiplication as a practical thing in life.

As another example, one of us was having a conversation with Jo during her planning period. Jo was asking for ideas to enrich her teaching and we were trying to understand why she habitually gave lots of worksheets and short assignments out of the textbook.

> *R:* One kind of interesting way to approach it would be to use

different topics with different themes and then have different groups of kids work on different themes.

Jo: I wish they were intelligent enough to do that.

R: If they haven't done it before, it takes learning how to do it.

Jo: The problem is they can't read ... I'm very specific about what I want and where to find it. And what must be done each day. If you don't give them a time limit, they'll take forever. So everything has to be laid out, and since I'm a little afraid of this grouping because they'll sit around and talk about sports, I have to lay it [assignment] out very specifically.

One teacher, Carlotta, who taught multiply handicapped students, talked about how her students' skill levels influenced her teaching by making her become more sensitive to their individual needs and learning styles.

I've really learned a lot from being with my kids because I think that their differences are so obvious that I've had to accommodate them. I think if I were to teach regular, it would be easier to see those differences and be able to meet the needs better than or easier than it would be for some other teachers.

In a few cases, kids acted as a determinant of how teachers taught by responding to a teaching strategy in such a way that the teacher altered his or her use of that strategy. In the following example, the teacher Tim reluctantly modified the way he taught for a short period based on a student's request.

A student came up to me and said, 'why don't you help us do this experiment?'. And I said, 'What do you mean?'. 'Well, do it with us.' And I said, 'Work right with you and take an answer sheet and fill out the answers?'. And she said, 'Well, not necessarily the answer sheet, but work right with us.' And I said, 'Well, what if somebody else needs help, what am I going to do? Should I just forget about them?'. 'Well, no, you can help them if they come and ask you for help.' So she went on with this a little bit further, and I said, 'O.K., I'll help you, but if somebody comes and asks for help I am going to help them too.' And she said, 'Well, that's O.K. I don't mind, but I want you to help us.' So I went back and started with them — there's three of them in a group — and I just participated in their group.

Another teacher increased her use of a teaching strategy due to student reactions. She had previously tried using small group discussions and projects, but had some difficulty making good use of this strategy due to lack of training, so she had begun to use a textbook from which students read and answered the questions. When we asked her how she felt about teaching this way, she said, 'Very comfortable. Kids accept textbooks. I can't believe it. They bring it every day. I say, 'Turn to Chapter So and So', and they do it. It's not like all my other classes, where the kids say, 'What are we doing today', they don't know what they're doing. It seems like the textbook is part of their school day.' We suspect that the students were complying with this teaching strategy because they were used to it, and since that made the teacher's job easier, she enthusiastically increased her use of it.

A few teachers said they had stopped giving homework because of student response. They reported that most students did not do the homework or bring it back to school, so they gave up assigning it.

Student interest did not seem to be an important determinant of what most teachers taught, but it was for a few. For example, we asked the vocal music teacher how he selected songs to teach. He replied, 'Well, first of all, songs that I think the kids would enjoy singing, because if they don't, they aren't going to sing.'

Student behavior was rarely cited as a determinant of what or how teachers taught. One teacher said she individualized her math program because of truancy, and another commented that misbehavior in the classroom limited what he could do. But aside from these comments, teachers did not mention student behavior as a determinant influencing them.

Administrative policies and procedures (for example, curriculum guidelines, IEPs) were cited by a few teachers as determinants of what they taught, and the Principal was cited by a few as a major determinant. The following statements illustrate how the Principal was discussed as a determinant:

The administration for all its faults really doesn't bug you too much once you start doing something.

I have one day a week that is library day. Two years ago Thomas realized that most of the kids did not know how to use the library. It was obvious, I guess, from SRA testing. He said he wanted us to work with teaching them how to use the library. I started last year.

Two teachers also suggested that previous administrative policies —
lay-offs and transfers — had caused them to feel angry and frustrated
with the school system, thereby influencing how they taught. But by
and large, teachers did not seem to see the school administration as a
strong determinant of their teaching.

Teachers rarely mentioned colleagues as determinants of what or
how they taught. The science teachers planned their curriculum as a
department, but other departments did much less departmental planning of what individual teachers taught. Teachers outside the science
department mentioned colleagues as a determinant mainly in relation to
their expectations of what students at a given grade level should know.

A few teachers specified organizational variables that influenced
how they taught. Class size was cited as a barrier preventing a few from
using a variety of teaching strategies. Two said that interruptions,
especially coming and going early in the semester and at the beginning
of each period, limited what they could do in the classroom. One told
us that scheduling procedures limited time to plan courses, since he
rarely knew exactly what he was teaching from one trimester to the
next. (We checked this with Jerry Springs, who handled the scheduling. According to Jerry, teachers requested courses they wanted to
teach and their requests were rarely turned down.)

Teachers only rarely mentioned time as a determinant of how they
taught. When they mentioned time, they said a lack of it limited the
amount of planning one could do, how much help one could give
students in class, or how many different resources one could find to use
in class.

In short, then, the teachers saw resources and students (mainly
student skill levels) as the main determinants of their teaching. From
this, one might conclude that they were free to do virtually anything
they wanted in the classroom, limited only by their own philosophies
and professional preparation. But philosophy and teacher preparation
were mentioned even less as determinants than the school-related
factors. Teachers rarely mentioned how their educational philosophies
influenced their daily teaching. One social studies teacher made a point
of saying that his Calvinistic upbringing, with its strong work ethic and
strong belief in democracy influenced how and what he taught. Also, a
few teachers said that their personal comfort influenced how they
taught. For example, they used large group instruction to satisfy their
own personal comfort more than anything else. But these were the
closest most teachers came to discussing a personal philosophy as a
determinant of their actions.

Teachers infrequently cited their professional development as a determinant of what or how they taught. Two teachers had recently begun to teach courses for which they had no training or background, and they saw this as a problem. A few teachers saw years of experience as a determinant of their teaching. For example, a veteran teacher who had been teaching for eleven years said his experience allowed him to teach effectively with few lessons that were 'busts'; a new teacher said she was running out of energy designing all her lessons for the first time. A few teachers said that prior experience in other schools had helped them learn to use certain teaching strategies effectively. We were surprised at how rarely professional readings or inservices were cited as determinants of what and how teachers taught. Aside from human relations workshops, it seemed that few teachers had a systematic plan of professional growth which influenced their daily teaching.

One might have expected to find the teachers cataloguing numerous restraints on their work, such as class size, period length, administrative guidelines, parent pressure and so forth. The Five Bridges teachers gave us few such complaints. Then why did they teach as they did? They seemed to base their practice on the world that is, and therefore were unaware of determinants that shaped their thoughts and actions. They took for granted what they should teach, how they should teach, how they should relate with students, and what they could expect from students. They felt constrained only when something differed from what they saw as the norm — when there weren't enough textbooks, when students could not read the textbooks, when assigned to teach something for which they had little background. We will come back to examine the world that is, and see how it was a determinant of their teaching after we examine determinants of the teachers' knowledge and actions related to human diversity.

How the Administrators Led

The administrators and counselors worked compatibly and well together. Given this, and their similar responsibilities and goals, we wondered if a common set of determinants shaped their jobs. We found that each described a different set.

Thomas said that his job was shaped mainly by district policies and by his own ideals and beliefs. District policies dictated what he had to do or was responsible for, gave him deadlines and paperwork, and made it difficult or impossible to do some things he might have liked. Thomas was also the Director of a Teacher Corps project, a job that cut the amount of time he could spend on his job as Principal, as well as placing additional guidelines and expectations on him. However, he said he had learned to 'work the system' — by-passing district level people who made it difficult to obtain his requests and working with people who had power and who he believed would support him. For example, an Assistant Superintendent was interested in seeing him develop a multicultural program at Five Bridges and supported him for this.

Thomas' beliefs and values also determined his actions. One of his strongest beliefs was that people are basically good and will work productively at things they enjoy.

> I'm a firm believer, if people are doing something that they like, they do a better job. Or if they understand why they are doing it, they'll do a better job. If they find success in what they are doing, that breeds success. This applies to both students and staff.

It was Thomas' faith in people to do well at what they enjoyed that caused him to employ the 'go with the goers' strategy with his staff — to look for signs of willingness and success and build on that, and to overlook resistance or apathy.

But his belief in the students competed with his belief in the teachers, because the majority of teachers would not 'go', causing teaching in general and affirmation of human diversity to suffer greatly. Perhaps Thomas wanted to respect the teachers as much as the students, and therefore did not push his ideas upon them. The question he faced was which group — the teachers or students — he should support. Since the teachers were not performing to the level of quality that the job required and the students were suffering for it, how would he be able to 'go with the goers' and still ensure that the students receive the best education available? Thomas did not clearly see the extent to which teachers were not 'going' because he spent little time in classrooms observing teaching.

For Jerry Springs career-related determinants were the main factors shaping his job. Since he wanted to attain a principalship one day, he took care to do his job well and consistent with the Principal's wishes so as not to jeopardize his chances for promotion and because he believed that was how administrators should function. His ideals and values regarding schooling were important to him, but he would not put aside his image of what an Assistant Principal ought to do, to pursue those ideals if they did not fit within the job as defined by administrative guidelines. This came through clearly when he discussed the school objective of education that is multicultural. He believed it was an important objective and was critical of Thomas' strategy for working toward it. But he told us that, 'The Assistant Principal's job is to support the Principal and carry out whatever the Principal directs you to do and to help him'. Thomas had delegated discipline and scheduling as Jerry's main responsibilities, so Jerry worked in those areas to the best of his ability, and supported Thomas as needed in other things that came up. It was primarily through discipline that he got to know the students and scheduling that he got to know the teachers.

Marjorie was influenced by a different set of determinants that revolved around personal concerns. She often talked about her image of responsibilities her job entailed and about educational administration courses she was taking. She said these courses were important to building her self-confidence and that confidence was a major determinant of how she worked. She said that her age and sex, and other people's reactions to them, strongly affected choices she made about courses of action. Communication with other staff members affected her attitude toward her job, which in turn shaped her work. She also said that her personal life was a determinant: 'Sometimes our personal lives are such that we don't care to that extent. It's not that we don't care, but we don't care to the extent that we're willing to put the extra effort in.'

Anthony said that the main determinants of his job performance were Thomas, the staff (interacting with Anthony's values), and the community.

> *Anthony:* I think a lot of it has to do initially with the leeway Thomas has given in working with kids. I would like to think he sees the value that I have here in the building. He has allowed me . . . to break the typical stereotypic role of a counselor. I'm kind of a combination of social worker, counselor, big brother, Assistant Principal kind of thing. . . .
>
> *R:* Are there other things that impact your job within this building, that either give you possibilities or limitations?
>
> *Anthony:* Attitudes of staff. We're doing some right things in the building, but I still think there are a lot of people on the staff that probably shouldn't be here, shouldn't be teaching altogether. My daily contact with them keeps me sharp to the point that I am always aware of what is needed or where I can help students. We have some members of the community, particularly the

upper bluff, who have particular ideas about what priorities the school should have, educationally and socially. Those things I think are good for me because they keep me on my toes and they don't allow me to day dream and become too idealistic.

The teachers' professional view of Anthony caused him to be more active at some times than at others in supporting the students. For example, when many teachers claimed that the school objective of education that is multicultural was 'Anthony's baby', Anthony backed off from promoting it because he did not want the teachers to use his involvement as an excuse for their ignoring it.

Finally, Sarah said that her job was determined mainly by events and problems that arose daily. She spent much of her time available to students in the counseling office so she could respond to their needs and concerns, and assist the administrators when needed.

> *Sarah:* We have kids that come in all the time, or I'll get a call from the office, maybe Thomas wants to talk to us or maybe Marjorie has a student she sends up or we are usually involved with kids.
> *R:* You never know exactly what the day is going to bring —
> *Sarah:* We don't know — and I like it.

We can best summarize by saying that Thomas was the single most important determinant of how the administrators and counselors did their jobs. Beyond that, each was heeding the beat of a somewhat different drummer. Each attended to and responded to things he or she saw as most important; no single set of determinants shaped their jobs.

Beliefs and Actions about Human Diversity

To understand why teachers and administrators viewed and responded to human diversity as they did, we asked them many 'why' questions. They cited determinants related to their backgrounds, their professional development, factors in their daily lives, and the school. We will examine each of these.

When they talked about their backgrounds and family lives, it was largely with respect to their views on race and sex. Most staff members had had little contact with members of other racial groups until adulthood. For example, one teacher told us,

I grew up in an all-white community. The only time I remember hearing anything at all, we had a person from the NAACP talk to us in my senior high. That's the only experience I had with a black.... In my senior year [of college], I had a roommate. She was black, and she and I are still close friends.

Another teacher mentioned that he had probably unconsciously incorporated some of his family's negative attitudes about race. Having had limited exposure to members of other racial groups as a young person he had had no basis to question those attitudes. Two white faculty members mentioned having minority in-laws, who had sensitized them to cultural differences and racism. Four more said that their travels abroad had sensitized them to cultural diversity and provided them with some knowledge of a foreign culture. The Hispanic staff members, on the other hand, saw their family backgrounds as strong determinants of their will to fight against racism, since racism had been a part of their lives.

Several of the faculty talked about their upbringing in relation to sex roles and sexism. While some experienced traditional sex role socialization at home, two who grew up on farms said that their backgrounds taught them that both sexes were in many ways equal.

> *Betty:* When I was 9 years old I couldn't wait to get my own calf. I had to wait until I was a little bigger because my dad said it was going to run me over. I remember just waiting for that because it was a really big thing. My brother was a year older and got his right away because he was much bigger than I was. I had to understand that rationale; I wasn't happy with it, but I got mine. It wasn't something that a girl doesn't get. In fact, I was always proud of the fact that I seemed to have good judgment in picking out calves because I always got the ones who won the awards and my brothers never did....
>
> *R:* So things were pretty equal?
>
> *Betty:* I guess they seemed to be. There wasn't a whole lot of talk about 'girls don't do this' and so forth.

Faculty members also learned about sex roles and sexism in marital relationships. Working out domestic chores with a spouse had helped shaped the thinking of some. For others, the process of divorce had made them see sexism in a particular way. For instance:

> I'm involved in a separation and a divorce right now, and I think sexism had a lot to do with it because I think my wife has more liberal ideas.... She no longer needs a husband, she earns

more money than I do and there's more opportunities for women with sexism coming through strongly, and I think that has a lot to do with divorces of many people. I've heard this said by many divorced men.

Teachers and administrators rarely mentioned their backgrounds as determinants of their knowledge of handicap or social class. The few who had a handicapped family member said their backgrounds were determinants of knowledge in this area. Only Anthony said social class was a barrier he had lived with and struggled against all his life. One teacher talked in some depth about her social class background only after reading a book on social class that helped her understand its impact on people's views of themselves and their opportunities.

The personal and family backgrounds of faculty members were important for the lack of exposure they provided to members of different cultural groups more so than for providing cross cultural contacts. A few teachers said that this limited their knowledge about human diversity and their ability to work toward the school objective of education that is multicultural. Some said they lacked knowledge about handicap because they had not been exposed to handicapped people before Five Bridges was mainstreamed. Others said they lacked exposure to teachers who were teaching from a multicultural perspective, or lacked knowledge about different cultural groups. For example:

> I think something that I would like to do more is to learn more about the history of the different groups so that I can throw things in every once in a while. I don't feel very confident yet of knowing enough, I guess, about Mexican backgrounds, but I think that would be very valuable.

Professional development at the in-service level was described by over half of the teachers and administrators as an important determinant of their interest in and knowledge about education that is multicultural. For example:

> *R:* Has anyone tried to help you learn how to implement education that is multicultural in your classroom?
> *Teacher:* I went to that three-day seminar that's offered at Franklin School. And the first day they just talked about what multicultural meant and where the problems came up in trying to implement it, and so it was like a class back in school — human relations. And so the first day was rather difficult for me because you're constantly bombarded with your own prejudice,

and pretty soon you just want to fight back and say,' All right, I'm not prejudiced, just leave me alone, I'll go back to my school and I'll do it my own way, but I don't want to sit here and listen to you badgering me'. And then the second day they got into a little more analytical vein, talking about analyzing instructional materials. And then the third day we spent talking about how to implement it in our lesson plans.

The workshops teachers described seemed to focus primarily on race. Social class, sexism and handicap were not often mentioned by teachers as receiving much attention in workshops. The administrators, on the other hand, seemed to have attended a wider variety of workshops: they discussed workshops on issues such as mainstreaming, sex bias in schools, and concerns of minority women. Teacher Corps meetings were a form of in-service the administrators found particularly important in broadening their understand of human diversity.

Many faculty members learned about human diversity through readings more than through in-service. The band director commented:

> I try to read newspapers every day, two different newspapers. I read *US News and World Report,* I read *Time* magazine, and several music magazines. . . . What I read I think influences me a lot, and of course in this day and age there's a lot of information on racism, sexism, pluralism, if you want to call it that, bring all groups together of all ethnic backgrounds.

What is typical about this comment is the nature of what teachers read — newspapers, popular literature and some professional literature. What is also typical is that they usually did not systematically pursue knowledge related to human diversity, but rather encountered bits and pieces of it accidentally.

Many teachers said that television was an important determinant of their knowledge about human diversity. For some, this was more important than what they read. Teachers said that they learned about different groups by watching TV shows, and became aware of stereotypes by reflecting on biases in what they were watching. For example, two teachers described to us TV shows:

> *Sam:* I watch a lot of TV, probably too much, and I've recommended a new series that's on now to the kids — the 'America' series by Alastair Cooke. The show brings up a lot of very good points that deal with multicultural education. The

first one was on Monday night and dealt pretty much with immigration to this country. It started, actually, with the Asians or the Indians crossing the Alaskan Peninsula.

Kay: *Saturday Night Live*, just sickening. Did you see that?
R: I see it sometimes.
Kay: Two weeks ago they had a panel called women's problems.
R: I didn't see that.
Kay: Oh, you're lucky you didn't, you would have been really mad. It was really sickening. And it wasn't even well done either. And they had men's problems which was just as insulting for women. They had a panel of men, this is called women's problems, a panel of men, and they were really sickening, all different types, like a cowboy and a truck driver and kind of macho types, and they were talking about women, how they see women's problems, and they were really superficial and disgusting, you know how crude they get, and then the next week they had men's problems, and they had these ladies who were, one was some kind of a phys. ed. type, you know really strong and masculine, and the rest were real demure and real meek and the things they said were real superficial too, so they knocked it all.
R: Did you see that as putting down women more than men?
Kay: No, I thought the first one kind of put down men, because the men were so bad, but I also thought, what they said put down women. They put down both. Now the other one wasn't so much a put down on men as it was on women, the one that was called men's problems with the women on the panel. Yeah, I think that maybe it was.

Thomas, Jerry, Sarah and Marjorie, plus a few teachers cited previous teaching experiences as determinants of their interest and knowledge about human diversity. For example, a teacher, Susan, who was Jewish told us about a previous teaching job in which she had been harassed for both her ethnicity and what she taught.

I taught in a German Catholic little town, and they had community vigilante groups of which the school board is made up. I taught Ethnic Studies in an eighth grade up there. I had some problems with community reactions on their kids. I resigned from there before school started this fall.

She pointed out that this experience had contributed to her interest in education that is multicultural, as well as having helped her develop knowledge about different ethnic groups. All the administrators except Anthony had previously worked in schools with a large minority population. They cited their experiences as very important in developing the awareness of racism and appreciation of cultural diversity that they brought with them to Five Bridges.

The community was mentioned as a determinant only by teachers who lived or had grown up in the community, and by Anthony. These teachers said that it was a determinant of their interest in the school objective of education that is multicultural. One who had not grown up there but had moved there recently also said that meetings with parents were a determinant of her knowledge about race and handicap.

We found, then, that faculty members mentioned factors outside Five Bridges as the main determinants of their interest in and knowledge about human diversity. The family was cited most often as influencing their knowledge of sexism and sex roles; professional development broadened their knowledge about race. Most teachers learned from experiences they encountered accidentally but rarely sought experiences that would broaden their understanding of human diversity. Even workshops were attended more because they were expected than because staff members had a thirst for understanding discrimination or inequality.

The main determinants of how teachers responded to diversity in their classrooms were school-related: resources, kids, colleagues, the administration and time. Many teachers named resources, but talked about them in different ways. Most of these teachers said that the lack of multicultural resources prevented them from doing anything multicultural in their classrooms.

> *Nell:* My biggest bogdown is finding the material. Or having it available. Material in science and math — even the library is very low. I don't think anything has been written from what I can see. And even at the workshop over at Franklin, we really had to dig to find anything.

A few teachers said that the availability of material and human resources in the school helped them bring attention to human diversity into their teaching. They also cited presence of Teacher Corps money for buying multicultural resources as enabling them to deal with diversity in their teaching. Two teachers who had tried to locate resources commented that the available material resources were a help, but that it was difficult to find as much as they would like, and saw this as limiting what they could do.

Most teachers did not directly say that the students at Five Bridges were a determinant of their interest, knowledge or actions related to human diversity. A few said that the racial mixture of the students interested them in the school objective of education that is multicultural; some of the administrators also indicated that this was the case. However, the students did not present the teachers with racial fights or tensions, so the teachers saw little pressing need to deal with race in their teaching. The librarian said that students were a determinant of her library book orders. Since the students were racially mixed she ordered some books that were about minority cultural groups. Students were reading these books, so she continued to keep their racial diversity in mind when ordering books.

A few teachers said that the presence of handicapped students in their classrooms caused them to be interested in and gain some knowledge about the handicapped. These teachers said they had not been around handicapped people before, and commented that one could not ignore the concept of handicap when one deals with one or two handicapped students every day. Jerry made the same observation with relation to his job as disciplinarian.

Teachers mentioned several ways in which colleagues influenced their actions related to human diversity. Two pairs of teachers shared a classroom and materials: a remedial reading teacher and her aide, and two EMR teachers. They all pointed out that teaching with a colleague who shared their interest in human diversity caused them to try to integrate it into their teaching. The colleague served as a source of ideas and materials as well as a source of moral support.

A few teachers said that Hispanic staff members provided them with knowledge and insights for working with Hispanic students or attending to racial diversity. For example, one teacher who had constructed several multicultural bulletin boards received an unsolicited critique from Anthony which she said caused her to rethink some unexamined stereotypes. A few other teachers asked Manuela and Claudio about classroom materials and teaching techniques for Mexican students; without these human resources in the building these teachers probably would not have learned things they did.

The reluctance and negative attitudes of colleagues was cited by several teachers as a major reason why the school did not make more progress with education that is multicultural. For example, when asked what they saw as the biggest barrier to progress with this school objective, two teachers replied:

> I think a lot of teachers' attitudes. Maybe they say they do stuff, but I don't think they do as much as they say.

> I think some of the teachers don't understand it, the program or the process, and I don't know what the reason for that is, because Thomas has done a lot to make it clear. I think some people, and you'll find this in business or wherever, are not willing to change, teachers are noted for that. I mean, everybody teaches in their own way, and has their own classroom, and I think sometimes it's difficult to change.

While teachers said that their colleagues' reluctance to change prevented progress, it is interesting that no one directly stated that his or her own attitudes or reluctance prevented him or her from acting.

Several teachers said that the school administration — especially Thomas — was a determinant of their interest in and actions toward implementing education that is multicultural. They commented that he openly supported it and conveyed enthusiasm for it, often brought it up at faculty meetings, sent people to workshops relating to it, and tried to encourage teachers while respecting their individual teaching styles. The following comment was typical:

> I wouldn't be doing it if I hadn't come to this school, and I think Thomas' role was encouraging me to do some of these things in multicultural, like the workshop and the January seminar. We talk about it in staff meetings and he constantly brings it up.

Thomas was probably the strongest determinant of what teachers did in the classroom related to human diversity; colleagues and available resources were also positive determinants for some. But the main determinant teachers said prevented from doing more than they did was time. When asked what hindered their efforts with education that is multicultural, they quickly and without hesitation or elaboration, said 'time'.

> *Betty:* I think just basically time, to be able to implement, and to find resources.

> *Meg:* I don't feel I have the time on a day-to-day basis to do all the researching. It's one of those things that's going to take time to get a wealth of information.

Bernice: Getting ideas and having the time to do it without feeling that you're being overworked and under-paid.

We found it interesting that teachers did not say time hindered their interest in or knowledge about human diversity. It mainly hindered them from acting on it in the classroom.

The Teachers: Representatives of the Status Quo

The teachers told us about factors they saw as determinants of their teaching and their responses to human diversity. We believe that, while these were influencing factors, they were not all strong determinants. The strongest determinants for the teachers were not mentioned much.

The teachers did not include personal backgrounds as determinants of their actions in classrooms. Several talked about incidents with people and social experiences that shaped their attitudes about race and sex, but otherwise spoke little of their backgrounds. Yet we know several things about the teachers' backgrounds that we believe are very important. Most were white and had been raised in totally or predominantly white communities. A little over half were from middle class backgrounds; few were from economically poor family backgrounds. Most those from blue collar homes did not talk about inequality based on class, or personal experiences with class. Most of the teachers were raised in homes in which the father worked and the mother stayed home. Most were married; several of the men had wives who stayed home, and some of the married women commented on their performance of traditional domestic chores in the evenings and on weekends. Few teachers had been around handicapped people very much before coming to Five Bridges. All had been educated in a school system that teaches knowledge mostly by and about white middle class males, and in which teaching strategies such as lecturing and assigning questions to answer from the textbook are more common than strategies involving students such as having students create and produce a dramatic enactment of an historic event. We are persuaded of the strong impact of teachers' backgrounds partly because the students' community life was such a strong determinant of their cultural knowledge. The students talked about it because it was part of their lives 'now'. The teachers' community and family experiences as young people were a part of their personal histories that seemed to have receded from their consciousness.

One teacher did begin analyzing the impact of her background on her outlooks, values, and goals during the course of this study. Marilyn read Sennett and Cobb's (1973) *Hidden Injuries of Class*. This helped her recognize and examine the impact of social class on her life, and helped her understand how she had learned to function in a classist society. At the same time, she began to be aware of sex bias in her background and daily life, and its influence in shaping feelings and ideas. She exemplified a teacher who can become conscious of the powerful effect of unequal social relationships based on race, sex, social class and handicap, as acted out daily through the years of one's personal background, on how one believes and acts as a teacher. We believe other teachers did not discuss their backgrounds because they no longer thought much about many past experiences, they did not wish to face their own acceptance of inequality, or because they took their backgrounds for granted and simply did not see them as determinants of what they were doing now.

The backgrounds of secondary level teachers are important for another reason. People who teach at the secondary level often enter teaching because they are interested in a subject area and teaching is an occupation they can pursue in that area. For example, science teachers in secondary schools often become science teachers because they love science, and choose teaching as a science-related career that fits with other life commitments and priorities. When they are in the classroom, they want primarily to help students become interested in and competent with the subject matter so dear to them. If students show little interest in it or little competence with it, a teacher may lose interest in teaching, and try simply to 'get through the period'. The issue is not necessarily whether the students have ability or interest in *some* area, or whether the students have personal goals. For the teacher whose primary teaching interest is subject matter, the students who are most rewarding to teach are those who share interest and ability *in that subject matter* the teacher finds interesting. Several of the Five Bridges teachers — especially those in the core areas — did express a love for their subjects; we suspect that a love for the subject more than a dedication to kids was the main motive for their entering teaching, and a major determinant of how and what they taught daily.

Let us now examine the determinants that the teachers did name. They talked somewhat about professional development, citing it mostly as a determinant of their interest in education that is multicultural. They did not cite it as a major determinant of how and what they taught on a daily basis. It could be that their pre-service and in-service education had not strongly influenced their teaching, and that they had developed their understanding of teaching 'on the job', by experience. It is more likely that teachers' beliefs about what and how to teach were based on their own experience as students in schools, as Lortie (1975) suggests, augmented by their professional training, and modified to suit what they saw as imperatives and problems specific to jobs they held as teachers.

For example, most of the core area teachers used lectures and textbook reading as principal teaching strategies. It is likely that these strategies were used by their own teachers and college professors, and thus were accepted as standard teaching procedures. In their pre-service training they probably had some practice using these and other strategies. On the job they reverted to using those strategies most familiar to them. Students were used to them (as Kay pointed out earlier in this chapter), and these were workable strategies for managing the flow of knowledge in classrooms containing about thirty students. The teachers' own experiences as students were probably as unexamined and taken for granted as most of their personal background experiences. Their pre-service training had occurred long enough ago that it was probably no longer consciously thought about. One can also wonder to what extent the teachers' pre-service training prepared them for a school like Five Bridges; for example, how well prepared were they to teach reading in the context of their subject matter?

What about in-service workshops as a determinant of how and what teachers taught? Human relations workshops seem to have been the most common form of in-service the teachers had experienced recently, so these were what the teachers talked about. Based on observations, however, we believe workshops had little impact on what teachers actually did in the classroom. When we say this, we are referring not just to human relations workshops. Shortly before we began our study, the staff had a workshop on cooperative learning put on by a nationally known authority on this subject at a neighboring university. In our classroom observations we saw very little use of cooperative learning as it had been presented in the workshop.

We are not even sure to what extent the human relations workshops had an impact on teachers' beliefs about human diversity. Most of the workshops teachers mentioned focused on race, but on the attitude survey we administered, as reported in Chapter 5, the teachers scored lowest on the race sub-scale. Quite likely what the workshops gave teachers was a vocabulary and set of concepts for talking about race and the feeling that they were doing something socially accepted toward dealing with racism by attending workshops — but little beyond that. The workshops may have had a greater impact on what teachers did in the classroom had the teachers been more highly skilled or more committed to combatting inequality, or had the workshops been of higher caliber or more intensive and ongoing.

Teachers mentioned the media — especially TV — as a determinant of their awareness and knowledge about human diversity. We believe that it is more accurate to say that the media helped teachers realize that what they had learned in the workshops was correct. For example, after having become more sensitized to sexism, Kay was angered by sexist skits on *Saturday Night Live.* In this sense, biases in the media can be useful because they enable teachers to practice recognizing stereotypes and biases.

The teachers did not mention the community as a determinant. However, we believe their perceptions of this community strongly influenced their teaching in two ways. First, since many of the parents were minority and most of the parents were working class, teachers were discouraged from wanting to live in the community or at least actively make contact with parents. Keeping themselves distant from the community had the unplanned effect, then, of reducing the probability that parents would exert pressure on the teachers. Second, the social class of the parents was probably what the teachers based their expectations of the students on. Teachers pointed to students' reading scores as indicators that they would not go to college, but it is likely that they expected the students to follow in their parents' footsteps, and thus were not surprised or alarmed by their low reading scores.

We found students to be a major determinant of how teachers taught, which agrees with what others have found (Jackson, 1968; Metz, 1978). The Five Bridges teachers said student skill and knowledge levels limited what and how they could teach. This to some extent was true. However, it should have raised important questions in the minds of the teachers before they planned the curriculum any further. Why were the students achieving poorly? Were they failing to learn because they didn't have the ability? What could be done to help the students achieve success? If the teachers concluded that the students did have ability and several of them believed this — we wonder why they did not try various teaching approaches until they figured out what approach would be best. Instead, they continued to teach the students as they had always taught them — boringly, and achieved the same degree of success — minimum.

The teachers seemed to have an image of what junior high students should know, and believed that one could assign students to levels of competence based on how much of this knowledge they had. This image probably developed from their own experiences as students in white middle-class schools, their experiences with other white middle-class students, and the content in texts written for the 'typical' white middle-class student. If students did not possess much of this expected knowledge, they were seen as low in academic ability, or at least deficient in knowledge and skills. Most teachers did not seem to consider the possibility that the students might have a complex fund of knowledge and skills that could be developed in school despite their low reading scores, and thus did not take student interests or 'non-academic' knowledge into account when planning lessons. Furthermore, the students were compliant with teacher requests. Like their parents, most did not rebel against or question what the teachers were doing.

Teachers said that resources were a major determinant of what they taught and why they did not attend more to human diversity in their teaching. That teachers see what to teach as given, and allow textbook publishers and other curriculum writers to determine what they will teach has been documented in other studies (Dreeben, 1970; Jackson, 1968; Tabachnick, *et. al.*, 1979). But even if we were to see teachers as disseminators of prepackaged content rather than as developers of content, we would have to acknowledge that there is more than one book or package for any given course. The question then becomes how teachers decide which text to use. At Five Bridges it appears that most teachers were deciding which resources to use based on what was immediately accessible and what they were already familiar with. How resources dealt with human diversity was a criterion some used for selecting resources, but many did not.

In fact, many said that a lack of resources prevented them from dealing with human diversity, which we believe was an excuse as much as it was an actual limitation, for several reasons. First, Thomas had secured extra money through several federal programs and was interested in seeing funds spent on multicultural resources. A few teachers ordered resources through Teacher Corps; most did not. Second, the librarian ordered multicultural resources of various sorts for the library. Some teachers used what she had ordered, but there was nowhere near a 'mad rush' on this material. She had also assembled a professional library for the teachers containing books about teaching and pluralism; few were checked out during the whole time we were there. Third, the teachers themselves developed a set of multicultural lesson plans which they assembled into a notebook and distributed to all staff members. However, when we asked teachers if they were using material in this notebook (we asked them repeatedly for about six months), the question became a joke because at most only two or three teachers had. The next year the notebooks were stacked on a shelf in the supply room where they collected dust during the remainder of the study. A few teachers did a commendable job of scrounging around for resources, and a few made many of their own materials when ready-made materials were inadequate or difficult to find. For example, Marilyn rewrote stories to make them non-sexist; Don videotaped movies from TV to use in class; Shelby and his students created newspapers and bulletins. But most teachers did not do this — they tended to stick with resources that were readily available and familiar.

The school administration can be constraint on what teachers do (Dreeben, 1970; McLaughlin and Marsh, 1975) but at Five Bridges it was not. The administration made suggestions and recommendations to teachers, but did not force or coerce them. Neither did district or Teacher Corps policies affect what teachers did; while guidelines, rules and regulations were suggested, no one checked to see what or how teachers were actually teaching in their classrooms. Perhaps PL 94–142 was the one 'down from above' factor that affected teachers the most, since it resulted in the placement of handicapped students in their classrooms.

Their colleagues were not determinants. Teachers said that they rarely saw each other teach, and believed each should be able to teach as he or she saw fit. Few seemed to have a philosophy of education that helped determine their work. Finally, teachers did not name organizational variables as important determinants of their work. While other researchers (for example, Lortie, 1975; Jackson, 1968; Metz, 1978) have written about the importance of organizational variables, and we believe that variables such as class size and length of periods do influence teachers, the Five Bridges teachers did not see these as major constraints.

In fact, the teachers seemed to have a great deal of autonomy in their classrooms. Neither parents, nor students, nor colleagues, nor administrators were pressuring them to teach in any certain way. What about time? Was it a determinant? The teachers said that it was when it came to doing something about human diversity, although they did not mention time when they talked about teaching generally.

We investigated the time they spent on school work. Most teachers arrived at school fifteen or twenty minutes early; some arrived as the bell was ringing; others arrived an hour early. By a half-hour after school was dismissed, teachers were hard to find.

It appeared to us that teachers were accustomed to allocating a certain percentage of their time to teaching. They structured their lives such that they were busy with other things, and when asked to increase their time on school work to change the way they were teaching or develop new curriculum, did not wish school time to encroach on their other pursuits. Paid time allocated by the school district for them to do this was very insufficient, putting the burden for finding time almost completely on their shoulders. Perhaps if responding affirmatively to human diversity had been more a priority with them, as well as improving their teaching skills in general, they would have dedicated more of their personal time to doing so. Which brings us back to the impact of the teachers' background on their teaching.

The teachers were probably quite comfortable functioning in the world as it is, with a few exceptions. The special education teachers, for example, appear to have been committed to bettering the world for 'their' kids, and often spoke of their students as if they were their own children. Shelby seemed genuinely interested in the lives and futures of his students, and often spoke of wanting them to be able to control their own worlds. Annette had a dedication to developing literary skills of the average and better readers, and put in extra time and effort to develop a program that would push them to learn more. But by and large, although the teachers were friendly with the students and liked them, they did not seem dedicated to seeing that the students attain the best in life, to providing students with the knowledge and skills to change society so that it can benefit oppressed people more, or to continually refining their teaching skills. At least, they were not dedicated to these things enough to rearrange their own priorities in order to do something for their students beyond 'business as usual'. They probably saw little need to do so, and without pressure from anyone — parents, students, colleagues, or administrators — that would at least make 'business as usual' uncomfortable, there was little motivation to change their teaching. For the most part, they taught material they were familiar with or considered standard for the subjects they were assigned to teach. They used teaching strategies that were comfortable and familiar. And they dealt with their students' diversity by becoming familiar with language and ideas related to human diversity, and by giving human diversity some vocal support, but not by changing their behavior in order to actively affirm it.

Institutionalized Dominance in the School Bureaucracy

The administrators provide an illuminating illustration of how dominance based on race, class, and sex is maintained and challenged in the administrative bureaucracy governing public education systems. Most administrative jobs in school systems are held by white men, especially those jobs that are in line for promotion (Adkinson, 1981). Thomas and Jerry are illustrative of two white males who were recruited into administration by their former principals, took the 'right' courses to qualify for administrative positions, and knew how to move up through the system. Both probably took for granted that if they worked hard enough they could 'make it' in school administration, since they had plenty of role models as well as access to the informal 'boys' club' (Adkinson, 1981; Stockard, *et. al.,* 1980).

However, Thomas did not think about people in the same way that most white males do. He was genuinely interested in promoting the interests of minorities and lower class people, and could have posed a threat to the values undergirding the system that had accepted and promoted him had his administrative style been more forceful. (Although we wonder whether he would have achieved the position he did if he had been an outspoken critic of race and class inequality in the school bureaucracy.) Then why was Thomas not more successful in upsetting traditional patterns of dominance even in his school?

Part of the problem rested with Thomas himself. He believed in the goodness of human nature — in adults as well as children — and in its eventual triumph. He was also reluctant to promote open interpersonal conflict, which may be why he was not perceived as a threat to the school's bureaucracy. Thomas was basically a caring person who believed in the empirical-rationale approach to change (Chin and Benne, 1976), which holds that since teachers are rational human beings, once they gain information about problems, concerns and needs of students, they will adapt their teaching accordingly. Thomas believed it was important to change teachers' attitudes first, and give them information about a problem, before dealing with their behavior. Therefore, he made a great effort to provide workshops and resources that would facilitate attitude change. But, since such change was slow in coming, according to situational leadership theory (for example,

Hersey and Blanchard, 1977) Thomas should have used a more hard-line approach with his staff. Although Thomas understood situational leadership theory, he did not commit himself to employing it. He commented to us that on the Hersey and Blanchard leadership scale, he was in the high-relationship low-task quadrant, and questioned whether that leadership style was actually appropriate for working with his staff, yet he continued to employ it. Also, he was knowledgeable of supervision procedures and processes (Goldhammer, 1969; Glickman, 1981; Cogan, 1973); nevertheless, he did not use these in working with his teachers. Thomas probably made minimal use of situational leadership and supervision to avoid open conflict with teachers.

Also important to Thomas' belief system was the idea that resources — human and material — should be available to help teachers become 'goers'. Thomas' ability to cut through bureaucratic red tape to get services for the school and his ability to secure government funding of programs readily attest to his administrative skills in procuring resources. (It is ironic that lack of resources was one of the main barriers teachers named to implementing the multicultural school objective.)

Jerry had views about human diversity similar to Thomas', but these were overshadowed by his desire and quite reasonable expectation that he could successfully attain an administrative position of power. Jerry could explain in clear terms how to get the teachers to teach basic skills and affirm human diversity more effectively, but he did not see his role as planning the administration's strategy for doing this. What he desired more than reforming the teaching at Five Bridges was the acquisition of a principalship. Jerry came along during a time of financial retrenchment, when administrative jobs were not as plentiful as they had been once. This probably made it seem even more imperative to him that he conform to the expectations of the system, to enhance his chances for success in it (which were already better than average, given his race and sex).

Anthony also eventually wanted to become a school principal. He recognized that his race could work against him, although if he appeared acceptable to those hiring, his race could help them fill affirmative action requirements. He wanted this position so that he could shape a school and its teachers for the benefit of students like those in Rivercrest. Without sacrificing his mission, he continually struggled to walk successfully the thin line between being acceptable enough to get hired without being coopted or silenced. In this way, he recognized that the administrative system operated to maintain its race and class bias, but also recognized the possibility of achieving some power within it.

Marjorie aspired to a career in administration — not because she had a cause to fight, like Anthony and Thomas, but because she was attracted by the work and the status and power that accompanied it. But she approached her quest with much less confidence than Thomas or Jerry, in part because she saw very few young women in school administration. Lacking role models and personal self confidence, she was not sure how to behave on the job — she was not even sure what shoes to wear, and opted for shoes that were stylish but uncomfortable. She (probably very accurately) believed that her competence would be questioned because of her sex and her age. Thomas had extended her a hand of sponsorship into the system, but it was not for a permanent job, so her future in administration was still uncertain. Therefore, to ensure her best chance at success, Marjorie did what she believed was expected of her with care and thoroughness. In no way did she attempt to rock the boat; rather, her main concern was to figure out which way the boat was rocking so she could adapt to it. She was aware of sexist biases in the system, but these biases multiplied her insecurity, so that she did not entertain the idea of seriously fighting sex bias, as that could be like slitting her own throat.

Chapter 9

A Critical Appraisal of What Happens After the School Bell Rings

In this book we have presented our observations about what happens at Five Bridges after the school bell rings from a number of vantage points. Here we synthesize and appraise what we've learned. And we return to a question raised at the beginning of this book: to what extent do schools maintain inequality, and to what extent do they promote equality? Finally, we discuss teaching — what differentiates excellence from mediocrity.

We hope to leave you with a clear understanding of what was happening at Five Bridges — and of what is often happening in many schools nationwide. We hope to appeal to your sense of social justice and shake your faith in schools to the extent that that faith is naive. We also hope to appeal to your belief in human goodness and potential for excellence, because we believe these were also present at Five Bridges. We do not wish to leave you in despair — this critical appraisal of schooling at Five Bridges will be followed by a chapter of recommendations that we believe can be implemented by those who truly wish to do so.

Students, Teachers and Administrators

We will begin this synthesis and appraisal by summarizing what we know about the students, the teachers and the administrators at Five Bridges. We will go beyond summarizing, however, offering a portrait that captures the essence of each of these role groups.

Like many junior high school students, the Five Bridges students were more interested in their social lives than schoolwork. In their social lives they were quite comfortable with and enjoyed the presence of peers who differed from one another visibly. Most visible differences among peers — with the exception of gender — did not form a basis for the structure of their social system. The attributes students used to structure their social system included gender, social behavior and common interests.

Students liked teachers who were pleasant to them personally, and disliked those who were not. They liked schoolwork that actively involved them, was immediately practical, or that they found inherently interesting. Most schoolwork did not fall into one of these categories and students classified it as boring. However, the students accepted the idea of school, believing they needed to pass their classes to succeed in later life, and they complied with and did both what they saw as boring and what they liked (although they complied in a mechanical, disengaged fashion).

The students did think about their futures. Most had an idea of what they wanted to do in the future and these ideas were in some cases not limited to the sorts of jobs they saw being filled around them. But few had worked out a plan for achieving their goals; they seemed to have faith that the future would take care of itself, and spent most of their time concerning themselves with day-to-day social and family activities.

The administrative team was comprised of five very decent, caring people who were concerned about the students and who put in a great deal of time at their jobs. They also worked well together, each pulling his or her own weight, and each being careful not to usurp another's responsibility or authority. They were an effective team for administering the school's daily operations.

They were much less effective as leaders of major school change. While all were 'for' maximizing student achievement and implementing education that is multicultural, only Thomas and Anthony were guided by a philosophy that had these as high priorities. Marjorie's and Sarah's actions were guided by daily happenings that required a response and Jerry's were guided by his adherence to responsibilities delegated by the Principal. Furthermore, none of the five had much previous experience actually raising depressed student achievement (especially reading), or implementing education that is multicultural in the classroom, much less leading a staff toward these goals. In addition, although Marjorie had taught English and Jerry had taught chemistry, the rest had little experience of any sort in core curricular areas — Anthony had not taught in the classroom, Sarah had taught physical education, and Thomas had taught industrial arts. Only Anthony had grown up in a pluralistic school setting; the others were still learning to deal with human diversity themselves. So, while they were good people who worked hard at their jobs and had excellent intentions, they collectively lacked the background and in some cases the intense commitment required for effectively doing what they set out to do with the school objectives.

The teachers were well-meaning people, but at best the great majority were average teachers who were not used to thinking in terms of pluralism and had little, if any, preparation for doing so. They came to Five Bridges with taken-for-granted ideas about who is where in the social structure and about people from backgrounds that differed from their own. Although they 'knew' that one was not supposed to be racist, classist, sexist or handicappist, this awareness did not penetrate the assumptions and actions they made on a daily basis outside the realm of face-to-face interactions. Thus, although the teachers were nice to the students and tried to treat them all equally, they seemed to assume, for example, that working class students could not be expected to achieve well in school, that racism and sexism were unrelated to what they taught. Even though they were explicitly and continuously asked to reexamine these assumptions by the administration, few teachers did — they did not seem to see a need to do so.

Furthermore, they did not seem to see a need to upgrade their teaching skills or re-examine their assumptions about education. The teachers had learned (more or less) to perform smoothly the actions average teachers traditionally perform, such as deliver lectures, assign reading and 'plug students into' worksheets. But most were not masters of teaching. They lacked a broad repertoire of teaching strategies from which to draw or a well-defined method of selecting and carrying out the best teaching strategy for any given situation. They did have reasons for why they taught what and as they did — but these reasons, such as 'this content is practical', 'the students cannot read', or 'we don't have enough materials', had not been questioned and examined. It was as though the teachers did not really believe that developing their teaching skills would pay off in increased student learning. And it was as though they did not recognize the mediocrity in most of their teaching. When the students did not learn much or did not seem interested in classwork, the teachers laid the blame on the students and their skill levels, rather than looking to their own teaching for part of the explanation.

Schooling and Inequality

We have described schooling at Five Bridges as it relates to inequality while sharing our findings in each of the previous chapters. But we have only suggested the extent to which the school was reproducing and/or challenging inequality based on race, sex, social class and handicap. We would like to do that now. We analyzed each 'ism' by examining who within each role group in the school was acting on behalf of the dominant group and who was acting on behalf of subordinate groups. We then examined what consequences the actions of each were having on relationships among groups in the school and in society as a whole.

Inequality Based on Race

The process by which inequality based on race was being reproduced and challenged at Five Bridges was complex and cannot adequately be presented in a word or two. The administrators acted on behalf of non-whites in challenging racial inequality by adopting the school goal of education that is multicultural. Beyond that, they did little as a group to challenge it, by not ensuring that this goal was actually implemented. Anthony continuously acted as a spokesperson for racial equality and for the interests of non-whites, but had too little power in the school to do much more than that. The commitment levels of the rest of the administrative team toward fighting racism varied, but their actions tended to maintain the status quo more than challenge it.

The teachers acted on behalf of non-whites by giving them equal access with whites to all courses and activities in the school — no one was being denied an education on the basis of race. The teachers also treated all students equally without regard to race. But the education they were offering the students was a mediocre one, not one that would enable students — white or non-white — to compete successfully for money, power, or status in society. Furthermore, the teachers were doing very little to broaden the students' understanding of racism or cultural pluralism — in fact, they were teaching the students to accept white culture and believe white interpretation of reality through their curricula. Even the few minority teachers were tacitly accepting this racist teaching by doing little to question or change it.

The students — both white and non-white — had constructed their own non-racist society, supported by non-racist beliefs about people. The students challenged their parents when their parents advocated racist beliefs. But they did not challenge racism in the school and were not well prepared to challenge racism in society, probably because they were unaware of the extent of its existence. Quite likely, the positive race relations they experienced among each other sheltered them from recognizing racism elsewhere.

Among each of the three role groups, then, there was some action on behalf of racial equality, but much on behalf of maintenance of the status quo. While the students were living a social system that challenges the status quo, they were not being given the knowledge or the skills in school to make a dent in race relations outside of their own neighborhood. In fact, there was probably enough that was occurring in Five Bridges on behalf of racial equality to give one the illusion that racism was succesfully being eliminated there, when actually the students were being taught to occupy a passive social role, to believe white interpretations, and to accept working class lives.

What response were non-whites at Five Bridges making to their own subordination? Of the four responses suggested by Deutsch (1973) and described in Chapter 1 — accepting subordination, escaping membership in the subordinate group, mobilizing to challenge sub-ordination and insulating themselves from the dominant group — it seems they were making a weak attempt to mobilize and challenge it. The students challenged racism at home, but were not prepared to challenge it elsewhere. In fact, they insulated themselves from racism in the school by dismissing it as boring and irrelevant and becoming much more engaged in their social lives outside of school. Anthony, working principally with Thomas, was attempting to mobilize a staff effort to challenge racism. But we wonder if Anthony's efforts were weakened because Thomas — a member of the dominant group who sympathized with non-whites, but had not experienced racial subordination — delegated himself as 'leader of the charge'. Perhaps efforts to mobilize a challenge to racism in the school would have been more effective had non-whites had more prominent leadership roles in this challenge.

There was racial conflict at Five Bridges, then, but it was not overt. The students were probably only dimly aware that a conflict of interests was being battled out there. The teachers were aware of the importance of showing respect for the racial diversity in the school, and did some things that gave the illusion of that respect without seriously challenging white dominance. The administrators were also aware of the importance of respecting the interests of minority people, but only Anthony, and to a lesser extent Thomas, were poignantly aware of how unsuccessful their challenge to racial inequality was. Probably the fact that conflict was not overt and hostile but was rather a conflict of interest kept the teachers from attending to race more. Since the great majority of the staff was white, they probably did not see the importance of restructuring race relations.

Inequality Based on Sex

The reproduction of inequality based on sex at Five Bridges was less complex than race because less was being done to challenge sexism. Challenging sexism was a component of the administrators' goal of education that is multicultural, but it was not a component they talked about very much. Marjorie and Anthony were dealing with sexism in their personal lives, but did not often openly challenge it. Sarah was interested in challenging sexism, but admitted she did not do much about it that was organized and on-going. Thomas and Jerry were not in favour of sexism if asked, but neither discussed nor actively challenged it on a day-to-day basis.

Neither was there an active champion of equality based on sex among the teachers. Several teachers were dealing with sexism in their personal lives, but they did not integrate attention to sexism into their teaching. A few teachers included some attention to sexism in their curricula, but none tried to do such things as organize a staff effort to combat sexism. While the staff as a whole attempted to treat boys and girls equally and offer them equal access to most courses, they saw sex segregation in classroom seating, sports, student social life and traditionally sex-specific electives as natural. They also did not question using curricula that included a preponderance of male interpretations, perspectives and concerns. It seems as though the women on the staff accepted inequality based on sex, or at least did not see it as a problem that had anything to do with schooling.

The students were confused about sexism. Most of the boys and some of the girls saw traditional sex roles (with women allowed to work in any job but still responsible for the home) as natural. Some of the boys and many of the girls challenged specific sexist practices, such as work roles at home or dating practices, and a few were aware that these conflicts were sexist in nature (as opposed to being individual conflicts without a basis in group membership). But among these students there was no organized challenge to sexism. In fact, it seemed as though some students who challenged one aspect of sexism, such as work roles at home, accepted other aspects of sexism, such as dating practices or the 'beauty' image associated with females.

Thus, dominance based on sex was being reproduced in the school to about the same extent as it is being reproduced in society at large. In fact, the school lacked the outspoken and organized resistance to sexism that is currently a force in society in the feminist movement. We could speculate that a few of the girls who were battling sexism in their own personal lives could eventually become active feminists, but there was little happening in the school that would propel them in that direction.

We believe the challenge to racism had a better chance at Five Bridges than the challenge to sexism. The challenge to racism had outspoken advocacy in the administration, and it had a non-racist student body supporting it. There was no active advocate for a challenge to sexism in the staff, little in teaching practices that challenged sexism (outside the treating of boys and girls equally), and the students were acting out sexism within their own social system more than they were challenging it.

Inequality Based on Social Class

To what extent was inequality based on social class being reproduced or challenged at Five Bridges? The strongest challenge to it came from Anthony and Thomas in the administrative team. Both advocated challenging the students to achieve in school and prepare for college, both advocated encouraging the students to consider a wide range of career goals, and both maintained that one's potential and ability level does not depend on one's social class. In addition, both saw strengths in the home backgrounds of the students and, although they recognized economic problems in the community, did not blame community members for their economic situation.

The other three members of the administrative team and the great majority of the teachers can be considered together. We believe they were very actively, but for the most part unconsciously, perpetuating inequality based on social class. When asked what classism was, they could not define it or describe it in much detail. In discussions of the students' home backgrounds and on the attitude assessment scale, they expressed many negative stereotypes related to social class, and were more open in voicing class stereotypes than race stereotypes. It seems as though their acceptance of an unequal social class structure was so entrenched that they did not regard it as inappropriate to hold and voice these beliefs. Furthermore, they did not check the truth or falsehood of stereotypes of the students' social class (as Annette did with her expectations for reading achievement).

The students were not very aware of social class or of the struggle poor people have waged to better their lives. They knew that family incomes varied, but did not seem aware of the extent of the gap in income and privileges received between rich, middle-income, and poor people and were not too aware of where they would fall on a national family income continuum. The students also seemed quite unaware of the social status and power that accompanies middle-to-upper income standing. The main exception to this was some of the boys who had some recognition of the wealth, prestige and 'coolness' that sports heroes have. We cannot say what response the students were making to their own economic oppression because their awareness of that oppression was so undeveloped.

The challenge Anthony and Thomas were making to classism seemed to be falling on deaf ears at Five Bridges. The teachers who came from family backgrounds similar in class to the students' had achieved some social mobility and tended to look down on people who did not appear to be striving for the same mobility. These teachers had dealt with their own economic oppression by escaping membership in the lower or working class. They, along with their colleagues from white collar backgrounds, defined themselves as middle-class and seemed to see themselves as better than or at least different from lower income people.

Also, few of the teachers were 'goers' or 'strivers' in academic or cultural pursuits in their own personal lives. In general, their command of high status knowledge was not above average, and their understanding of the relationship among social, economic and political stratification was rudimentary. Furthermore, most were not active learners and pursuers of on-going interests and explorations, or active participants in cultural and social events in the city. At least, if they were, they rarely brought this into the school. We rarely saw teachers sharing their own lives with the students — their own interests, their own pursuit of knowledge, their love of learning and the excitement of a challenge, their own academic travels, and so forth. Most teachers taught skills in a drill and practice fashion and passed on information for the students to learn. There were exceptions to this, such as Don's class on Future Studies which was based on his own ongoing pursuit of knowledge in this area — but the exceptions were few.

We therefore do not believe the teachers were well equipped to broaden the students' horizons and prepare them to be economically mobile. Even less were the teachers prepared to teach the students about class and to help them question a social and economic structure which is based on inequality. We do not see these as impossible tasks — but we do not believe the teachers at Five Bridges had the backgrounds, attitudes or insights to carry out these tasks in spite of Anthony's and Thomas' concerns. Instead, they dealt with Anthony by calling him 'too academic', and with Thomas by saying they were already doing what he was asking by enrolling the students in courses that drilled them on reading skills.

Inequality Based on Handicap

This form of inequality was probably being challenged by the school more successfully than the other three forms of inequality we have discussed. There were many vocal advocates for eliminating inequality based on handicap (especially physical impairment) among all three role groups in the school, as well as outside advocates who made an impact on the school. Outside of the school PL 94–142 was being responded to seriously at the district level — seriously enough that Five Bridges was renovated to make it accessible to wheelchairs, and staffing and facilities were provided for physically impaired students. Parents of handicapped students also constituted an advocate group who met periodically with teachers and administrators to voice their concern and support the education of their children.

The main advocate on the administrative team was Jerry. Although he had little prior experience with handicapped people, he was enthusiastic about mainstreaming, and enjoyed his administrative role on the IEP Committee. Among the teachers there was a sizeable contingency of special education staff who constituted an organized and vocal advocate group for all handicapped students. The interest of the rest of the teachers ranged from high to low — many were not interested in mainstreaming, but many were interested and tried to work positively with the special education teachers in the interests of special education students.

The regular students, for the most part, were at least receptive to handicapped peers. Most still held some negative stereotypes about them and did not quite see them as equals, but they had made considerable progress since mainstreaming started. The main response the physically impaired students made to their oppression was to challenge it. Doug tried to escape membership in the group by associating with non-impaired students, and a few physically impaired students may have tried to insulate themselves from the regular students, but most openly confronted hostility and stereotypes in their peers and were doing so with some success.

Therefore, we are quite optimistic about the school's challenge to inequality based on handicap. We suspect this form of inequality was being so successfully challenged in part because it is usually non-threatening to people's own social standing and personal relationships. In the US today PL 94–142 is regarded as humane, though costly. People do not seem to fear being 'taken over' by the handicapped, and do not seem to see the handicapped as posing a challenge to their own lifestyles and values. Therefore, in a school such as Five Bridges, there is a willingness to support it where the willingness to confront, in contrast, sexism may be weak or absent. Furthermore, the existence of special education and PL 94–142 brings with it teachers (usually more than one per school) trained to teach students with handicaps, committee structures for involving staff and parents in their education, and financial support for the education of these students. This is in sharp contrast to educational laws and programs that deal with race, sex, or social class which *may* provide a building with a trained teacher or two and some resources, but rarely a cadre of trained staff and a legally based committee structure and set of procedures for involving a whole school.

We wonder how things may have gone for the LD, ED and EMR students at Five Bridges had there been a stronger academic emphasis. As it was, most of the students were below grade level in academic skills and many were in special programs one or two periods per day, so students in these special education classes did not stand out. In a school with a more academic thrust, teachers often group students by what they see as academic ability, so special education students more often end up on the 'bottom of the pile'. Given the lack of flexibility in the Five Bridges teachers' teaching, we suspect they would not have attempted to teach to diverse skill levels and learning styles if they saw the student-body as a whole as more able, but would, rather, have tracked them into different 'ability' levels, at least in the core area classes. This might have stigmatized the LD, ED and EMR students in the eyes of their peers, but it might not. We can only speculate on this.

Dominance at the Institutional and Individual Levels

Five Bridges illustrates to us how dominance is maintained and perpetuated at the institutional and individual levels. The school is situated within an institutional structure that is staffed by people with commitments and perspectives that enable them to serve the institution and that has its own ways of operating.

Let us imagine we were standing in the Principal's office at Five Bridges, surveying the school's institutional context. Looking within the school, we would see some institutionalized features of inequality that could be manipulated by the Principal, although probably not without encountering resistance. In schools, especially at the secondary level, knowledge is divided into packets called courses, each being taught by a teacher who has been trained to view certain kinds of knowledge as legitimate to teach in that course, and who may have a very hard time conceiving of anything else as legitimate. This structure is similar from one school to the next, and from one level of schooling to the next. Furthermore, what should be taught in each course is standardized not just by what teachers know to teach, but also by what is in textbooks printed for standard courses. Within this institutionalized organization and selection of knowledge are many biases which are widely recognized today — textbooks are biased, elective courses structure in sex stereotypic roles, and so forth. As a Principal, one would need to decide what to do about this. What Thomas did was to add on courses about people of colour, add a bilingual program, procure multicultural text materials (which teachers were encouraged but not mandated to use), encourage members of both sexes to enroll in courses that still taught sex stereotypic content. What he did not do was restructure what knowledge was taught within the courses that were there. For example, it was taken for granted that what is usually taught in junior high science courses was worth teaching as science to the Five Bridges students. What was not done enough was to ask how other cultures such as Native Americans have learned about and related to nature, for example, or how the students learn about their world on their own, or what actions women have taken in history that fall within the domain of scientific thinking.

Also institutionalized within the building was the privacy of teaching. Teachers were not observed by their peers or even by an administrator when they taught. They rarely exchanged ideas and never had to justify to another adult why they taught as they did; neither did they have the help of another adult to draw on. This institutional structure was changed by a few teachers (for example, Marilyn and Paula) who chose to team teach, but otherwise was left intact. It probably could have been changed relatively easily for the purpose of adding flexibility and quality to how teachers taught, but this was not done.

Now let us look outward from the school. Within the school district administration and school board we see a preponderance of whites, of males and of middle-class people. They have set down the district's criteria for selecting teachers and procedures for staffing the schools. They have set the criteria for graduation and have suggested courses and texts that would be suitable. They also have the power to build, tear down and renovate buildings as they see fit and their budget permits. It is interesting to compare the district's response to different forms of human diversity, specifically as it related to Five Bridges. The school institution at the district level, with federal support, was interested in reducing inequality based on physical impairment. Therefore, the district chose to renovate the physical plant of Five Bridges, relocate the program for physically impaired students, provide the school with staff trained to teach them, mandate that the students be mainstreamed into regular classes, and mandate that staff be involved in planning educational programs for these students. Although additional steps could have been taken to further reduce handicappism (for example, mandating that extra curricular activities be accessible to the handicapped, mandating that curricular materials include people with handicaps), still the steps that were taken effectively changed many handicappist practices at the school level and made a very noticeable impact on the students' cultural knowledge about handicap.

The district did very little like this with respect to race, sex or social class. It did desegregate its schools racially (but not necessarily by social class) and it did mandate that both sexes be provided with sports and with an opportunity to take the same courses. But it did not, for example, change criteria for hiring teachers to ensure those hired would have a commitment or background for fighting racism, sexism or classism. It did not place pressure on individual schools to provide students with exposure to and preparation for a wide variety of postgraduation future options, as another example. Also, it did not give the Principal enough power to do what was necessary to get the job done, such as firing or relieving teachers of their duties at the school. In these ways, inequality based on race, sex and social class was perpetuated within the institutional structure of the schools — by the people who held power at the school district level and who had both the power to change practices in the district, as well as the choice as to how and whether that power would be exercised.

At the individual level, inequality is perpetuated when individuals do not consider it as a problem worth their attention or when they overtly accept it. The Five Bridges staff encountered human diversity every day in their classrooms, in the form of the student body. But this particular student body did not present diversity to the teachers as a problem. The students by and large got along well, although they maintained sex segregation which the teachers saw as natural rather than socially conditioned. The students also got along with the teachers — they complied with teacher demands and were nice to teachers who were nice to them, even if they saw classwork as boring. From the teachers' perspective, this probably seemed like a successful school in its treatment of human diversity, because diverse people were treating each other humanely on a face-to-face basis. The teachers may have even believed that they were promoting social equality because there was relatively little inequality among the students and in the way the teachers treated the students.

Did this mean that the teachers were unaware of inequality based on race, sex, and social class in society, or that they saw no relationship between inequality and schooling? Probably not, but it does suggest that most were unconcerned with these things and gave them little thought. Quite likely they even avoided thinking about social inequality because this would be personally threatening. Since most of the teachers were white, they did not see racial inequality as their problem. The teachers were middle class, either by birth or by escaping the lower class through their own efforts, so they did not see class as their problem. Half were women, but they were comfortable dealing with sexism on a personal level only — the women for the most part did not seem to see themselves as members of an oppressed group that needs to take collective action to change its oppressed status. Since they did not see social inequality as a personal concern, most of the teachers did not think about it. When asked by the administration to deal with it, they looked to the nature of human relationships in their own classrooms, and maintained that there was no problem worthy of their time and attention.

We are tempted therefore to say that the teachers did not really care about or respect the students. Another response would be to say that they liked the students but did not see them as equal to themselves. They cared in a paternalistic way like the missionary cares for the native inhabitants. In this way the teachers justified their actions, even though they were actively perpetuating inequality in the way they performed their jobs.

In Chapter 1 we raised a question concerning what respect for human diversity means. We believe that respect needs to include a belief that all people should have an equal chance at obtaining the resources in this country. Respect does not tolerate inequality among people based on group membership. Therefore, people who truly respect human diversity are actively seeking ways to change practices and structures that continue to perpetuate inequality. It is not enough to be nice to people in face-to-face interactions, since one can be nice but still see others as inferior, or as unfortunate because 'chance' rather than group dominance has blocked their access to resources.

Quality of Education

We have described earlier how the teachers taught. Most teachers who taught basic skills used ditto sheets, workbooks, reading kits and some easy-reading high-interest materials. These materials were used with the students daily. They made up the major part of the teachers' attack on the students' underachievement in the basic skills. As materials for *helping* to raise achievement, these are good; but when they are used in the same fashion every day without being supplemented with other approaches, such as language experience, they become, as the students appropriately described them, dull and boring. Simply put, we believe that students' basic skills could have been improved, but diverse approaches were needed to rekindle students' desire to learn — a desire that had burned out by the overuse and abuse of prepackaged materials. Teachers were mainly giving out assignments, not teaching, and there is a big difference between the two.

We can compare the way basic skills were taught with the way baseball was played by a major league Midwest team. The management knew the fans would turn out regardless of how well the game was played, in the same way that the administration knew the Five Bridges students would show up for basic skills instruction. But the team's mangement was not oriented toward winning. They may have acquired one or two exceptionally good players on the team, but did not have a strategy for building a winning team. Their main concern was to put on an adequate show for the fans — which consistently resulted in a poor win-loss record. Similarly, at Five Bridges few people had high expectations for students to achieve well in school and go on to professional careers. One or two basic skills teachers performed better than average, but the team as a whole was not striving for the championship. And there was no administrative plan to recruit an excellent team of basic skills teachers who together could have significantly raised students' achievement levels.

The content area teachers also, by and large, had low expectations for the students' learning and did not challenge them or adjust their teaching strategies enough to compensate for the students' low reading levels. Most used the same few teaching strategies — strategies they knew were not those the students preferred. Most relied on reading and writing as vehicles for teaching content even though they knew most students were poor in these skills. An alternative approach would be first, to involve students in learning activities such as simulations, interviewing, and hand-on projects, which do not require much reading; and second, to use reading and writing assignments specifically to support basic skills development as well as teach content. This would require close collaboration between the basic skills teachers and the content area teachers. We did not see much of this being done — it was mainly done by special education teachers regarding mainstreamed students. The content area teachers responded to the students' low skill levels mainly by 'watering down' the content to a level of complexity they thought the students could grasp. In the process, they bored the students with routine teaching processes that put students in a passive role.

It seemed as though most of the teachers developed some technical competence doing a limited range of 'teacherly' things, then learned to justify what they were doing without critically examining why they were doing it. For example, teachers said they dictated notes so that students would have something to study for tests. But they did not say why they believed reproducing information on tests was worthwhile or what purpose (beside passing the test) this information would serve for the students, why that purpose was worth striving for, and why that particular teaching strategy was the best from among a range of alternatives. In short, reasons most teachers gave for why they taught as they did seemed unexamined, not deeply thought about. Few of the teachers gave evidence that they had worked out a set of values and beliefs defining what school is for, what they hoped to accomplish as teachers, why, and what and how one would do that best. Lacking a philosophy to give structure and guidance to what they were doing, most of the teachers were busy 'doing' in a mediocre fashion, and did not have a tool to help them reflect on their actions and develop their professional competence. Rather than being guided by a set of beliefs, they were guided by a limited repertoire of strategies they knew, materials available to them, and problems they encountered in their classrooms that required a response.

An illustrative exception was Shelby. Shelby told us that his teaching was guided by his belief in democracy and in an educated public. Guided by that belief, he thought about what one would teach to students and how one should teach in order to help create an educated, reflective public for a participatory democracy. Shelby then went about developing technical competence as a teacher in doing this. While we would like to see his philosophy specifically address unequal social relationships among groups, even if it did only tangentially, Shelby still taught well and did it with conviction.

Had all the teachers approached teaching by developing, defining, and justifying the basic beliefs grounding their craft, then learned the technical competence required to actualize their philosophies, we believe they would have offered the students a better education. And, had their philosophies included consideration of how their actions related to social inequality, some may have become interested in changing those actions. At least, having a philosophy that guided their thought would have helped the teachers intelligently discuss and think about what they were doing and how that related to the students' present and future place in society.

What would quality education mean in a school like Five Bridges? Can one offer a quality education without actively dealing with cultural diversity? The recent reports on education would have us think so, since these do not address cultural diversity beyond advocating that all students have equal access to the same curriculum. We believe quality education involves much more than this — it has to take account of race, class, gender and handicap.

At Five Bridges, the students brought with them to school identities that were rooted in their membership in social groups. At home and in the community they had learned who they were *as* males and females, Rivercresters, Mexicans, whites, Puerto Ricans, Egyptians and so forth. They had also learned a view of society that took into account these features of their own identity. For example, they had learned that racism was a problem more among older people than their contemporaries — they were prepared for a world in which race relations were like race relations in Rivercrest. They had learned expectations and roles for males and females, and were trying to grow up in such a way that they could successfully handle those roles. In order to control their own destinies in a society that is biased against minorities, women, lower class, and handicapped people, they would have to learn to negotiate the barriers they would face; and they would have to learn to see those barriers not as 'givens', but as social arrangments that are changeable even if they are well entrenched. A school program that ignored these realities in relationship to its students would not be providing them an education of the highest quality — an education that would further their interests.

Quality education recognizes and deals with the complexity of human experience, and excellence as it has been manifest in diverse contexts. For example, a quality history class recognizes that historic events have been shaped by different groups of people interacting with each other, who have different perspectives about a given event. The acquisition of Texas by the US government is usually taught from the perspective of Anglo landholding males. A quality history class does not assume this is the only perspective, but views that event as a struggle among conflicting groups, and examines it as such. Similarly, a quality literature class recognizes that people have historically developed literary traditions within different cultural contexts. People have used somewhat different sets of criteria for defining what their best literature is. Circumstances have in part dictated the form that literary tradition took. If one reads only the literature written by white middle class men, or judged as good by such men, one is missing a large part of the human literary experience. Historically schools in the US have omitted, oversimplified, stereotyped. Text materials today still do this. To discuss educational excellence without addressing this need is tacitly to accept the biased and simplified view of the world that schools have generally taught.

Quality education, finally, is tailored to ensure that all students perform well. At Five Bridges, this means that students are not written off because their basic skills are poor; it means that instruction is designed for those students to help them learn to perform well. Instructional programs cannot be designed in the abstract and then imported into a school and put to work. They must be developed with relationship to the students in a particular school and drawn from a wide repertoire of strategies that have shown success. And they are put into practice by teachers who sincerely believe in the capability of their students.

Chapter 10

A Plan for Action

After spending three years observing and learning in a school, it can probably be assumed that we have some suggestions to make to educators. In fact, some may argue that, given the poor state of education today, we have an obligation to do so. Obligation or not, we wish to use what we have learned as a springboard to discuss a modest but challenging plan to improve the quality of education young people receive.

Before we suggest the plan, however, let us stress that this study be given serious attention. Like several previous studies (for example, Ogbu, 1978; Rist, 1970; Metz, 1978; Everhart, 1983) it documents that schools do help to reproduce structural inequality in some very specific, identifiable ways. But it goes beyond previous studies by examining how a school was addressing several forms of diversity — race, social class, sex and handicap — based on data collected over a period of time. It also goes beyond previous studies in pointing out factors that were actually promoting equality. Thus, it provides an analysis of the school as a very complex institution that has a net effect of reproducing the status quo, but that contains the elements of social change. It also points out how race, sex, social class and handicap are perceived and responded to somewhat differently by the various members of the school.

Equally important, this study documents specific school-related factors that educators need to deal with to raise the chances of success for children who are members of oppressed groups. Within education circles there has been for several years a debate concerning who is to blame for the lack of school success experienced by many minority children and lower class children. The home backgrounds of these children are frequently cited as the primary cause for their failure (for example, Coleman, 1966), rather than the school. Or, some educators look to the job market and the economic structure in pointing the finger of blame (for example, Bowles and Gintis, 1976). What concerns us is not that the home or the job market may not influence children's success in school, but rather that educators often divest themselves of responsibility for oppressed children when they think the die has already been cast. And yet, teachers and administrators daily play a very significant role in determining the success of their students in the school, as our study of Five Bridges has documented. We believe that educators must focus attention on the school and its day to day processes, in addition to looking outside the school, because schools *do* make a difference and it is the school that educators can most directly influence and change.

What do we believe educators should do? We will present a plan for action that has four main parts: self-examination on the part of educators, building a power base for change, up-grading the quality of teachers in schools and making some significant changes in the curriculum and instruction in schools.

Self-examination

If we had directly asked staff members at Five Bridges whether they were actively helping to reproduce inequality, it is safe to assume that few would have responded in the affirmative. Most would have been quick to show us what they were doing in the name of reducing racism, sexism or handicappism — and, in fact, usually reponded that way whenever we asked them how their curriculum and teaching were responding to multiculturalism. Yet, as we watched what they were actually doing, it became apparent that most were helping to perpetuate the status quo rather than change it. Most of the staff members were wearing blinders. They did not see biases in their taken-for-granted assumptions about children, learning, teaching, what is worth knowing and so forth. When we analyzed the determinants of what the staff members did and believed it became apparent that their own backgrounds and positions within the social structure were very important, and to a large extent provided the blinders they wore. What staff members viewed as problems, what they viewed as given, the sorts of actions they viewed as appropriate, the ways of investing their energies they viewed as worthwhile were based to a large extent on how they had experienced the world as members of their own racial groups, social classes, genders, age groups and so forth.

Most Five Bridges teachers wore blinders in another area as well.

Most seemed to consider the teaching methods they used appropriate or comfortable and their skill as teachers good. They were able to justify why they taught as they did and usually appeared satisfied with the justifications they gave. They placed problems with their teaching on other factors such as resources or students' home environment, not on themselves. White middle-class teachers who teach lower-class or minority students are not alone in doing this. We would venture to say that many other teachers who are members of oppressed groups, or who are sensitive to racism, sexism, classism or handicappism have also not examined their own teaching skill and continue to reproduce the status quo as a result. Teachers need to examine their own knowledge about teaching and the reasons why they teach as they do. For example, is the lecture method being used because it is really the best way to actualize one's instructional goals or because it is the method one is most familiar with? Are ditto sheets being used because they are the best material for maximizing student learning or because they are convenient? Are students being asked to read a particular textbook because that is the best way for them to learn a body of concepts, or because textbook teaching is the norm and this particular book is available? Is the school's policy toward homework based on sound instructional procedures or limited expectations of what students will do outside school?

We believe that no educator is exempt from such blinders. The experience of Five Bridges illustrates the way unexamined personal biases and actions greatly overshadow good intentions when educators act.

We therefore recommend that educators — including researchers and administrators as well as teachers — examine their actions and their own backgrounds and interest. We will not detail a plan for how this should be done, since plans have been suggested by others elsewhere (for example, Chin and Benne, 1976; Grant and Melnick, 1977). But we do challenge educators, including the reader, to confront personal biases — to find out from members of oppressed groups how their actions actually appear to those who are struggling daily against oppression. We also challenge educators to examine their teaching skill and the reasons they use to justify how they do their work.

Building a Power Base

Frequently people who are personally committed to promoting a more equitable society and school experience feel overwhelmed by the task and alone in their own institutional settings. At Five Bridges we found this true of individuals such as Anthony and Marilyn. To such people we suggest it is necessary to mobilize a collective power base drawing on others who are potential allies. For example, at Five Bridges there were several individuals who could have formed a power base were they not divided by personality differences and personal commitments to reducing different forms of inequality.

In mobilizing to fight oppression and institute quality education in the school, individuals who are struggling against sexism, classism, handicappism, racism and educational mediocrity need to form coalitions that can work together. This may mean putting aside personality conflicts and compromising somewhat on action priorities, but it also means increasing the number of allies one has, and increasing the number of role groups in a school system to which one has access. At Five Bridges, a coalition of the special education teachers, Thomas, Anthony, Shelby, students and community members could have been a powerful base to institute change. It did not form because individuals were not sufficiently aware of their common concerns, and allowed personal conflicts to get in the way. Educators who want to promote change need to learn from examples such as Five Bridges how to be politically astute, and to recognize that change is a political process which requires a power base that can be built in most institutional settings.

This idea can be applied at the school district, state and national levels as well. For example, many states are currently attempting to revise their standards, requirements and procedures for public instruction. Educators who are concerned about educational mediocrity, and about race, class, gender and handicap need to coalesce and work together to make sure that their concerns and interests are not being left out or undermined. It is particularly crucial in a time of conservatism to pool resources and energies in order to form as strong an interest group as possible.

At the national level there is considerable public debate about the condition of education in this country and how it can be improved. But much of that debate is being shaped by white males (Sleeter, 1982). Educators and citizens who are not white, and who are female, lower-class, handicapped — or who support the interests of oppressed people — need to put aside their differences in order to ensure that their collective voice is strong enough to be heard. This requires actively listening to each other and being willing to support each other's concerns. It also requires being willing to speak out and become involved.

Now we will propose two major changes for schools. The first regards the staff, and the second regards the content and process of the curriculum.

Quality of Staff

We believe that education in America is a vital enterprise that is understaffed with talented, thinking people who are committed to developing their teaching skill. Schools are also too often staffed by teachers who have burned out and teachers who are lazy and just want to get through the day. Teacher salaries are low, teachers are not pushed to excellence, teaching conditions and job security are often far from desirable, and good teachers are not rewarded for their excellence. We believe that these conditions deter America's talent from entering teaching, since good salaries and working conditions, and recognition for work well done are more abundant in other professions. Five Bridges provides an example.

At Five Bridges the administration had set raising reading and math achievement as a major school goal, in addition to providing an education that is multicultural. Raising achievement levels at a school in which achievement historically had been depressed should require, one would think, teachers with excellent teaching skills and a commitment to teaching. Yet Thomas had few such teachers to work with. In addition, he was able to offer little incentive for teachers to put extra effort into upgrading their work. Teachers who simply put in time in the classroom were being paid on the same salary scale and offered the same rewards as those who took the time to develop better curriculum, individualize their instruction, get to know more about their students and so forth. The quality of the staff he had to work with was a major hindrance in Thomas's efforts to improve the quality of education Five Bridges students were receiving.

Hiring and Retaining Quality Teachers

Communities need to demand and be willing to pay for excellent teachers. For example, taxpayers could make a bargain with the school district. Under the terms of this bargain, the taxpayers would support higher salaries for teachers *if* and *only if* the district would: (i) recruit and hire only the best teachers; (ii) establish a procedure for weeding out incompetent teachers (current procedures are so cumbersome they deter any but the most daunted administrator from trying to dismiss any but the most utterly incompetent teacher); and (iii) establish a plan for meaningfully rewarding teacher excellence.

These new teachers and administrators should represent diverse racial groups, both sexes and different handicapping conditions; and all should be genuinely concerned about creating schools that will contribute to a more just society. In addition, they need to have a commitment to kids and a faith in kids, regardless of race, sex, social class or handicap. Communities need to be choosy — to seek demonstration of this understanding and commitment. It is not enough to be satisfied with staff members who use vacuous phrases such as 'needs of the students' and 'bias-free tests' without being able to demonstrate what they mean. There are many people who have learned a few catch phrases without having developed a philosophy of education to guide their practice. Administrators like Thomas and Anthony need more support from teachers and other administrators who care about human diversity and who understand the nature of institutional oppression. They need active support, not lip service.

One of the most interesting aspects of the Five Bridges staff was the special education teachers. They were committed to 'their' kids, educated to teach them, and understood many realities of handicappism in society. Collectively they made an impact on Five Bridges. Teachers need to be trained, hired, and distributed in such a way that schools will have at the least a strong nucleus of minority teachers and other teachers who are committed to combatting racism, sexism and classism, as well as handicappism.

Today there are many people seeking teaching jobs. Some of these people are excellent; many have a record of mediocrity. There are also talented students in the colleges and universities trying to decide what degree or professional training to pursue. In addition, there are teachers who would take time off to pursue advanced degrees but are discouraged from doing so because, when it comes time for them to be rehired, they are aware of a tendency to hire those who come most cheaply — teachers with no experience and bachelors degrees only. These people need to know that intellectual talent is needed and will be paid for, and the citizens need to know that their tax money will not be wasted on more mediocre teachers. We would like to stress that the salaries of all good teachers need to be raised — not just of those in subject areas where there is a teacher shortage, such as math and science. Good teachers in *all* areas are valuable, and their compensation needs to reflect their value.

Schools also need to look critically at their leadership and recruit and prepare strong leaders. There is a difference between administering the daily functions of a school and leading it toward excellence, especially when the school has not demonstrated a history of excellence. Communities should ensure that the Principal and the district administrators have strong, assertive leadership skills in addition to administrative competence. As with teachers, good intentions are not sufficient — good intentions and mediocre leadership skills will not build an excellent school program.

We will leave it to the district to decide how to dismiss incompetent teachers, but we would like to offer a suggestion about recognizing teacher excellence. Proposals for merit pay or other forms of recognition often get bogged down over disagreement on criteria or procedures for teacher evaluation. Yet, if one steps into a university, one sees faculty members evaluating and promoting each other, based on criteria they have established. School districts could establish teacher ranks and appoint teacher committees to decide what criteria earn promotion, how teachers are to be evaluated, and who should do the evaluating. In universities it is common knowledge that faculty members desiring promotion put a full effort into their publications, or teaching record, or whatever is being evaluated in that institution. We might expect teachers to do the same thing — to expend their best effort at teaching, knowing their work will be recognized and rewarded by their peers.

Preparing Quality Teachers

It is in the college or university, we believe, that quality is theoretically and, in part, practically defined. We would be among the first to suggest that teachers' pre-service education needs major improvement.

There needs to be active recruitment of students who demonstrate social sensitivity and academic excellence. The practice of allowing anyone who wants to teach into the program without establishing some means for screening out mediocrity needs to stop. Screening out only the least academically able is not sufficient — standards for recruitment and retention must be based on academic excellence, willingness to work, commitment to all students and willingness to learn about cultural diversity and social inequality in America.

Students often say they want to become teachers because they love kids and want to help kids (Grant, 1981; Lortie, 1975). Pre-service preparation programs need to make certain that these good intentions are translated into a clearly defined teaching philosophy, a strong knowledge base and skill in the use of various teaching methods and procedures of instruction. Let us comment briefly on each of these.

Philosophy requires that one learns to be specific in defining what one means and learns to examine critically the assumptions and facts one uses to justify a belief. It means knowing what one is attempting to do in the classroom and why. It means analyzing and reflecting on teaching practices of all kinds to determine the extent to which these are justifiable. Learning to do philosophy about teaching must begin early in the pre-service program, and must be an integral part of the entire program.

Pre-service students need a strong knowledge base about subject matter, teaching and learning, and students of diverse backgrounds. Those preparing to teach at the elementary level need depth in an academic discipline. They should have at least five or six courses in a discipline (for example, history, biology), some of which are at the junior-senior level. Pre-service students preparing to teach at the secondary level need a major in an academic area. The purpose of this is to give the student a strong grounding in both the basic concepts of a field of knowledge as well as the thinking processes used by scholars in that field. As we will argue later, one goal of schooling should be to develop children's thinking skills. This requires that teachers learn to use the mode of thinking employed in at least one disciplinary area. We will also argue later that teachers play an active role in deciding what knowledge to teach — this cannot be done well unless teachers have studied a field in depth.

Pre-service students need a strong knowledge base about learning, teaching and schooling as a social institution. The education literature contains a wealth of conceptual and research knowledge in these areas. For example, much of value to the teacher has been written about theories of learning and their implications for teaching. Students will assuredly not acquire much of this knowledge through 'on the job' training or experience. They need to learn to use the research literature, as well as learning a solid foundation of knowledge about teaching, schooling and students before they teach. They should be challenged and held accountable for learning — they should not be allowed to teach until they have mastered this knowledge base.

Teachers also need a strong knowledge base about students who differ from them based on home culture, gender and handicap. They need to know what the concept of culture means, and they need some knowledge about and experience with American cultures other than their own. This will require such experiences as reading about other people, interacting with other people and enjoying aspects of other cultures like literature or language. It will also require studying what schools have done historically to reproduce dominance by whites, males and the wealthy. This will entail learning about areas such as cultural bias in school knowledge, materials and testing, or the development of math anxiety in women.

Finally, pre-service students need to develop skill in the classroom. Teacher educators, working in concert with school personnel, must see to it that pre-service students receive field experience with teachers who will encourage them to become analytic and reflective about what and how they teach. We are not necessarily advocating *more* field experience. More field experience in and of itself may only produce new teachers who are just like the ones we have. Field experiences need to be carefully selected with three criteria in mind. They should provide students with experience teaching pupils of diverse race and class backgrounds and pupils who are handicapped. They should provide students with models of excellent teaching, not models of mediocrity. Finally, they should provide students with experience in classrooms where they are supported in their efforts to practice skills learned in the college or university.

We would like to make one additional point about the preparation of teachers. At the college or university level only part of it occurs in the department or school of education. Much of it occurs in the liberal arts courses. In those courses what knowledge are students being taught on which they will based their curricula? Are they being encouraged to think, to reflect, to wonder and question? What image of society are they being encouraged to adopt? Are they acquiring an in-depth understanding of any discipline? This is an area that cannot be overlooked when considering teacher preparation.

Curriculum and Instruction

We believe that some major changes are in order in Five Bridges and probably most other schools, These are changes in both general orientation as well as daily practice. They are not piecemeal changes that can be tacked onto an otherwise intact existing school program, but changes that would transform the program.

Most Americans would say that schools exist primarily for the purpose of developing young people intellectually — helping them learn to think and acquire knowledge and skills. But if we probe into what schools actually do, we will be quite dismayed. At Five Bridges, what intellectual development meant in practice in most classrooms was to pump students with rote knowledge that they would be able to reproduce on tests. Developing thinking skills, curiosity or learning skills either took a distinct backseat or was left behind altogether. We know Five Bridges is not unique in this regard (Goodlad, 1984).

We are also concerned about the tendency on the part of many to assume that schools, although situated within society, are neutral toward it. Educators talk about preparing the young for their adult lives, to take their place in society, to contribute to society — but often fail to help the young to develop an understanding of what that could mean to them personally. At Five Bridges most of the staff simply assumed that the students would occupy jobs like their parents', and did not picture the students as leaders in the world of the future. Furthermore, they did not help the students to develop skills to create a society or a place in society that would be more desirable or rewarding than that the students would inherit from their parents.

These considerations prompt us to suggest four main goals for schools. We will discuss each of these goals in relation to their implications for curriculum and instruction.

Develop Learning and Thinking Skills

All children come to school with some skills for learning and thinking, but all children should continue to develop these skills throughout their schooling. We will explain what we mean by learning and thinking skills, then offer a few thoughts on teaching them. One area includes skills in acquiring, using, and communicating knowledge. We are not simply proposing the three R's, because we see these as too limiting. We would add a grounding in computer literacy, oral literacy and literacy in aesthetic expression. We would also add skills we forget to teach in school, such as code-switching from one dialect or cultural context to another, and reading non-verbal social communication. The aim should be to maximize each child's ability to express himself or herself, and to understand others.

Another area includes skills in higher level thinking. For example, students should practice organizing ideas, interpreting ideas, relating ideas, producing new knowledge, synthesizing knowledge, applying principles and evaluating ideas. Skills in memorizing and recalling information are important, and were emphasized at Five Bridges, as they are in most schools. But practice in these lower level skills should not replace or crowd out practice in more complex thinking skills.

We would like to see students begin to develop the enquiry skills embedded within each academic discipline. The disciplines are distinct primarily because each involves a somewhat different set of processes for stating questions and seeking knowledge. Commonly in the schools and even in college, students are taught only information gained as a result of enquiry within a discipline, rather than the mode of enquiry itself. For example, in history they may be taught about historic events without being taught the process of historical inquiry. Shelby's oral history class was the only example we found at Five Bridges of a teacher structuring that entire course around the enquiry process rather than content derived from that process. We are suggesting that young people should learn to do history, do natural science investigation, do social science investigation, do literature — as well as learning content within these different areas (which we shall address shortly).

Developing learning and thinking skills requires practice and feedback. People do not develop thinking skills very effectively by listening to teachers talk for extended periods of time, copying notes or filling in dittoes. Interestingly, the kinds of teaching strategies the Five Bridges students preferred were those that involved them in mental activity. We suspect most students enjoy activities that develop their skills as long as they are at an appropriate level of difficulty.

Teachers can integrate the development of thinking and learning skills into almost any content area. How the teacher teaches is more important for this goal than what the teacher teaches. The important thing is that the students are genuinely involved. Therefore, teachers need to take care that the content within which they work on thinking skills is motivating to the students. All people want to think and learn about things of concern or interest to them, but may appear lazy or 'slow' when asked to think about things they have no interest in. For this reason it is important that teachers get to know what interests their students and use that interest to motivate learning and enquiry.

Teach Knowledge

A second goal of education is to teach knowledge — ideas, concepts and factual information that has value. We do not believe that a single body of knowledge can be defined to be taught to all students — students and teachers bring with them into the school different interests and backgrounds of experience and live in environments that present different opportunities for learning. These are important and need to be taken into account when deciding what knowledge to teach. But at the same time, children should not shoulder the entire responsibility of deciding for themselves what basic knowledge they will need. Further, our common citizenship in one society demands that we share some common knowledge. Therefore, children should be taught in school knowledge that broadens their horizons and provides them with an information base shared by others. We offer the following recommendations in selecting that knowledge.

The knowledge taught in schools should be grounded in the various disciplines: language arts (English and at least one other language), social science, mathematics, natural science, the expressive arts and physical education. Whether the curriculum is organized into discipline-specific subject areas or into interdisciplinary studies is up to the local school, but it should include knowledge from these disciplines all the way through the grades. Exactly what is taught should be selected on the local level by the teachers and principals. Earlier we recommended that only well qualified, well educated teachers teach. Teachers who have had extensive study within a discipline would be well able to decide what is worth teaching from that discipline. Not all teachers will find the same knowledge worthwhile. We believe that is healthy — children have a right to experience different points of view. Teachers within a building may decide to coordinate their efforts so that the students experience some continuity — we would recommend that they do, in fact. But we believe it is important that teachers who know their area well be given decision-making power over what to teach because this will involve them fully in thinking about their discipline, which is ultimately what they will want their students to do also.

The knowledge taught in schools should build on the students' home language, life experiences and community background. At Five Bridges it was very obvious that students were learning much more from their world outside school than that in the school. The teachers too seemed to have learned about people, about teaching, and about subjects of interest to them based on personal experience more than coursework. This is not meant to imply that knowledge about the world outside one's experience is unimportant. While students need to know much more than they would otherwise learn in their home communities, teaching should start with, and build directly on, their interests and experiences. Knowledge requires a base of sensory experience to be meaningful (Eisner, 1982), and that base needs to rest on students' life experiences.

The knowledge taught in schools must include the perspectives and contributions of a plurality of cultural groups, social classes and both sexes. Historically in schools it has not. Today, although some curricula and texts attempt to be multicultural, what is usually done is to add contributions of minority men and white women to a standard curriculum, still interpreted mainly from a white middle class male perspective. For example, we would argue that all American students should learn knowledge about the Civil War. But they should learn the truth about what happened then from the perspective of black as well as white people, women as well as men, poor people as well as political and military leaders. We would argue that all American students should learn about women's historic struggle for equal rights — a struggle that usually occupies no more than a page at most in history texts. They should also learn why this struggle has been dominated by white middle-class women and how minority and working-class white women have viewed that. These are examples of what gets left out of most curricula and of what is part of the truth American students need to know.

Finally, the knowledge taught in schools needs to be selected in such a way that all students have equal access to high status knowledge. Whether they come from suburbia, the ghetto or the farm, all students have a right to 'get through the system' and go on to college or wherever they want to go. As we explained earlier, in order to do so people need to acquire the kind of knowledge that is on tests and that is expected of an 'educated' person. We would like to see that knowledge be redefined so that it includes America's cultural diversity, but until it is, teachers need to recognize that it exists and that some students have more access to it outside school than others. Furthermore, students have a right to know the value of high status knowledge. For example, students who do not personally enjoy the literature of Hemingway and who see it as alien to the literary traditions of their community should still know that familiarity with Hemingway may pay off when they are taking SAT's or trying to succeed in college. We suspect many students get turned off and bored by such knowledge in schools partly because

they do not understand its practical use, and that they would learn it if
for no other reason than to 'make it'.

Developing Respect for Self and Others

A third goal is to learn knowledge of and respect for self and others. So
much of the thinking about education today relates to students
developing their academic prowess. Discussions of education that relate
to students developing their personal and social selves seem to be
abandoned thoughts of yesterday. Yet, we all know that education is
interactive. It involves the self in relationship to one's environment and
to other people. Self esteem, respect for others, affirmation of human
differences, are goals that are just as important as any of the school's
other goals, for they are pillars upon which our society rests.

Students must have the kinds of experiences in school that allow
them to get to know themselves better. Experiences must encourage
exploration into the self. Although a good deal of schooling has
students reacting to events and experiences so that they can be sorted
and selected for future work roles, these kinds of experiences thwart
self-respect probably more often than they foster it. For example, the
student who is not deemed 'college material' is not seen as an important
person in the eyes of many schools. Students need an environment in
which personal interests and talents can come into being, develop and
be taken seriously. We must be careful that teaching the 'basics' or
stressing a narrow range of human achievement does not become the
most important purpose of the school.

Respect for self and others has implications for the curriculum. For
example, the curriculum should allow students to gain an understanding of the history of their own people, and the economic, political and
social events surrounding that history. The curriculum should help
students learn to relate to others by taking seriously and including the
interests and perspectives of different students in the class. It should
also include things such as the art, music and literature from the various
racial and cultural groups and both sexes, in the US specifically and the
world generally.

Students need to be allowed to set many of their learning goals,
and with guidance, experiment with processes for accomplishing those
goals. Personal and collective interests and talents should be explored
and shared in school. Human experiences should be shared through
literature and the arts. Feelings, wishes, and passions should be allowed

to flourish in school, as these propel us to further learning and to understanding one another.

Social Action

Our final goal is to develop ethical and reflective social action. Action that is not informed by learning and thinking is not necessarily responsible. And teaching knowledge as if it had no social context is often not ethical. People like to see congruence between thought and behavior, but too often see action as an inappropriate concern of education. Yet at the same time we lament people who do not or cannot 'practice what they preach' or what they have learned. But in life outside of school, we know that action and learning quite often feed one another.

Therefore, we propose bringing action into the school and giving it a social focus. For example, students should practice government in the school and classroom, not simply study about it. That practice should revolve around real issues of student life, such as the operation of the school or the setting of school goals. If being responsible for one's own behavior and creating a more just society are important, students' actions need to concern their social world.

Students also need to learn to use ethical reasoning, so that they can learn to make responsible and informal value judgments when taking action that involves themselves personally and other people. Students need to learn to judge the impact of their actions on their own lives as well as the lives of other people. Americans frequently forget that majority rule is not always just, for example. Students need to learn to be sensitive to instances in which the wishes of the majority adversely affect or simply ignore the rights or needs of the minority.

Schools can encourage social action by sponsoring or organizing student projects in their local community. Such projects could be part of the classwork for a course. For example, students could identify a local problem, research it, propose a way of solving it, then involve themselves in attempting to do so. Teachers will probably find that involvement in a real-life problem of immediate concern to students will not only help them develop social action skills but will also provide the motivation for developing thinking skills, foster respect for self and others and provide a focal point for learning new knowledge and ideas.

Can you imagine the impact that the sort of education we are proposing would have on the students at Five Bridges? It would greatly enhance the quality of their own lives, not to mention the lives of the teachers; it would probably also greatly increase the likelihood that they could make contributions to society that would benefit many. Imagine the impact this kind of education would have on the children in your neighborhood; imagine how society would benefit if all young people received this education. Can we afford not to provide it to them?

Methodology for the Study

We would like here to provide a detailed description of procedures we used to collect and analyze data. Essentially, our goal was to collect enough data so that patterns that initially seemed new and tentative became well-documented. To accomplish this, we designed many of the specifics of our data collection strategy as the study proceeded, and terminated our data collection only when we felt we had learned as much as we could about race, social class, gender and handicap at Five Bridges during the time period of interest to us.

Data were collected between August 1978 and June 1981, by a three-member research team composed of ourselves and a colleague. It is important to point out that this research team brought a variety of backgrounds and perspectives to the study. One member was black, two were white; two were female, one was male. Among the three of us, we had taught almost every grade level K-12; one of us had also been a school administrator, one had been a special education teacher. These differences in our backgrounds enabled us to question assumptions made by each other, to ask questions other members of the team had not thought to ask, and to offer interpretations others had not made. We found that this helped to check the biases that we all brought to the task, and forced us to rely on the data, recheck data and collect new data to support or challenge our thinking. In addition, all three of us had had previous teaching experience in multiracial schools, which prepared us to feel comfortable in Five Bridges, and sensitized us to issues that may lie beyond surface appearances in the school.

Our visits to the school began with a two-week visit. After that, we made twenty-three visits that each lasted two to three days. During the first year of the study, visits occurred approximately every two weeks; after that they became more widely spaced. We collected data based on observation, interviews, examination of artifacts (for example, textbooks), and administration of questionnaires. Each will be described separately.

Observation

We conducted both site-specific and person-specific observations. Site-specific observations were made in classrooms, the lunch room, hallways, teachers' coffee rooms and the library. A total of 160 hours were spent observing in twenty-three classrooms, including most of the English, social studies, science, special education and music classrooms; half of the home economics, industrial arts and remedial classrooms; and about one-third of the math and foreign language classrooms. During each observation extensive notes were taken on a five-page, semi-structured observation schedule that focused on content of lessons, instructional materials, room environment, teaching strategies, seating patterns and interaction patterns. We rotated which researcher observed which classroom to ensure that aspects of classrooms were not overlooked or misinterpreted due to individual researcher bias. In a number of cases two of us attended the class together. After each visit to the school we compared notes, focusing particularly on previous visits to same classrooms, to note any patterns emerging and to determine inter-observer reliability.

Person-specific observations were made by shadowing an individual for part of the day, keeping running notes. All five administrators were shadowed, about ten teachers were shadowed and about twelve students were shadowed. During shadowing, the researchers wrote down what the individual did, and asked questions to elicit his or her interpretation of events. Individuals always knew when they were being shadowed and usually carried on a running dialogue about what they were doing and thinking.

We conducted less structured observations in other parts of the school and during three in-service sessions. We visited the lunchroom periodically and charted the race and sex composition of seating patterns. We regularly (about once a month) drew diagrams of bulletin boards and displays in the halls. We sat in the teachers' coffee room, drawing diagrams of its contents and taking notes on conversations. We followed students to the auditorium for a couple of assemblies and made running notes. We sat in the main office during every visit, and noted comings and goings. During in-service sessions we made running notes of what transpired, and interviewed teachers afterward.

Interviews

Interviews were conducted with the five administrators, twenty-six teachers, nine aides, about fifty students, two district-level administrators and five adult community residents. Most of these people in the school were interviewed on at least four occasions; interviews were tape recorded and ranged in duration from 20 minutes to over an hour. Most interviews were guided by semi-structured interview schedules designed for that visit; separate interview schedules were constructed for teachers, students and administrators.

We used two main types of interviews. One type was in-depth, designed to elicit an emic perspective about the school and the individual's life in school (Pelto and Pelto, 1970). These interviews normally lasted over an hour. They were structured around a small number of general 'grand tour' questions, such as 'Tell me what it's like to be a student here'. Interviewers phrased and ordered questions in a manner that fit the flow of conversation. Probes were used to encourage the interviewee to explain what he or she meant, compare areas of meaning, and elicit components of a category of knowledge, such as 'You have described four kinds of students here; are there any more?' (We followed interview procedures described by Spradley and McCurdy, 1972.) These in-depth interviews were conducted with all five administrators, a sample of nine teachers in different subject areas and a sample of twenty-eight students.

Shorter, more structured interviews were conducted with all interviewees. For these, questions were more specific, designed to collect perceptions (usually from many people) about specific things. For example, teachers were asked about their participation during Black History Week, or about their expectations of what students would do after high school. Interviews with teachers usually took place immediately before or after an observation, and several questions were directed specifically toward the lesson (for example, 'Why did you decide to teach the content I observed?'). We also talked with teachers before visiting their class to discuss the nature and objectives of the lesson.

Questionnaires

Two questionnaries were given to the teachers and administrators, and one to the students. A short questionnaire was given to teachers and administrators to collect demographic information. It asked about matters such as where the person grew up, occupation of his or her parents, where he or she attended college, and number of years teaching experience.

The second was a survey that previously had been designed by one member of the research team to assess attitudes about race, social class, gender, handicap and age. This survey consisted of two parts. The first was a list of 100 statements asking respondents to indicate the degree to which they agreed or disagreed on a Likert-scale answer sheet. Two sample items are: (i) men should be willing to work for women supervisors; (ii) the reason that there are few stories about minority members is that minority groups have so few stories. The Hoyt reliability for this survey is .97.

The second part is designed to assess teachers' recognition of bias in curriculum. It consists of five tasks. On the first, individuals are given a list of human characteristics, headed by the name of a racial or ethnic group. The individual is asked to circle words he or she believes best describe that group (the 'right' answer is not to circle any). For the second task, individuals are asked to write a response to a paragraph written from a culturally or gender biased perspective. The intent is to assess the individual's ability to recognize bias. The third task asks individuals to make at least one curriculum modification to a traditional history lesson about the Vietnam War (the lesson is traditional in that it focuses on battles and uses text material as the main source of information). The fourth task asks individuals to write a lesson plan that would encourage students to do a thoughtful piece of work. Finally, the fifth task asks individuals to examine an excerpt from a teachers' guide that includes illustrations from a film used to teach an economics lesson. The excerpt and illustrations contain many stereotypes of ethnic, gender, age and handicap groups; individuals are to list comments and questions they would want to discuss with their students before showing the film. These last three tasks assess ability to modify or develop curriculum in a way that takes into account human diversity.

Finally, students were given a short questionnaire asking about their future plans and their perceptions about social class. This was used for two reasons: (i) to verify data gathered in interviews about future plans; and (ii) to have students respond to a simple visual diagram regarding degree of family wealth.

Documents

A wide variety of documents were examined during the study. Textbooks in classrooms were analyzed for bias by counting illustrations and names by race and sex. Samples of students' work were examined to find out about the classwork students were given as well as student skills in writing. Administrative memos regarding the school objectives and in-service sessions were collected. Teachers assembled for each of us a red notebook they constructed during an in-service session containing ideas for integrating multiculturalism into their teaching. We attempted to collect lesson plans but most teachers did not write plans. We collected a set of student newspapers; the journalism class made a habit of saving a copy of each issue for us. We also examined library resources available to students and teachers and resources in the teachers' coffee room (including a ditto file).

In addition to collecting documents from within the school, we collected documents on the community. We gathered city census data, and we located a series of local newspaper feature articles about the community. We read issues of a newsletter produced in the community for local residents. We also gathered documents produced by the city regarding the school's desegregation and mainstreaming program.

Data Analysis

We analyzed most of the data using two procedures. One procedure was to develop individual portraits of administrators, teachers and students. For each individual who had been interviewed in depth, a componential analysis of the individual's cultural knowledge was constructed. This involved identifying the categories each individual used to describe various aspects of life at Five Bridges, and charting on a diagram the components and sub-components of each category (see Frake, 1980; Goodenough, 1956). This resulted in a diagram depicting how each individual viewed life at Five Bridges; these diagrams were inspected by the individuals they represented, who verified their accuracy or in some cases suggested modifications they saw as appropriate. See Sleeter (1981) and Boyle (1982) for the diagrams. For each individual teacher and administrator portrait, we also compiled observation data to construct a summary of how the person performed his or her job. These were also inspected for accuracy by individuals they represented. In the majority of cases, accuracy was confirmed; where there were questions, we collected further data.

A second procedure was a topic analysis. For this, we cut and pasted copies of observation notes and interview transcripts according to topic or question asked. We constructed separate folders on topics. We then examined the contents to determine, for example, during what percentage of observed classtime lécture was being used, or what students said about homework. Observation and interview data were analyzed separately, then compared to determine the extent to which they were mutually supportive.

Related to the topic analysis was our concern for allowing unexpected patterns or trends to emerge, and following up on these. For example, the pattern of interracial dating was suggested casually by a few students in the context of answering interview questions about related topics. During our next visit we made this an area for interview questions, and it became a topic of interest to us in understanding the students, social structure and race.

We also filed copies of data chronologically, intending initially to examine the implementation of building objectives over time. There was such negligible change over time that we abandoned this form of analysis after the first year and a half.

Data from documents were not analyzed separately, but rather were used to substantiate data collected through observations and interviews. For example, during interviews with students we sometimes discussed specific assignments, and examined their written work and/or texts they had used. Sometimes data from documents and artifacts suggested areas in which further observation and interview data should be collected.

An earlier draft of the completed manuscript was reviewed by two members of the school. For the most part, they confirmed its accuracy; they were also encouraged to offer corrections or raise questions about things they believed might have been misinterpreted. Based on their review, we believe the data and our analysis of it is highly accurate.

Bibliography

ACHOR, S. (1978) *Mexican-Americans in a Dallas Barrio*, Tuscon, University of Arizona Press.

ADKINSON, J. (1981) 'Women in school administration: A review of the research', *Review of Educational Research*, 51, pp. 311–43.

ADLER, M.J. (1982) *The Paideia Proposal*, New York, Macmillan.

ANYON, J. (1981) 'Elementary schooling and distinctions of social class', *Interchange*, 12, pp. 118–32.

APPLETON, N. (1983) *Cultural Pluralism in Education*, New York, Longman.

BARBAGLI, M. and DEI, M. (1977) 'Socialization into apathy and public subordination', in KARABEL, J. and HALSY, A.H.(Eds), *Power and Ideology in Education*, New York, Oxford University Press, pp. 423–31.

BECKER, W.C. (1977) 'Teaching reading and language to the disadvantaged — What have we learned from field research?' *Harvard Educational Review*, 47, pp. 518–43.

BISSINGER, H.G. (1980) 'West side stories', *St.Paul Sunday Pioneer Press*, 11 May.

BLOOM, B.S. (1971) (Ed), *Taxonomy of Educational Objectives, The Classification of Educational Goals, Handbook I: Cognitive Domain*, New York, David McKay.

BOURDIEU, P. (1977) 'Cultural reproduction and social reproduction', in KARABEL, J. and HALSEY, A.H. (Eds), *Power and Ideology in Education*, New York, Oxford University Press, pp. 487–510.

BOURDIEU, P. and PASSERON, J. (1977) *Reproduction in Education, Society, and Culture*, London, Sage.

BOWLES, S. and GINTIS, H. (1976) *Schooling in Capitalist America*, New York, Basic Books.

BOYER, E.L. (1983) *High School*, New York, Harper and Row.

BOYLE, M. (1982) *Teaching in a Desegregated and Mainstreamed School: A Study of the Affirmation of Human Diversity*, unpublished PhD dissertation, University of Wisconsin-Madison.

BOYLE, M. and SLEETER, C.E. (1981) 'In-service for a federally-mandated educational change: A study of PL 94–142', *Journal of Research and Development in Education*, 14, pp. 79–92.

BRAKE, M. (1980) *The Sociology of Youth Culture and Youth Subcultures*, Boston, Routledge and Kegan Paul.

BRUININKS, V.L. (1978) 'Peer status and personality characteristics of learning disabled and non-disabled students', *Journal of Learning Disabilities*, 11, pp. 29–34.

BRYAN, T.H. (1977) 'Learning disabled children's comprehension of nonverbal communication', *Journal of Learning Disabilities*, 10, pp. 36–42.

BUTTERFIELD, R.A., DEMOS, E.S., GRANT, G.W., MOY, P.S., and PEREZ, A.L. (1979) 'Multicultural analysis of a popular basal reading series in the International Year of the Child', *Journal of Negro Education*, 48, pp. 382–9.

CAREW, J.V. and LIGHTFOOT, S.L. (1979) *Beyond Bias: Perspectives on Classrooms*, Cambridge, Mass, Harvard University Press.

CENTERS, L. and CENTERS, R. (1963) 'Peer group attitudes toward the amputee child', *Journal of Social Psychology*, 61, pp. 127–32.

CHIN, R. and BENNE, K.D. (1976) 'General strategies for effecting changes in human systems', in BENNIS, W.G., BENNE, K.D., CHIN, R., and COREY, K.E. (Eds.), *The Planning of Change*, 3rd edn, New York, Holt, Rinehart, and Winston, pp. 22–45.

CLEMENT, D.C., EISENHART, M., and HARDING, J.R. (1979) 'The veneer of harmony: Social race relations in a southern desegregated school' in RIST, R.C. (Ed.), *Desegregated Schools: Appraisals of an American Experiment*, New York, Academic Press, pp. 15–64.

COGAN, M.L. (1973) *Clinical Supervision*, Boston, Houghton Mifflin.

COLEMAN, J.S. (1961) *The Adolescent Society*, New York, The Free Press.

COLEMAN, J.S. (1966) *Equality of Educational Opportunity*, Washington, D.C., U.S. Government Printing Office.

COLLINS, R. (1977) 'Functional and conflict theories of educational stratification', in KARABEL, J. and HALSEY, A.H. (Eds), *Power and Ideology in Education*, New York, Oxford University Press, pp. 118–36.

COLLINS, R. (1979) *The Credential Society*, New York, Academic Press.

COSER, L. (1956) *The Functions of Social Conflict*, New York, The Free Press.

CUSICK, P.A. (1973) *Inside High School*, New York, Holt, Rinehart, and Winston.

CUSICK, P.A. and AYLING, R.J. (1974) 'Biracial interaction in an urban secondary school', *School Review*, 82, pp. 486–94.

DAHRENDORF, R. (1959), *Class and Class Conflict in Industrial Society*, Stanford, Stanford University Press.

DEUTSCH, M. (1973) *The Resolution of Conflict*, New Haven, Conn, Yale University Press.

DREEBEN, R. (1970) *The Nature of Teaching: Schools and the Work of Teachers*, Glenview, Ill, Scott Foresman.

ELKIN, R. and WESTLEY, W.F. (1955) 'The myth of adolescent culture', *American Sociological Review*, 20, pp. 680–4.

EVERHART, R. (1983) *Reading, Writing, and Resistance*, London, Routledge and Kegan Paul.

FORCE, D.G. (1956) 'Social status of physically handicapped children', *Exceptional Children*, 23, pp. 104–7.

FRAKE, C.O. (1980) *Language and Cultural Description: Essays*, Stanford, Stanford University Press.

FRAZIER, N. and SADKER, M. (1973) *Sexism in School and Society*, New York, Harper and Row.

FULLER, M. (1980) 'Black girls in a London comprehensive school', in DEEM, R. (Ed.), *Schooling for Women's Work*, London, Routledge and Kegan Paul, pp. 52–65.

GARRETT, M.K. and CRUMP, W.D. (1970) 'Peer acceptance, teacher preference, and self-appraisal of social status among learning disabled adults', *Learning Disability Quarterly*, 3, pp. 42–8.

GASKELL, J. (1984) 'Gender and course choice: The orientations of male and female students', *Journal of Education*, 166, pp. 89–102.

GERARD, H.B. and MILLER, N. (1975) *School Desegregation: A Long-Term Study*, New York, Plenum Press.

GIROUX, H. (1981) *Ideology, Culture, and the Process of Schooling*, Lewes, Falmer Press.

GLICKMAN, C.D. (1981) *Developmental Supervision*, Alexandria, VA, Association for Supervision and Curriculum Development.

GOLDHAMMER, R. (1969) *Clinical Supervision: Special Methods for the Supervision of Teachers*, New York, Holt, Rinehart, and Winston.

GOODENOUGH, W.H. (1956) 'Componential analysis and the study of meaning', *Language*, 30, pp. 195–216.

GOODENOUGH, W.H. (1963) *Cooperation and Change*, New York, Sage.

GOODLAD, J.I. (1975) *The Dynamics of Educational Change: Toward Responsive Schools*, New York, McGraw-Hill.

GOODLAD, J.I. (1984) *A Place Called School*, New York, McGraw-Hill.

GOODMAN, H., GOTTLIEB, J., and HARRISON, R.J. (1972) 'Social acceptance of EMR's integrated into a nongraded elementary school', *American Journal of Mental Deficiency*, 76, pp. 412–7.

GORDON, W.C. (1957) *The Social System of the High School*, Glencoe, Ill, The Free Press.

GOTTLIEB, J. and BUDOFF, M. (1973) 'Social acceptability of retarded children in non-graded schools differing in architecture', *American Journal of Mental Deficiency*, 78, pp. 15–19.

GRAMSCI, A. (1971) *Selections from the Prison Notebook*, trans and ed HOARE, Q. and SMITH, G. New York, International Publishers.

GRANT, C.A. (1981) *Bringing Teaching to Life*, Boston, Allyn and Bacon.

GRANT, C.A. and MELNICK, S.L. (1977) 'Developing and implementing multi-cultural in-service teacher education', in COLLINS, J. and WILSON, A. (Ed.), *State Action for In-Service Education*, Syracuse, NY, Syracuse University Press.

GRANT, C.A. and SLEETER, C.E. (1985) 'The educational reform reports in the 1980's: A critique of their treatment of equity', in ALTBACH, P.G., KELLY, G.P. and WEIS, L. (Eds), *Excellence in Education: Perspectives on Policy and Practices*, Buffalo, NY, Prometheus.

HALE, J.E. (1982) *Black Children: Their Roots, Culture, and Learning Styles*, Provo, Ut, Brigham Young University Press.

HARGREAVES, D.H. (1967) *Social Relations in a Secondary School*, New York, Routledge and Kegan Paul.

HELLAND, K.I. (1978) 'Chicano/Latino study report', unpublished report for the Center for Urban and Regional Affairs, Minneapolis/St. Paul, Minnesota.

HERSEY, P. and BLANCHARD, K.H. (1977) *Management of Organizational Behavior*, 3rd edn, Englewood Cliffs, NJ, Prentice-Hall.

HOLLINGSHEAD, A.B. (1949) *Elmtown's Youth*, New York, Science Editions.

IANO, R.P., AYERS, D., HELLER, H.B., McGETTIGAN, J.F., and WALKER, V.S. (1974) 'Sociometric status of retarded children in an integrative program', *Exceptional Children*, 40, pp. 267–71.

JACKSON, P.W. (1968) *Life in Classrooms*, New York, Holt, Rinehart and Winston.

JENCKS, C. (1973) *Inequality: a Reassessment of the Effect of Family and Schooling in America*, New York, Basic Books.

KANDEL, D.B. and LESSER, G.S. (1972) *Youth in Two Worlds*, San Francisco, Jossey-Bass.

LACEY, C. (1970) *Hightown Grammar*, London, Manchester University Press.

LEACOCK, E.B. (1969) *Teaching and Learning in City Schools: A Comparative Study*, New York, Basic Books.

LEITHWOOD, K.A. and MONTGOMERY, D.J. (1982) 'The role of the elementary school principal in program improvement', *Review of Educational Research*, 52, pp. 309–39.

LIPHAM, J.M. and FRUTH, M.J. (1976) *The Principal and Individually Guided Education*, Reading, Mass, Addison-Wesley.

LONGSTREET, W.S. (1978) *Aspects of Ethnicity*, New York, Teachers College Press.

LORTIE, D.C. (1975) *Schoolteacher: A Sociological Study*, Chicago, University of Chicago Press.

McLAUGHLIN, M.W. and MARSH, D.D. (1975) 'Staff development and school change', *Teachers College Record*, 80, pp. 69–94.

McPHERSON, G.H. (1972) *Small Town Teacher*, Cambridge, Mass, Harvard University Press.

McROBBIE, A. (1978) 'Working class girls and the culture of femininity', in Women's Studies Group Centre for Contemporary Cultural Studies (Eds.), *Women Take Issue*, London, Hutchinson, pp. 96–108.

MARX, K. and ENGLES, F. (1947) *The German Ideology*, New York, International Publishers.

METZ, M.H. (1978) *Classrooms and Corridors: The Crisis of Authority in Desegregated Secondary Schools*, Berkeley, University of California Press.

MICHELS, R. (1959) *Political Parties: A Sociological Study of the Oligarchical Tendencies of Modern Democracies*, trans PAUL, E. and PAUL, C., New York, Dover Publications.

NATIONAL COMMISSION ON EXCELLENCE IN EDUCATION (1983) *A Nation at Risk: The Imperative of Educational Reform*, Washington, D.C., U.S. Government Printing Office.

NOBLIT, G.W. (1979) 'Patience and prudence in a southern high school: Managing the political economy of desegregated education', in RIST,

R.C. (Ed.), *Desegregated Schools: Appraisals of an American Experiment*, New York, Academic Press, pp. 65–88.

OGBU, J.U. (1974) *The Next Generation*, New York, Academic Press.

OGBU, J.U. (1978) *Minority Education and Caste*, New York, Academic Press.

OGBU, J.U. (1982) 'Cultural discontinuities and schooling', *Anthropology and Education Quarterly*, 13, pp. 290–307.

PELTO, P.J. (1965) *The Study of Anthropology*, Columbus, Ohio, Charles E. Merrill.

PELTO, P.J. and PELTO, G.H. (1970) *Anthropological Research*, Cambridge, Cambridge University Press.

PETRONI, F.A. and HIRSCH, E.A. (1970) *Two, Four, Six, Eight, When You Gonna Integrate?* New York, Behavioral Publications.

PHI DELTA KAPPA, INC. (1979 and 1980) *A Decade of Gallop Polls of Attitudes Toward Education 1969–1978*, and Annual Gallop poll of the public's attitudes toward the public schools, *Phi Delta Kappa*.

PHILIPS, S.U. (1983) *The Invisible Culture*, New York, Longman.

POLK, R.L. and CO. (1978) 'Dynamics of households', unpublished report for the City of St. Paul, Minnesota.

PURKEY, S.C. and SMITH, M.S. (1982) 'Effective schools: A review', *Elementary School Journal*, 83, pp. 427–52.

RICHARDSON, S.A., RONALD, L. and KLECK, R.E. (1974) 'The social status of handicapped and non-handicapped boys in a camp setting', *Journal of Special Education*, 9, pp. 143–52.

RIST, R.C. (1970) 'Student social class and teacher expectations: The self-fulfilling prophecy', *Harvard Educational Review*, 40, pp. 411–51.

RIST, R.C. (1978) *the Invisible Children*, Cambridge, Mass, Harvard University Press.

RIST, R.C. (1979) (Ed)., *Desegregated Schools: Appraisals of an American Experiment*, New York, Academic Press.

RUTTER, M., *et al.* (1979) *Fifteen Thousand Hours*, Cambridge, Mass, Harvard University Press.

SAPON-SHEVIN, M. (1982) 'Mentally retarded characters in children's literature', *Children's Literature in Education*, 13, pp. 19–31.

SCHERER, J. and SLAWSKI, E.J. (1979) 'Color, class and social control in an urban desegregated school', in RIST, R.C. (Ed.), *Desegregated Schools: Appraisals of an American Experiment*, New York, Academic Press, pp. 117–54.

SCHOFIELD, J.W. (1983) *Black and White in School*, New York, Praeger.

SENNETT, R. and COBB, J. (1973) *The Hidden Injuries of Class*, New York, Vintage Books.

SERBIN, L.A., O'LEARY, K.D., KENT, R.N., and TONICH, I.J. (1973) 'A comparison of teacher responses to the preacademic and problem behavior of boys and girls', *Child Development*, 44, pp. 796–804.

SHARP, R. and GREEN, A. (1975) *Education and Social Control: A Study in Progressive Primary Education*, London, Routledge and Kegan Paul.

SHOTEL, J.R., IANO, R.P., and McGETTIGAN, J.F. (1972) 'Teacher attitudes associated with the integration of handicapped children', *Exceptional Children*, 38, pp. 677–83.

SLEETER, C.E. (1981) *Student Friendships and Cultural Knowledge Related to Human Diversity in a Multiracial and Mainstreamed Junior High School*, unpublished Ph.D. dissertation, University of Wisconsin-Madison.

SLEETER, C.E. (1982) 'Secondary education in the 1980's: A review of the research', *NASSP Bulletin*, 66, pp. 69–81.

SPINDLER, G.B. (1982) 'General introduction' in SPINDLER, G.D. (Ed.), *Doing the Ethnography of Schooling: Educational Anthropology in Action*, New York, Holt, Rinehart and Winston, pp. 1–13.

SPRADLEY, J.P. and McCURDY, D.W. (1972) *The Cultural Experience*, Chicago, Science Research Associates.

SPRING, J. (1976) *The Sorting Machine*, New York, Longman.

STOCKARD, J., SCHMUCK, P.A., KEMPNER, K., WILLIAMS, P., EDSON, S.K., and SMITH, M.A. (1980) *Sex Equity in Education*, New York, Academic Press.

TABACHNICK, B.R. *et al.* (1979) 'Teacher education and the professional perspectives of student teachers', *Interchange*, 10, pp. 12–29.

VALLI, L. (1983) 'Becoming clerical workers: Business education and the culture of femininity', in APPLE, M.W. and WEIS, L. (Eds), *Ideology and Practice in Schooling*, Philadelphia, Temple University Press, pp. 213–34.

WALKER, S. and BARTON, L. (1983) *Gender, Class, and Education*, Lewes, Falmer Press.

WAX, R. (1976) 'Oglala Sioux drop-outs and their problems with educators', in ROBERTS, J.I. and AKINSANYA, S. (Eds), *Schooling in the Cultural Context*, New York, David McKay Co., pp. 216–25.

WEBER, M. (1947) *The Theory of Social and Economic Organization*, trans HENDERSON, A.M. and PARSONS, T. ed PARSONS, T. Glencoe, Ill, The Free Press.

WEBER, M. (1968) *Economy and Society*, New York, Bedminster Press.

WILLIE, C.V. (1978) *The Sociology of Urban Education: Desegregation and Integration.* Lexington, Mass, Lexington Books.

WILLIS, P. (1977) *Learning to Labour*, Westmead, England, Saxon House.

YOUNG, M.F.D. (1977) 'An approach to the study of curricula as socially organized knowledge', in BELLACK, A.A. and KLIEBARD, H.M. (Eds), *Curriculum and Evaluation*, Berkeley, McCutchan, pp. 254–85.

Author Index

Subject Index

voting rights 197

wealth 4, 5, 6, 57
welfare 77, 108
wheelchair sports 179
wheelchair students 38–9, 44, 123,
146, 173, 193
wheelchairs 122, 195, 241
white collar backgrounds
teachers 240
white middle class
cultural capital 63–7
Wilson, Thomas 70, 72, 73, 75, 76,
77, 78–9, 81, 83, 84, 85, 86, 87,
87–8, 90, 91, 94, 97, 98–100, 119,
120, 210, 212–13, 230–1, 232, 234,
237, 238, 239, 240, 241, 243, 254,
255, 256
women 87, 96, 122, 129, 197, 243,
263
careers 104
place in society 184
traditional role 83
working 195

women teachers 238
women's rights 130
Wonder, Stevie 130
woodshop, 197
work
aspirations 79
work aspirations 57–9
work roles 198–9
gender and 53–4, 79
workbooks 161, 246
working class 151, 182, 200, 205, 226,
235, 240
working women 195
workplace, sexism 130
worksheets, 137, 165, 166, 208, 235
workshops, human diversity 217–18,
220
World Languages and Cultures
Magnet Program 20
writing 12, 208, 247

Ziegler, Sarah 74–5, 76, 77, 80, 81,
82–3, 84, 85, 87, 90, 91, 92, 93, 94,
96, 97, 215, 219, 234, 238